Character
Introductions

Mile (Adele)

The current incarnation of a Japanese girl named Kurihara Misato, who was reborn into a fantasy world. She prayed to have "average" abilities in her new life, but instead was granted fantastic powers. During her time at Eckland Academy she was "Adele," but now at the Hunters' Prep School, she goes by "Mile."

Reina

A fifteen-year-old mage. Goes by the title "the Crimson Reina" and specializes in attack magic. She and Mile become roommates at the Hunters' Prep School. Though she has a forceful personality, she worries a great deal for her friend.

Mavis

A seventeen-year-old swordswoman. Comes from a long line of knights. She aimed to become a knight herself, but her family opposed her, so she ran away from home and enrolled at the Hunters' Prep School. She became roommates with the other three and is the leader of their group.

Pauline

A fourteen-year-old mage specializing in healing magic. The daughter of a merchant's mistress. She has a relaxing presence that envelopes others in worm feelings. She has an incredibly sweet disposition, and yet...?!

Marcela (Middle), Aureana (Left), Monika (Right)

Mile's best friends from Eckland Academy. Marcela, the daughter of a mid-ranking noble family; Monika, the daughter of a merchant; and Aureana, a commoner. At first, they were envious of Adele, who stood out at the academy, but after Adele taught them magic--among other things-- they became close friends.

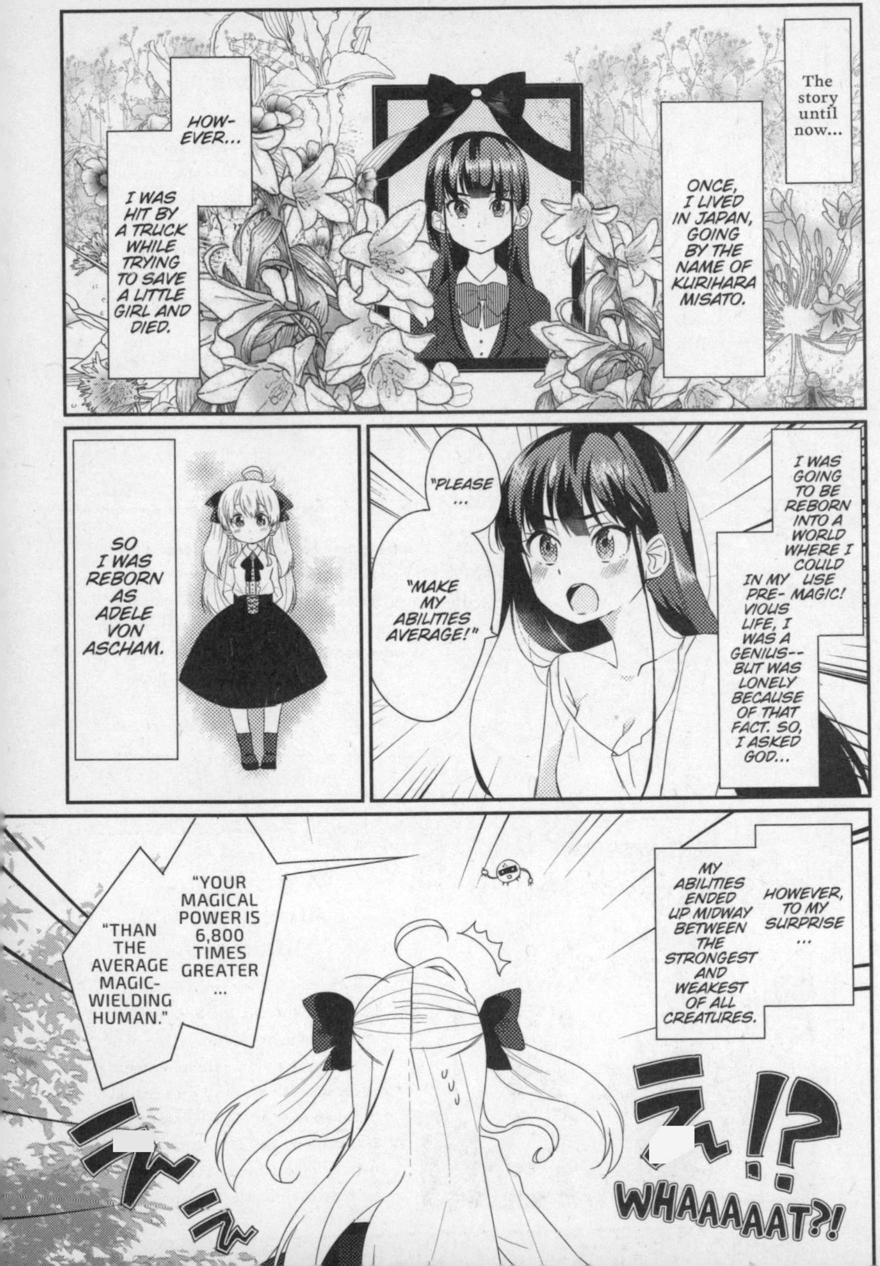
The story until now...
ONCE, I LIVED IN JAPAN, GOING BY THE NAME OF KURIHARA MISATO.
HOW-EVER...
I WAS HIT BY A TRUCK WHILE TRYING TO SAVE A LITTLE GIRL AND DIED.
I WAS GOING TO BE REBORN INTO A WORLD WHERE I COULD USE MAGIC!
IN MY PRE-VIOUS LIFE, I WAS A GENIUS--BUT WAS LONELY BECAUSE OF THAT FACT. SO, I ASKED GOD...
"PLEASE...
"MAKE MY ABILITIES AVERAGE!"
SO I WAS REBORN AS ADELE VON ASCHAM.
HOWEVER, TO MY SURPRISE...
MY ABILITIES ENDED UP MIDWAY BETWEEN THE STRONGEST AND WEAKEST OF ALL CREATURES.
"YOUR MAGICAL POWER IS 6,800 TIMES GREATER...
"THAN THE AVERAGE MAGIC-WIELDING HUMAN."
WHAAAAAT?!

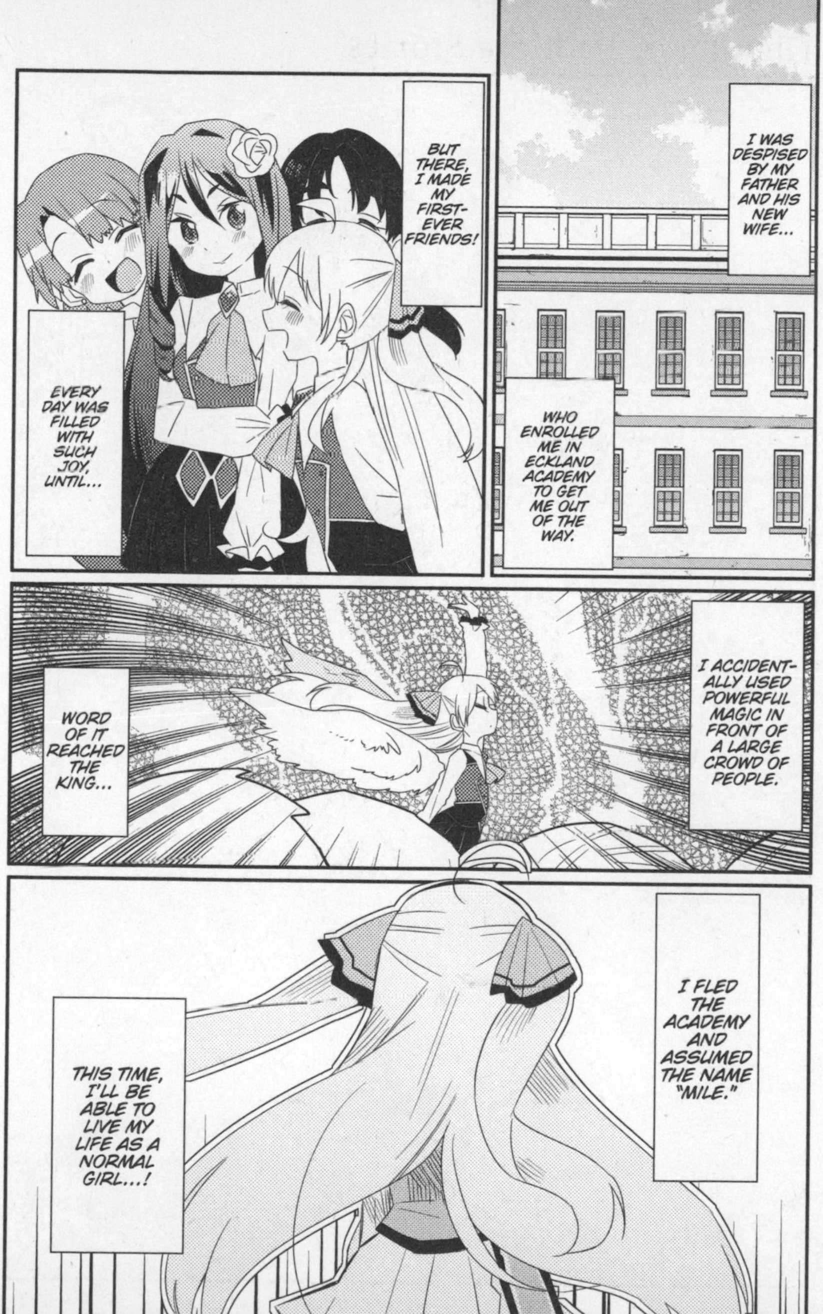
I WAS DESPISED BY MY FATHER AND HIS NEW WIFE...
WHO ENROLLED ME IN ECKLAND ACADEMY TO GET ME OUT OF THE WAY.
BUT THERE, I MADE MY FIRST-EVER FRIENDS!
EVERY DAY WAS FILLED WITH SUCH JOY, UNTIL...
I ACCIDENT-ALLY USED POWERFUL MAGIC IN FRONT OF A LARGE CROWD OF PEOPLE.
WORD OF IT REACHED THE KING...
I FLED THE ACADEMY AND ASSUMED THE NAME "MILE."
THIS TIME, I'LL BE ABLE TO LIVE MY LIFE AS A NORMAL GIRL...!

Chapter 7: Bedtime Stories

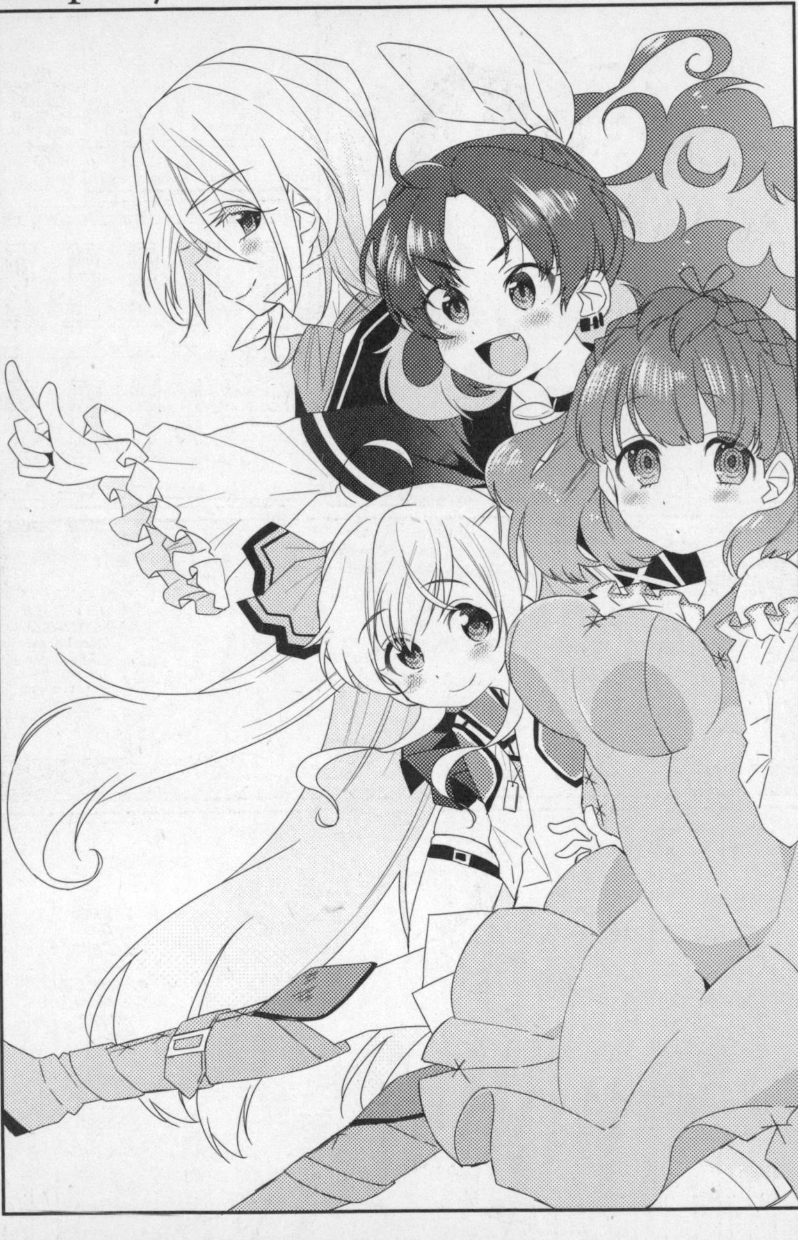

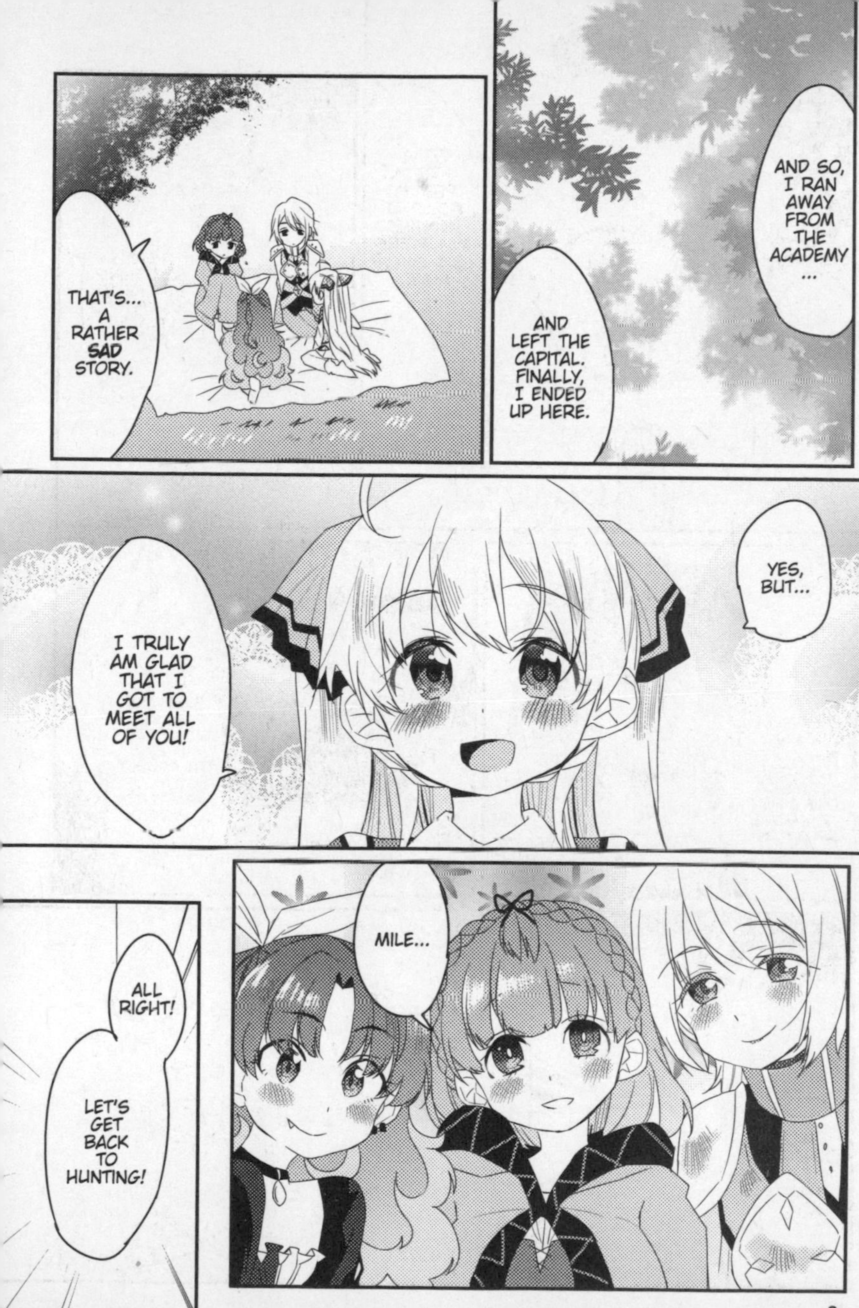
AND SO, I RAN AWAY FROM THE ACADEMY ...
AND LEFT THE CAPITAL. FINALLY, I ENDED UP HERE.
THAT'S... A RATHER SAD STORY.
YES, BUT...
I TRULY AM GLAD THAT I GOT TO MEET ALL OF YOU!
MILE...
ALL RIGHT!
LET'S GET BACK TO HUNTING!

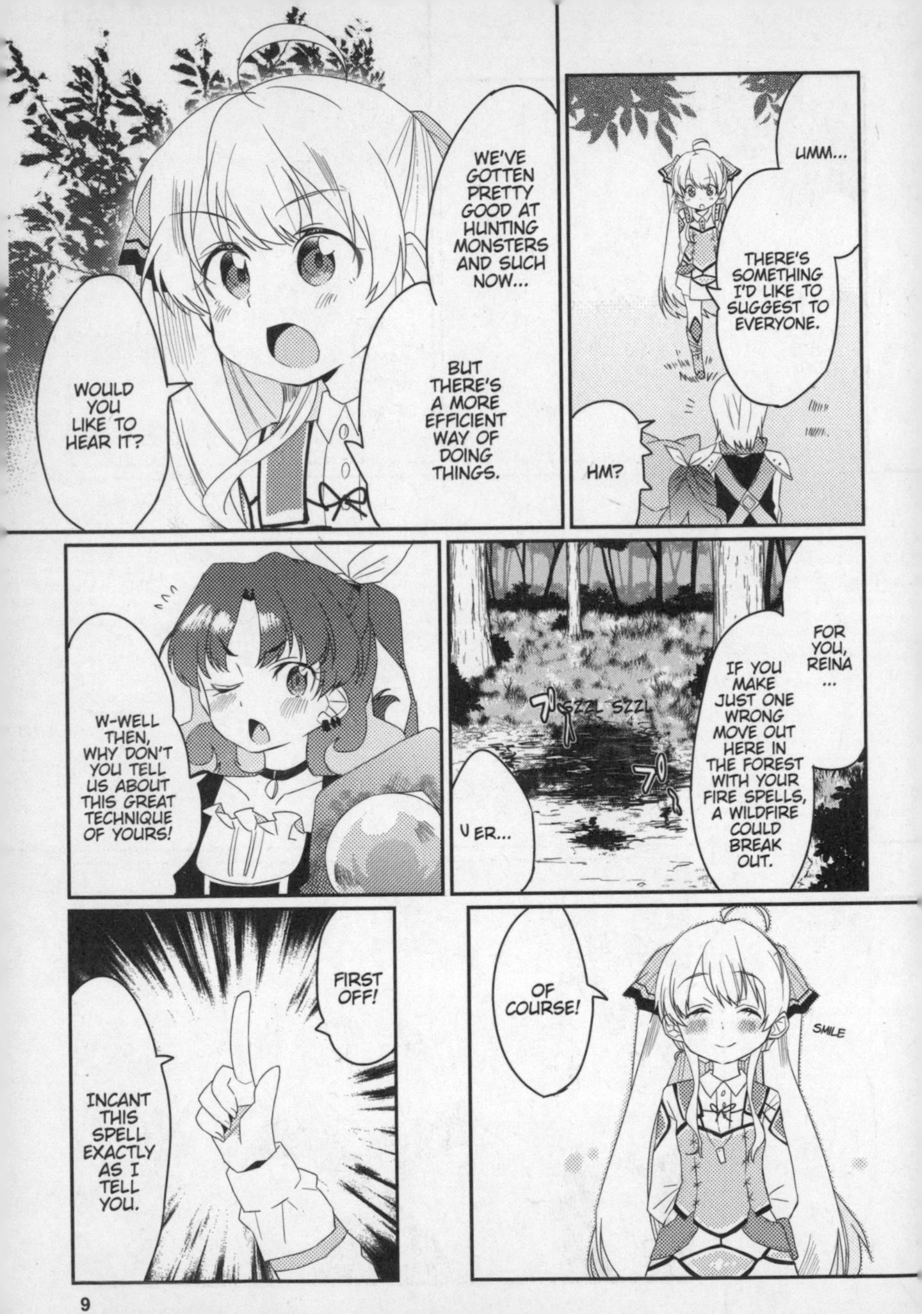
UMM...
THERE'S SOMETHING I'D LIKE TO SUGGEST TO EVERYONE.
HM?
WE'VE GOTTEN PRETTY GOOD AT HUNTING MONSTERS AND SUCH NOW...
BUT THERE'S A MORE EFFICIENT WAY OF DOING THINGS.
WOULD YOU LIKE TO HEAR IT?
FOR YOU, REINA...
IF YOU MAKE JUST ONE WRONG MOVE OUT HERE IN THE FOREST WITH YOUR FIRE SPELLS, A WILDFIRE COULD BREAK OUT.
SZZL SZZL
ER...
W-WELL THEN, WHY DON'T YOU TELL US ABOUT THIS GREAT TECHNIQUE OF YOURS!
OF COURSE!
SMILE
FIRST OFF!
INCANT THIS SPELL EXACTLY AS I TELL YOU.

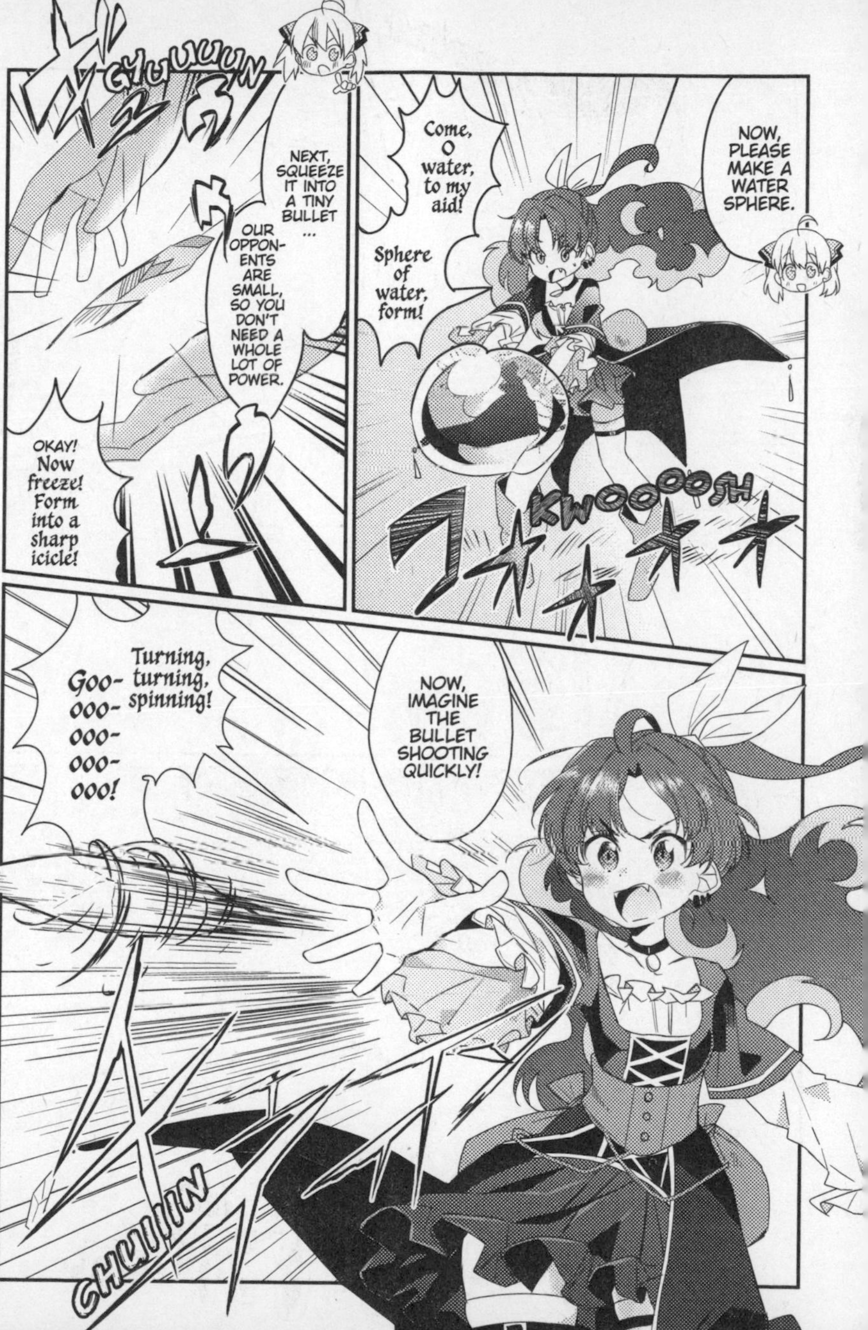
NOW, PLEASE MAKE A WATER SPHERE.
Come, O water, to my aid!
Sphere of water, form!
KWOOOOOSH
GYUUUUUN
NEXT, SQUEEZE IT INTO A TINY BULLET ...
OUR OPPONENTS ARE SMALL, SO YOU DON'T NEED A WHOLE LOT OF POWER.
OKAY! Now freeze! Form into a sharp icicle!
NOW, IMAGINE THE BULLET SHOOTING QUICKLY!
Turning, turning, spinning!
Goo-ooo-ooo-ooo-ooo!
CHUIIIN

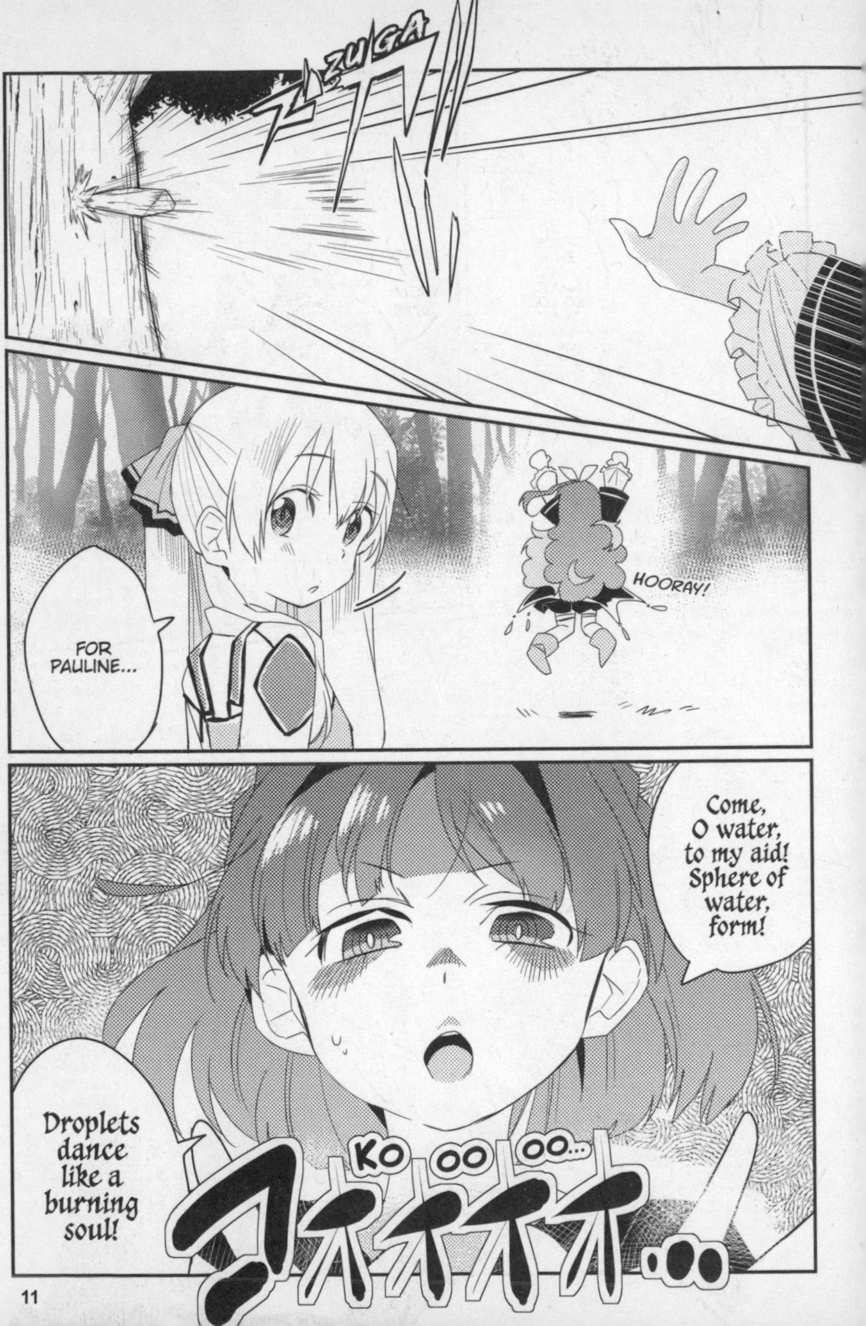
ZUGA
HOORAY!
FOR PAULINE...
Come, O water, to my aid! Sphere of water, form!
Droplets dance like a burning soul!
KO OO OO...

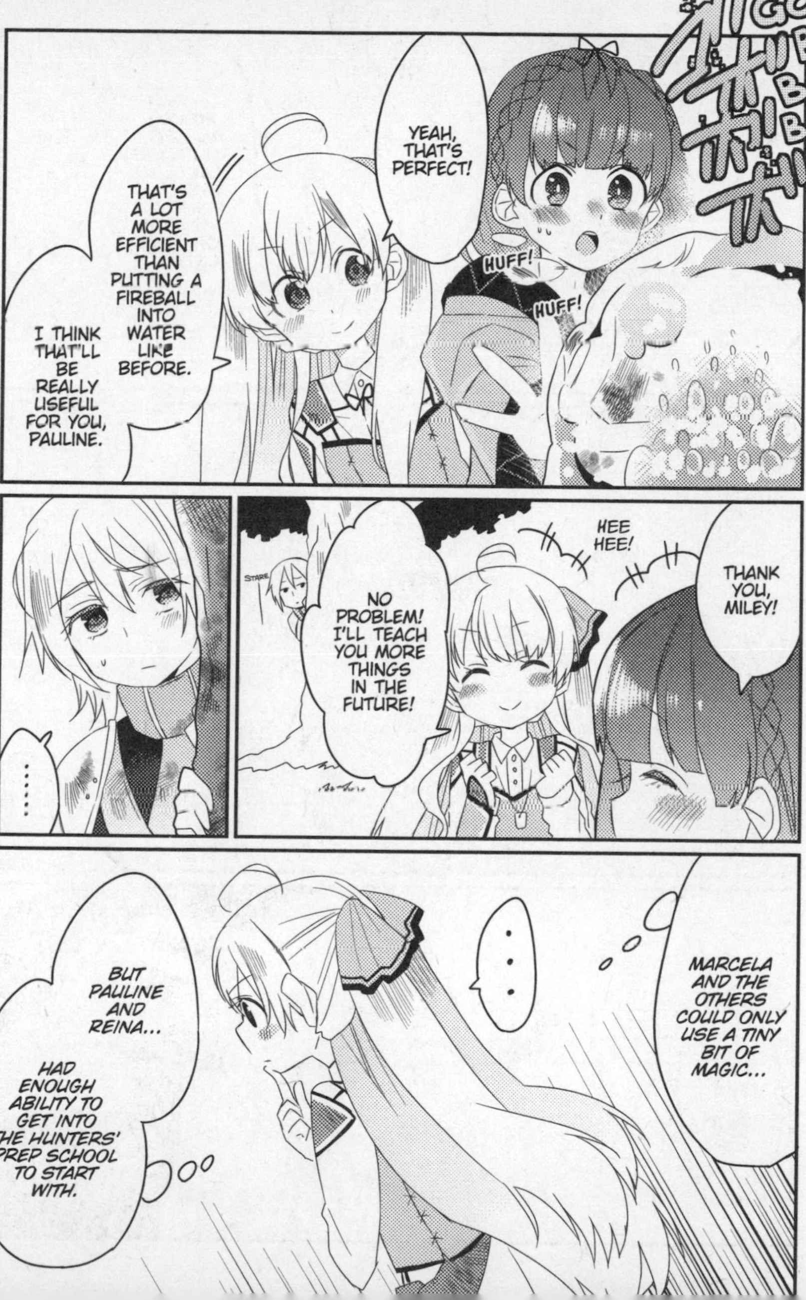
GO BO BO BO
YEAH, THAT'S PERFECT!
HUFF!
HUFF!
THAT'S A LOT MORE EFFICIENT THAN PUTTING A FIREBALL INTO WATER LIKE BEFORE.
I THINK THAT'LL BE REALLY USEFUL FOR YOU, PAULINE.
THANK YOU, MILEY!
HEE HEE!
NO PROBLEM! I'LL TEACH YOU MORE THINGS IN THE FUTURE!
STARE
......
MARCELA AND THE OTHERS COULD ONLY USE A TINY BIT OF MAGIC...
...
BUT PAULINE AND REINA...
HAD ENOUGH ABILITY TO GET INTO THE HUNTERS' PREP SCHOOL TO START WITH.

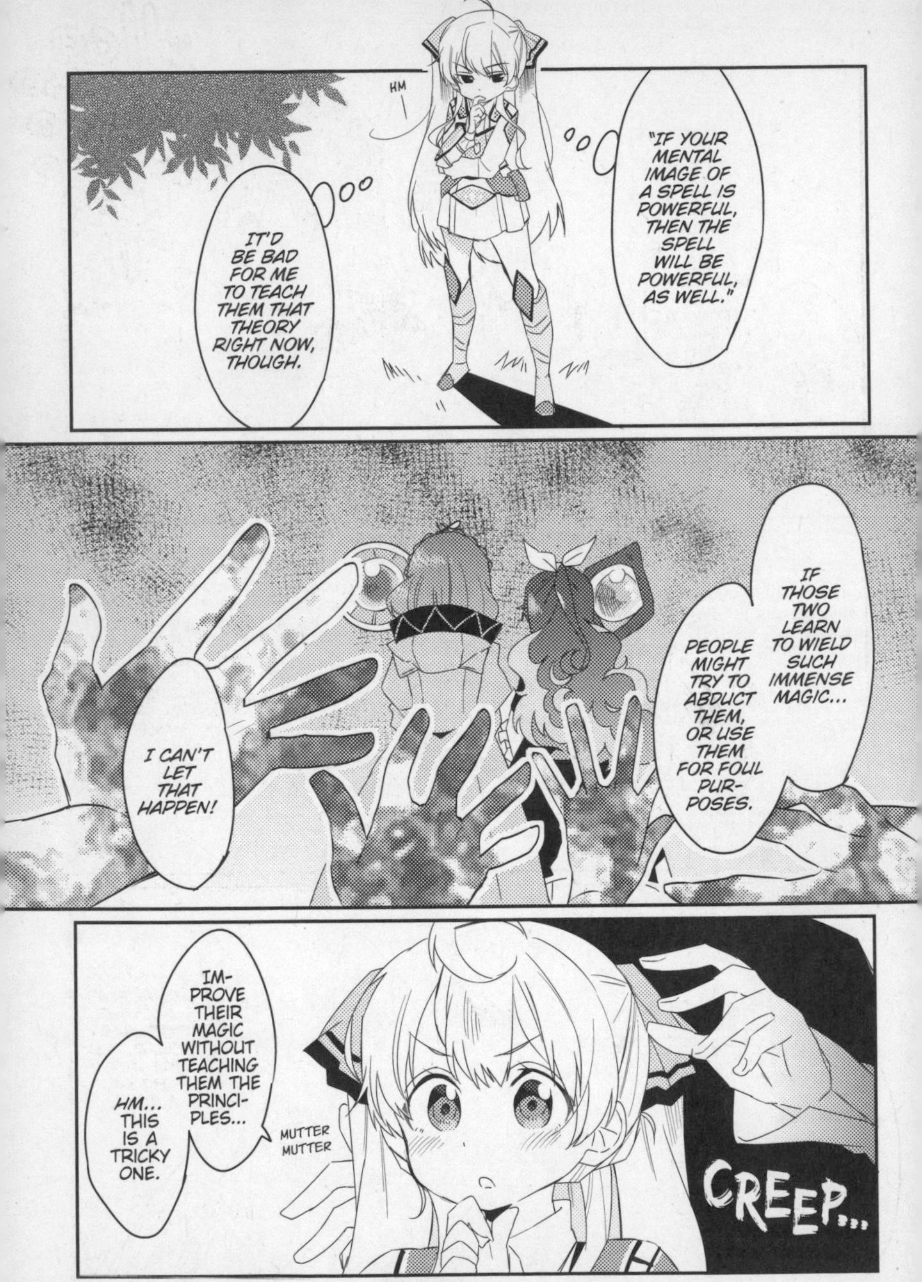
"IF YOUR MENTAL IMAGE OF A SPELL IS POWERFUL, THEN THE SPELL WILL BE POWERFUL, AS WELL."
HM
IT'D BE BAD FOR ME TO TEACH THEM THAT THEORY RIGHT NOW, THOUGH.
IF THOSE TWO LEARN TO WIELD SUCH IMMENSE MAGIC...
PEOPLE MIGHT TRY TO ABDUCT THEM, OR USE THEM FOR FOUL PURPOSES.
I CAN'T LET THAT HAPPEN!
IMPROVE THEIR MAGIC WITHOUT TEACHING THEM THE PRINCIPLES...
MUTTER MUTTER
HM... THIS IS A TRICKY ONE.
CREEP...

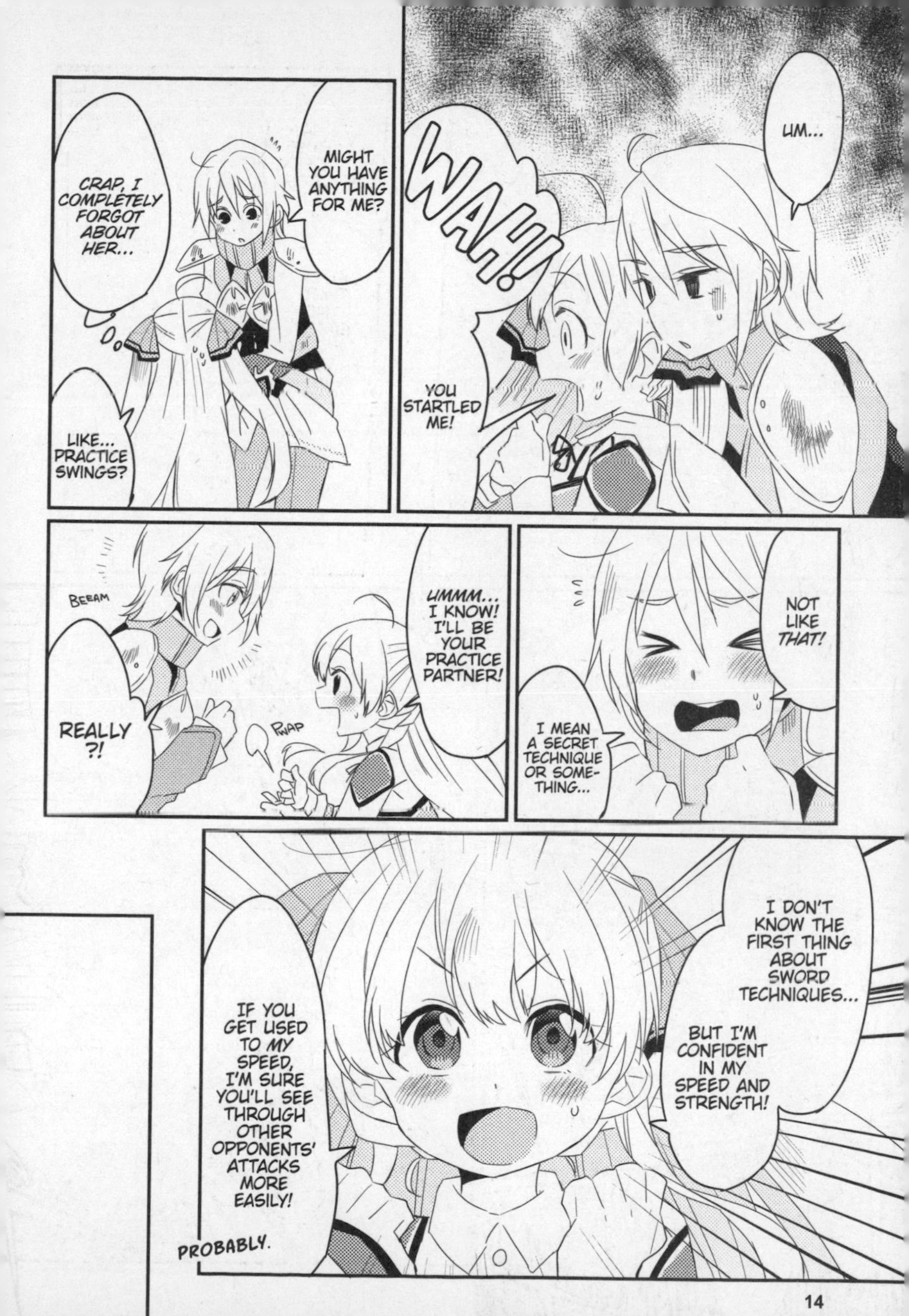
UM...
WAH!
YOU STARTLED ME!
MIGHT YOU HAVE ANYTHING FOR ME?
CRAP, I COMPLETELY FORGOT ABOUT HER...
LIKE... PRACTICE SWINGS?
NOT LIKE THAT!
I MEAN A SECRET TECHNIQUE OR SOMETHING...
UMMM... I KNOW! I'LL BE YOUR PRACTICE PARTNER!
BEEAM
REALLY?!
PWAP
I DON'T KNOW THE FIRST THING ABOUT SWORD TECHNIQUES...
BUT I'M CONFIDENT IN MY SPEED AND STRENGTH!
IF YOU GET USED TO MY SPEED, I'M SURE YOU'LL SEE THROUGH OTHER OPPONENTS' ATTACKS MORE EASILY!
PROBABLY.

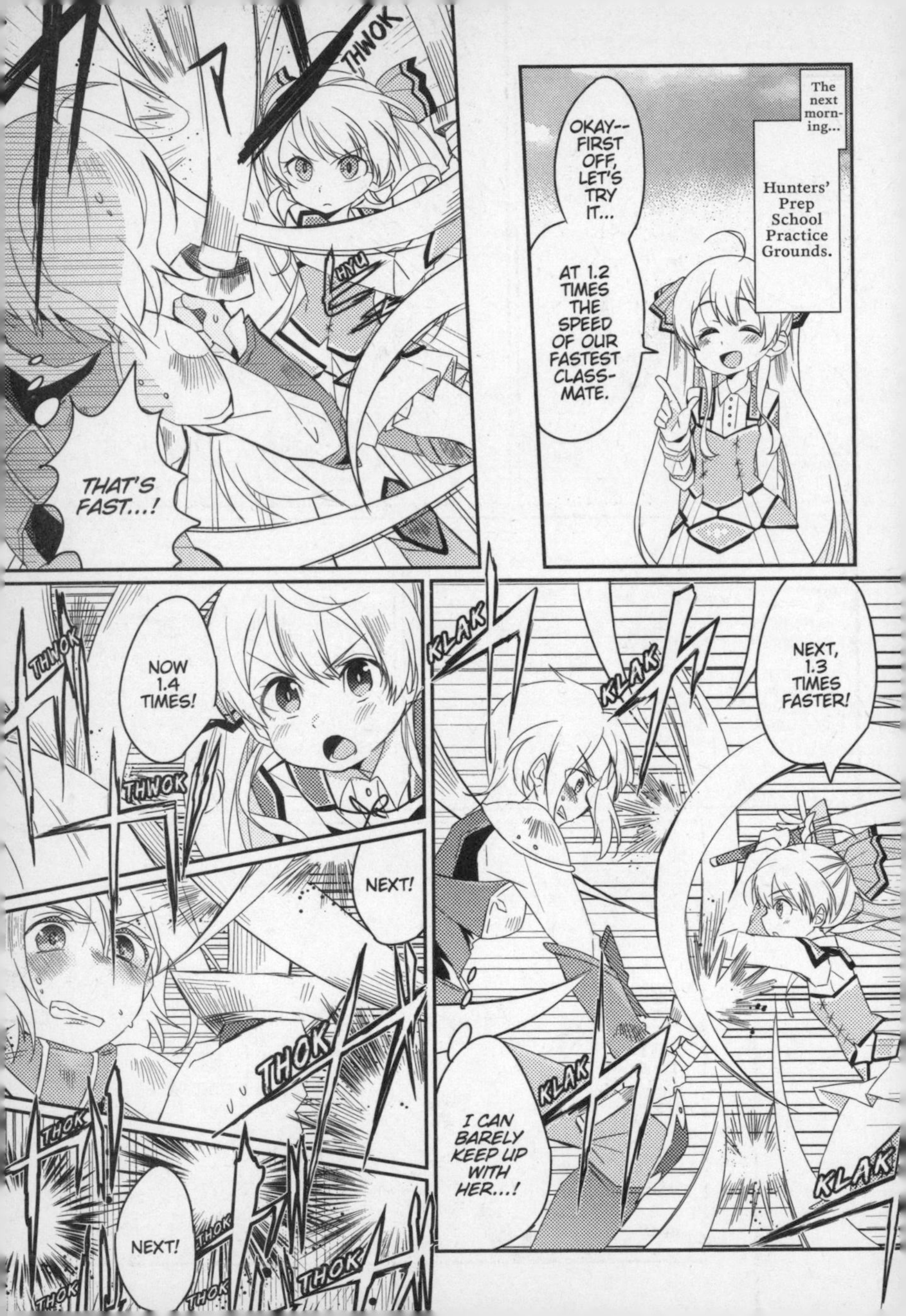
The next morning...
Hunters' Prep School Practice Grounds.
OKAY--FIRST OFF, LET'S TRY IT...
AT 1.2 TIMES THE SPEED OF OUR FASTEST CLASS-MATE.
THWOK
HYU
THAT'S FAST...!
NEXT, 1.3 TIMES FASTER!
KLAK
KLAK
KLAK
I CAN BARELY KEEP UP WITH HER...!
KLAK
NOW 1.4 TIMES!
THWOK
THWOK
NEXT!
THOK
THOK
NEXT!
THOK
THOK
THOK
THOK

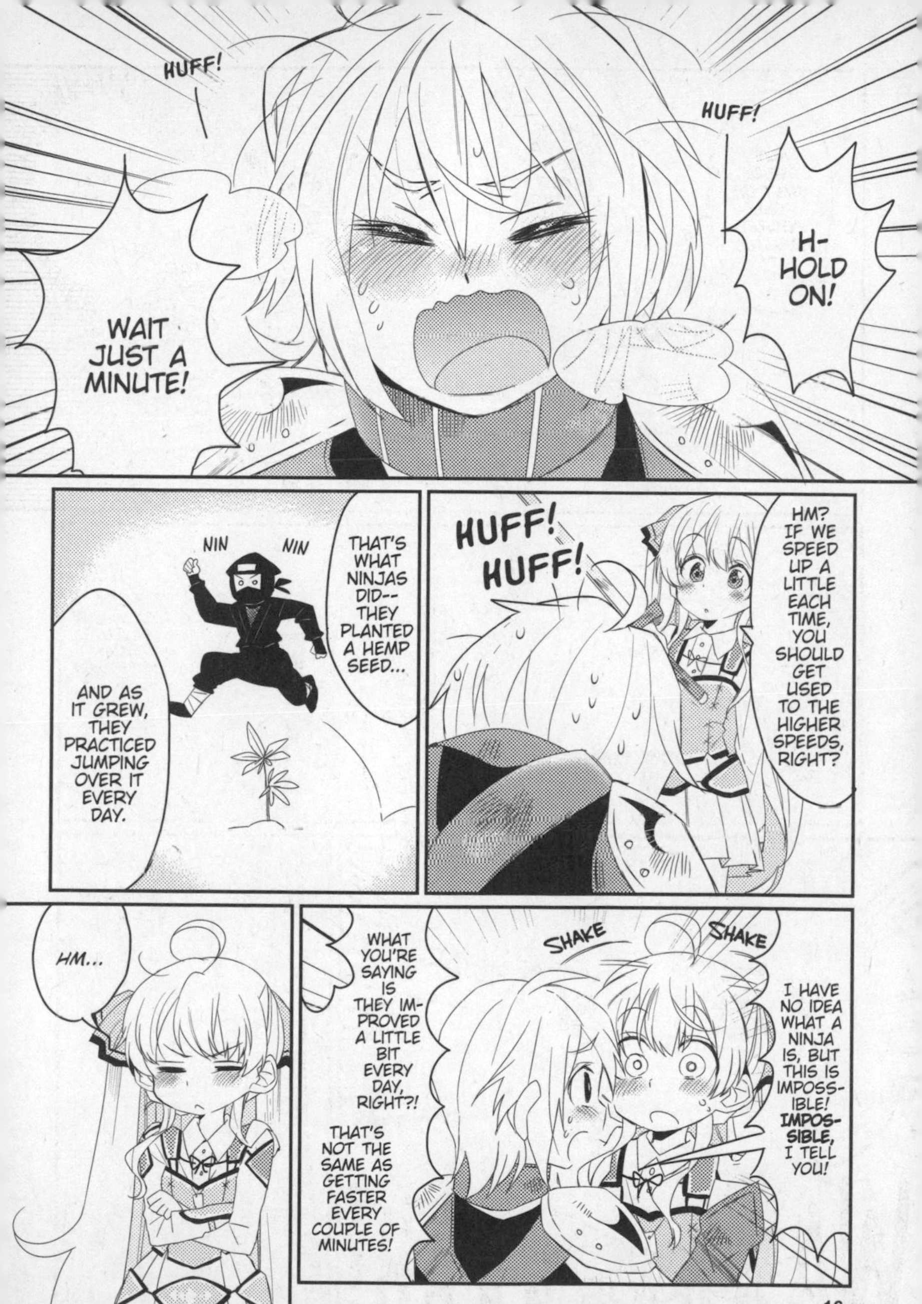
HUFF!
HUFF!
H-HOLD ON!
WAIT JUST A MINUTE!
HM? IF WE SPEED UP A LITTLE EACH TIME, YOU SHOULD GET USED TO THE HIGHER SPEEDS, RIGHT?
HUFF! HUFF!
THAT'S WHAT NINJAS DID--THEY PLANTED A HEMP SEED...
NIN NIN
AND AS IT GREW, THEY PRACTICED JUMPING OVER IT EVERY DAY.
SHAKE SHAKE
I HAVE NO IDEA WHAT A NINJA IS, BUT THIS IS IMPOSSIBLE! **IMPOSSIBLE,** I TELL YOU!
WHAT YOU'RE SAYING IS THEY IMPROVED A LITTLE BIT EVERY DAY, RIGHT?!
THAT'S NOT THE SAME AS GETTING FASTER EVERY COUPLE OF MINUTES!
HM...

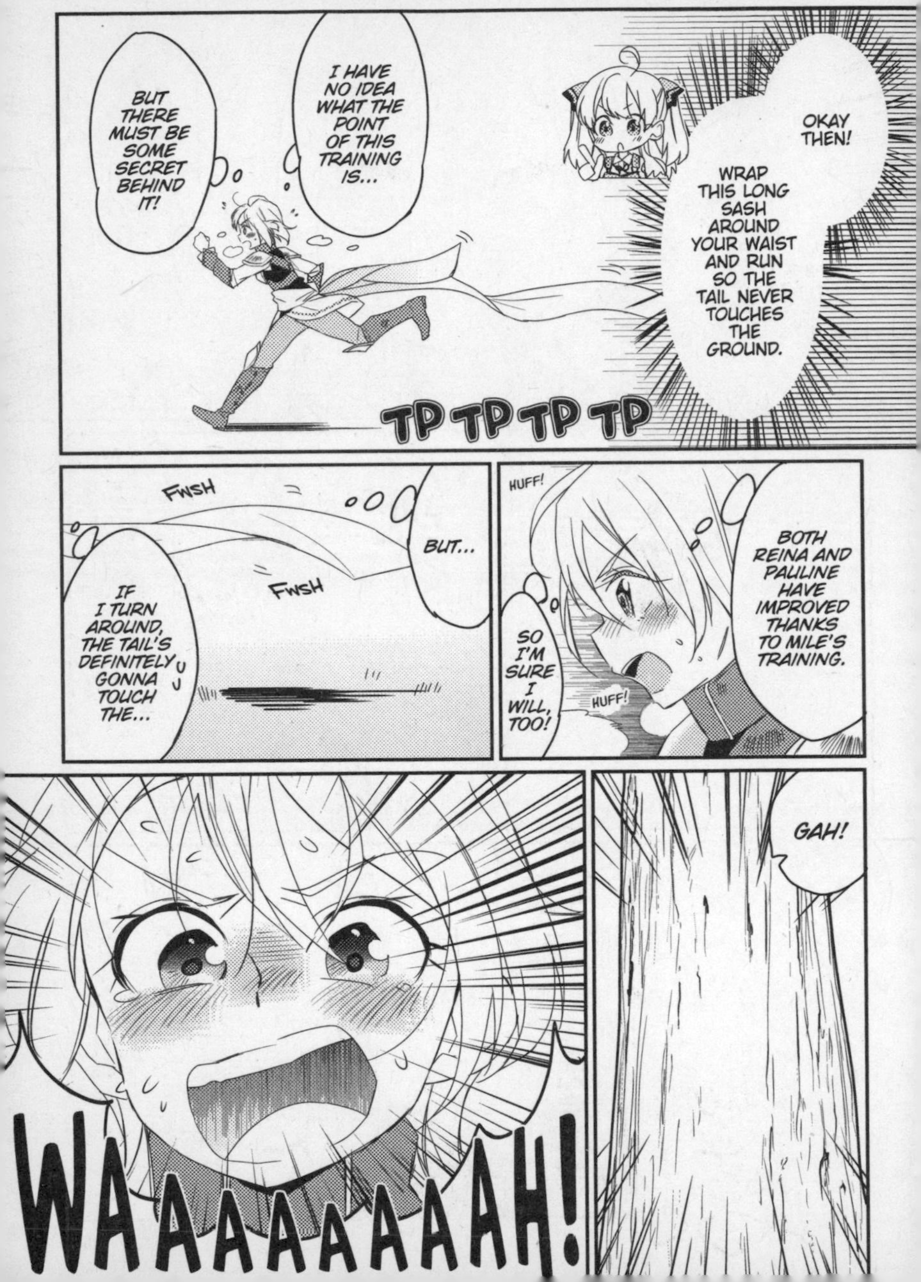
OKAY THEN!
WRAP THIS LONG SASH AROUND YOUR WAIST AND RUN SO THE TAIL NEVER TOUCHES THE GROUND.
I HAVE NO IDEA WHAT THE POINT OF THIS TRAINING IS...
BUT THERE MUST BE SOME SECRET BEHIND IT!
TP TP TP TP
HUFF!
BOTH REINA AND PAULINE HAVE IMPROVED THANKS TO MILE'S TRAINING.
SO I'M SURE I WILL, TOO!
HUFF!
FWSH
BUT...
FWSH
IF I TURN AROUND, THE TAIL'S DEFINITELY GONNA TOUCH THE...
GAH!
WAAAAAAAAH!

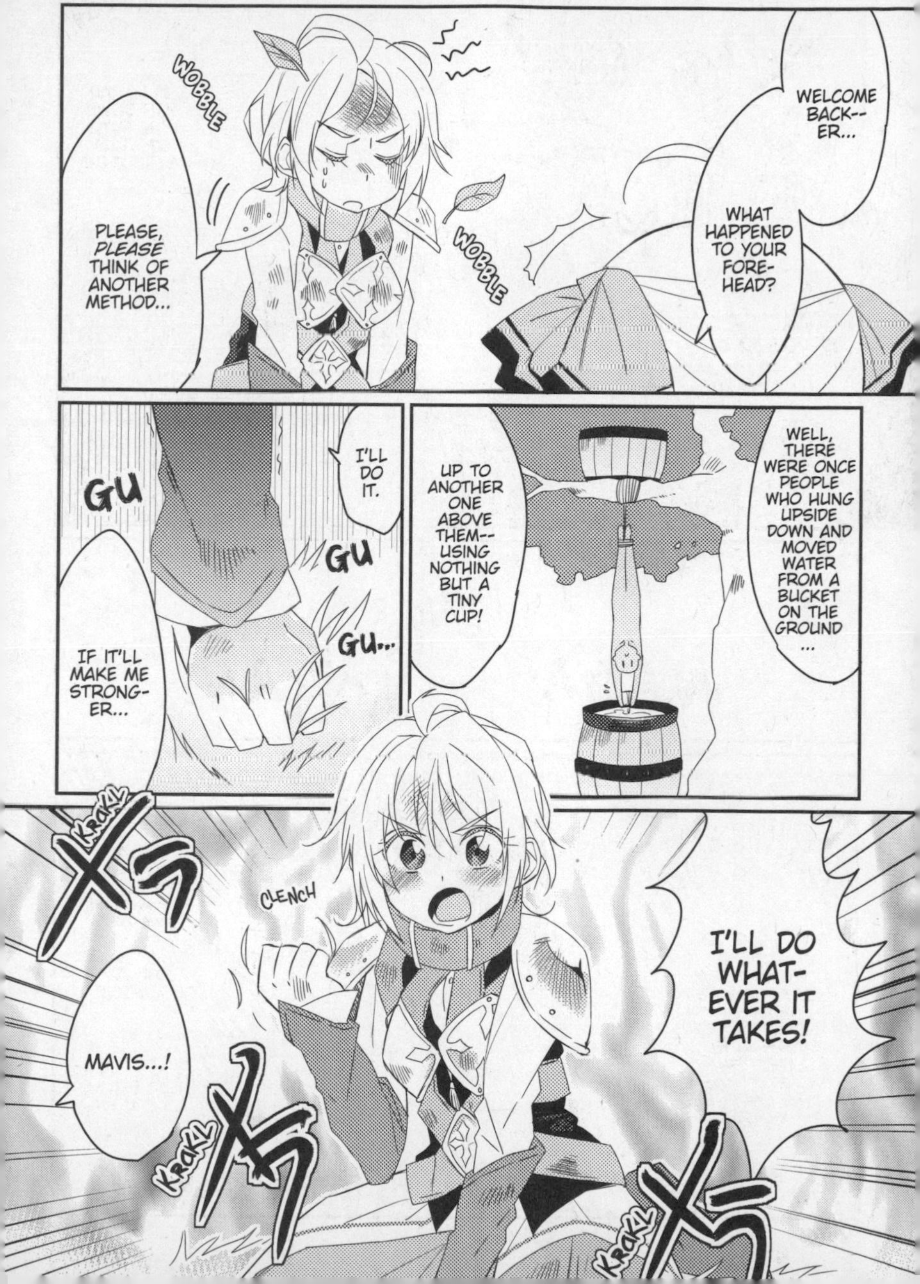
WELCOME BACK--ER...
WHAT HAPPENED TO YOUR FOREHEAD?
WOBBLE
WOBBLE
PLEASE, *PLEASE* THINK OF ANOTHER METHOD...
WELL, THERE WERE ONCE PEOPLE WHO HUNG UPSIDE DOWN AND MOVED WATER FROM A BUCKET ON THE GROUND ...
UP TO ANOTHER ONE ABOVE THEM--USING NOTHING BUT A TINY CUP!
I'LL DO IT.
GU
GU
GU...
IF IT'LL MAKE ME STRONGER...
I'LL DO WHATEVER IT TAKES!
CLENCH
MAVIS...!
KRAKL
KRAKL
KRAKL

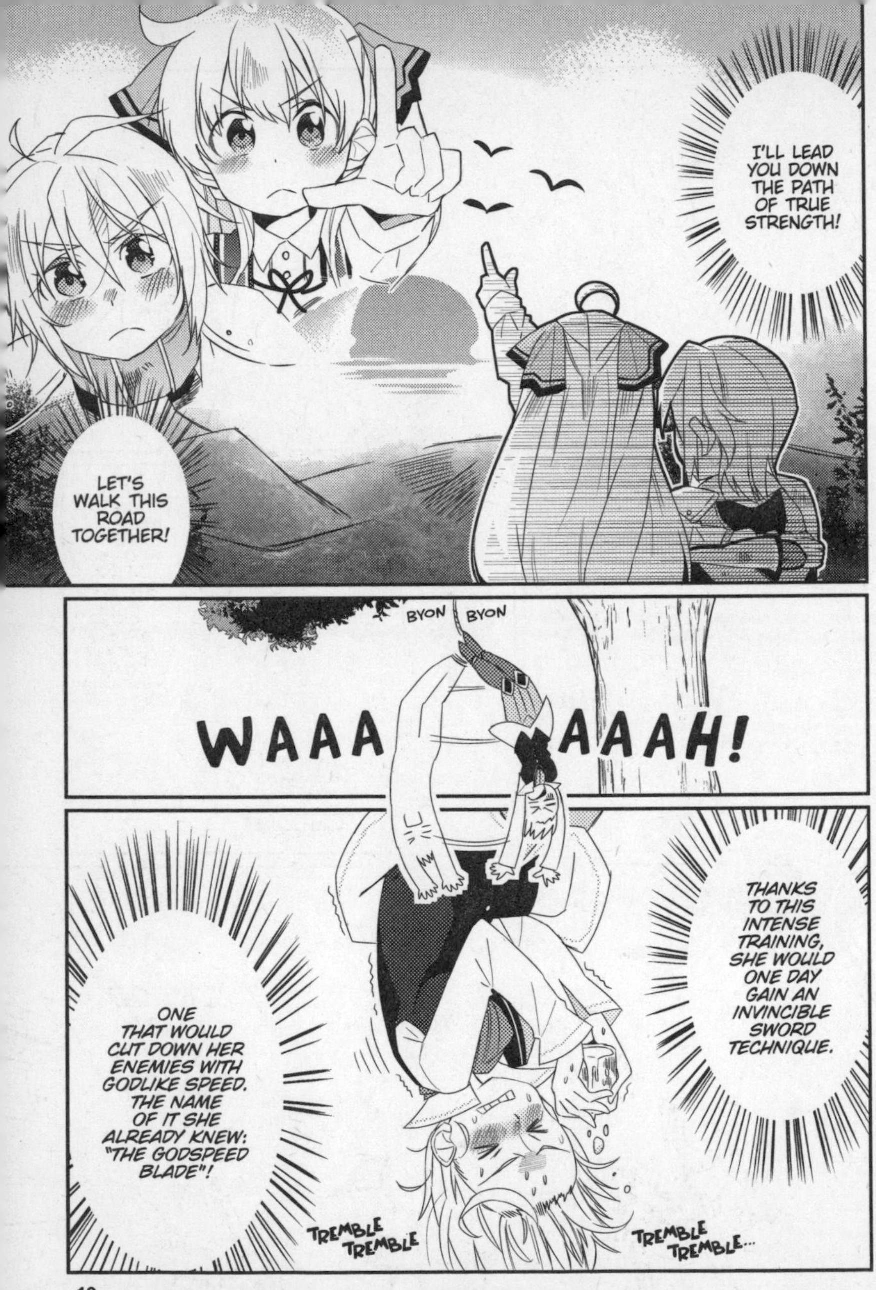
I'LL LEAD YOU DOWN THE PATH OF TRUE STRENGTH!
LET'S WALK THIS ROAD TOGETHER!
BYON BYON
WAAAAAAH!
THANKS TO THIS INTENSE TRAINING, SHE WOULD ONE DAY GAIN AN INVINCIBLE SWORD TECHNIQUE.
ONE THAT WOULD CUT DOWN HER ENEMIES WITH GODLIKE SPEED. THE NAME OF IT SHE ALREADY KNEW: "THE GODSPEED BLADE"!
TREMBLE TREMBLE...
TREMBLE TREMBLE

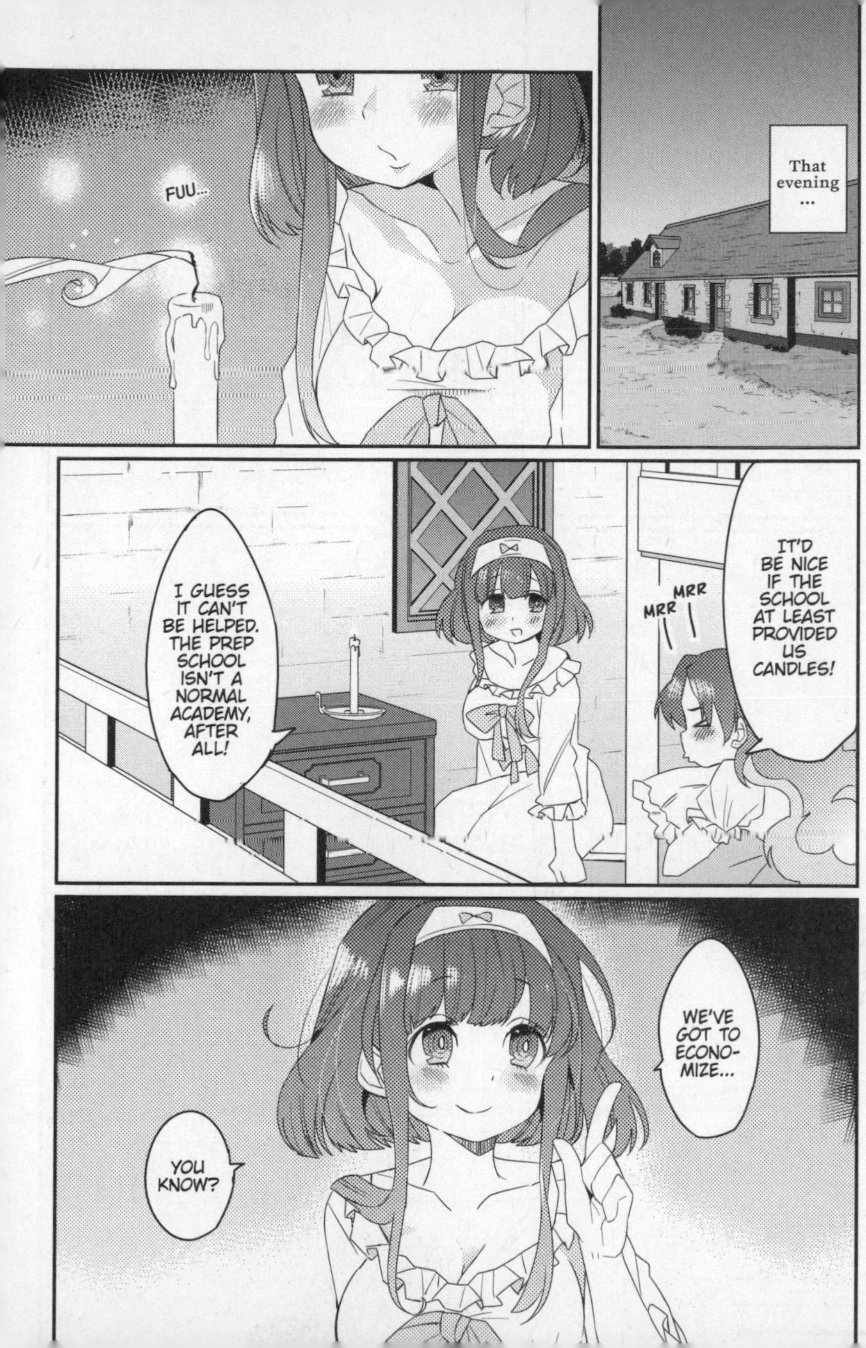
That evening ...
FUU...
IT'D BE NICE IF THE SCHOOL AT LEAST PROVIDED US CANDLES!
MRR MRR
I GUESS IT CAN'T BE HELPED. THE PREP SCHOOL ISN'T A NORMAL ACADEMY, AFTER ALL!
WE'VE GOT TO ECONO-MIZE...
YOU KNOW?

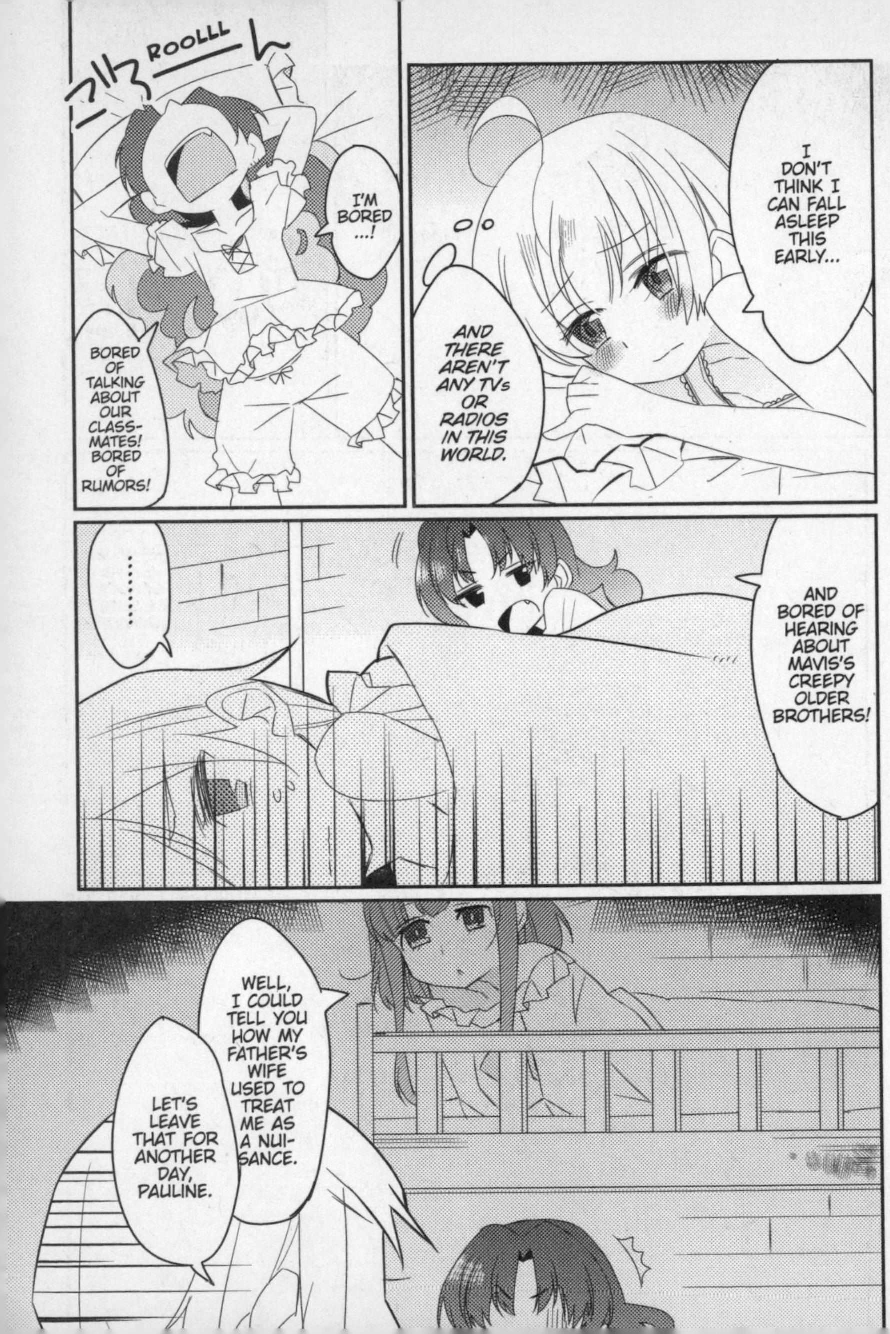
I DON'T THINK I CAN FALL ASLEEP THIS EARLY...
AND THERE AREN'T ANY TVs OR RADIOS IN THIS WORLD.
ROOLLL
I'M BORED ...!
BORED OF TALKING ABOUT OUR CLASS-MATES! BORED OF RUMORS!
AND BORED OF HEARING ABOUT MAVIS'S CREEPY OLDER BROTHERS!
......
WELL, I COULD TELL YOU HOW MY FATHER'S WIFE USED TO TREAT ME AS A NUI-SANCE.
LET'S LEAVE THAT FOR ANOTHER DAY, PAULINE.

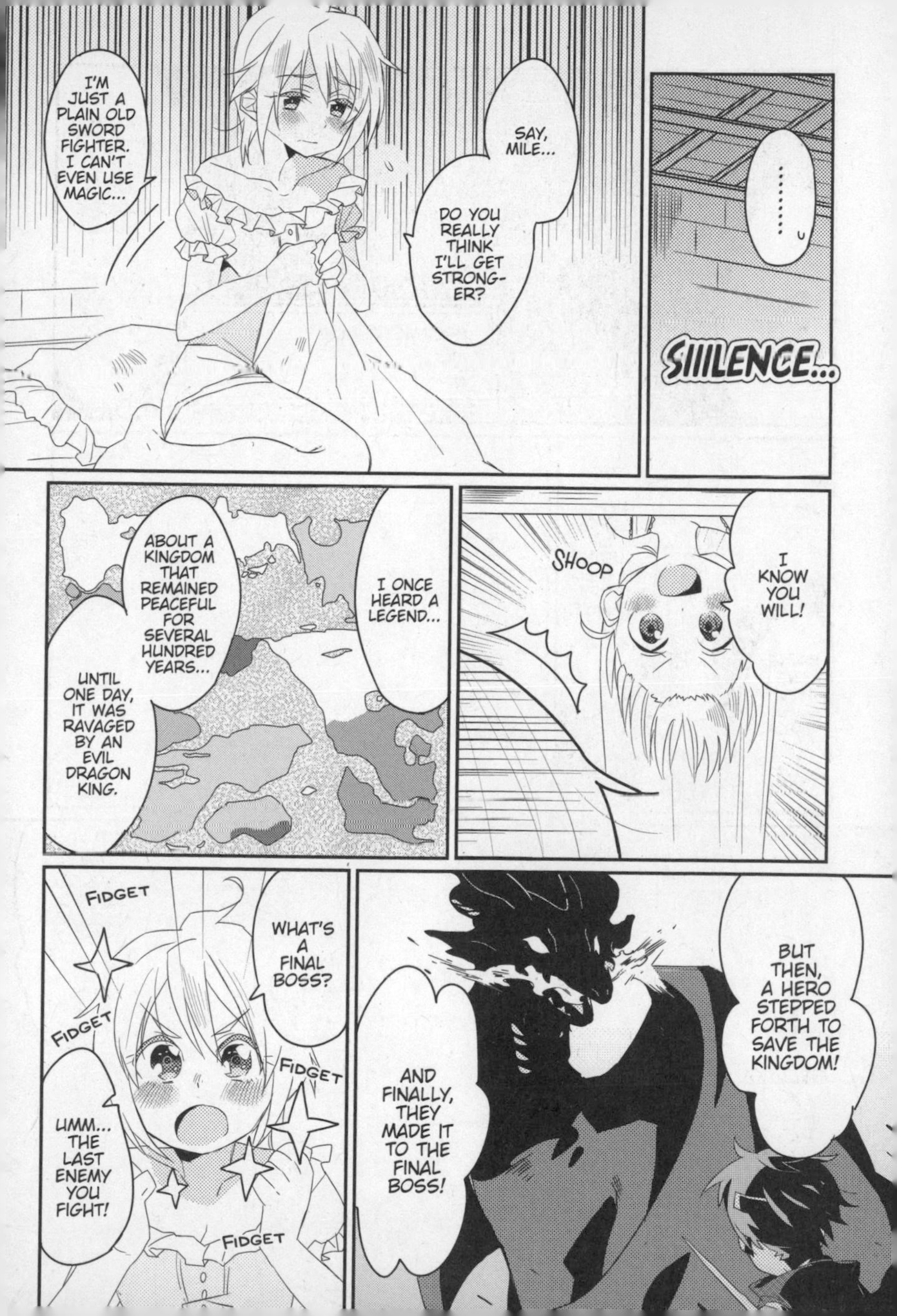
......
SIIILENCE...
SAY, MILE...
DO YOU REALLY THINK I'LL GET STRONGER?
I'M JUST A PLAIN OLD SWORD FIGHTER. I CAN'T EVEN USE MAGIC...
I KNOW YOU WILL!
SHOOP
I ONCE HEARD A LEGEND...
ABOUT A KINGDOM THAT REMAINED PEACEFUL FOR SEVERAL HUNDRED YEARS...
UNTIL ONE DAY, IT WAS RAVAGED BY AN EVIL DRAGON KING.
BUT THEN, A HERO STEPPED FORTH TO SAVE THE KINGDOM!
AND FINALLY, THEY MADE IT TO THE FINAL BOSS!
FIDGET
WHAT'S A FINAL BOSS?
FIDGET
FIDGET
UMM... THE LAST ENEMY YOU FIGHT!
FIDGET

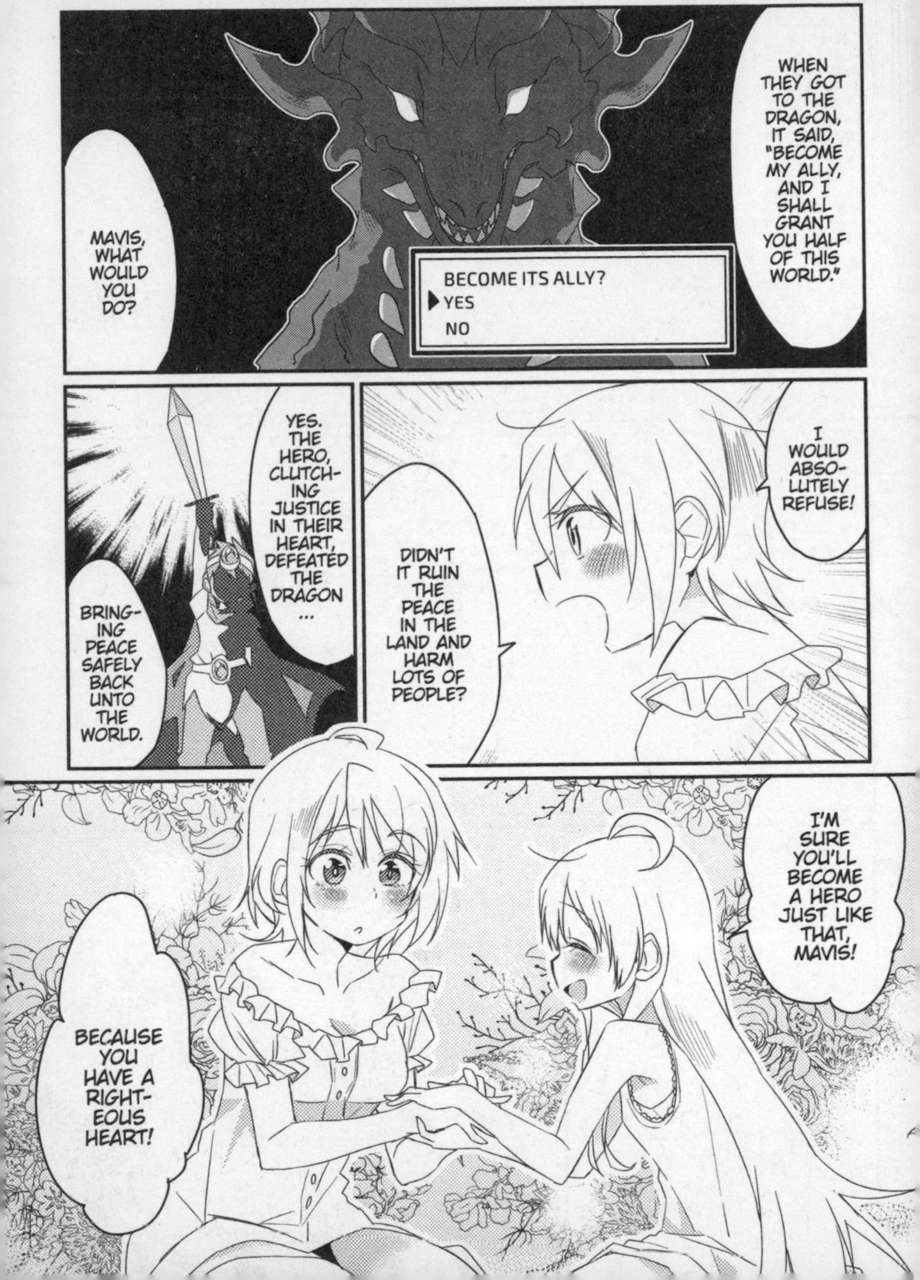
WHEN THEY GOT TO THE DRAGON, IT SAID, "BECOME MY ALLY, AND I SHALL GRANT YOU HALF OF THIS WORLD."
BECOME ITS ALLY?
▶YES
NO
MAVIS, WHAT WOULD YOU DO?
I WOULD ABSOLUTELY REFUSE!
DIDN'T IT RUIN THE PEACE IN THE LAND AND HARM LOTS OF PEOPLE?
YES. THE HERO, CLUTCHING JUSTICE IN THEIR HEART, DEFEATED THE DRAGON...
BRINGING PEACE SAFELY BACK UNTO THE WORLD.
I'M SURE YOU'LL BECOME A HERO JUST LIKE THAT, MAVIS!
BECAUSE YOU HAVE A RIGHTEOUS HEART!

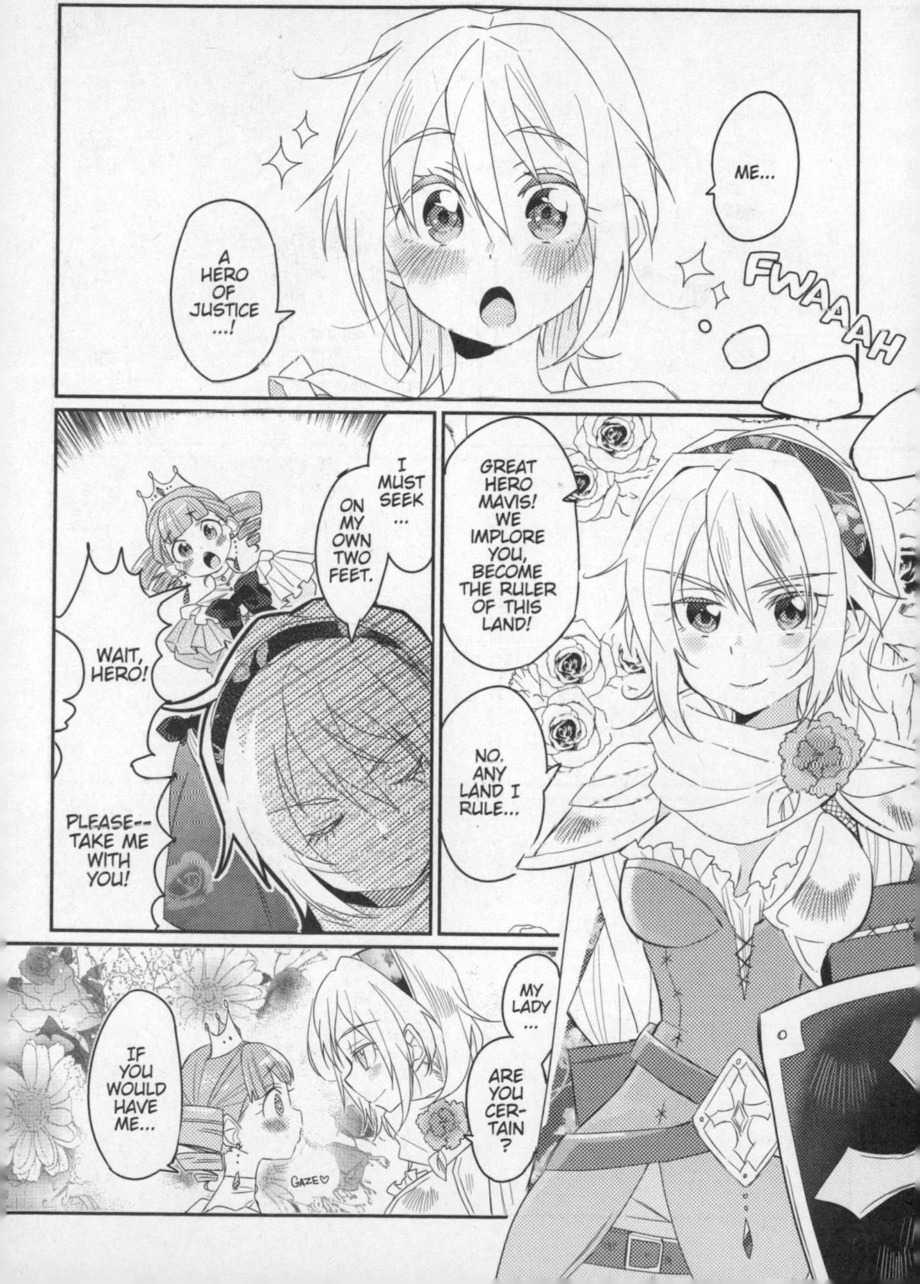
ME...
FWAAAAH
A HERO OF JUSTICE ...!
GREAT HERO MAVIS! WE IMPLORE YOU, BECOME THE RULER OF THIS LAND!
NO. ANY LAND I RULE...
I MUST SEEK ... ON MY OWN TWO FEET.
WAIT, HERO!
PLEASE-- TAKE ME WITH YOU!
MY LADY ...
ARE YOU CER-TAIN ?
IF YOU WOULD HAVE ME...
GAZE♡

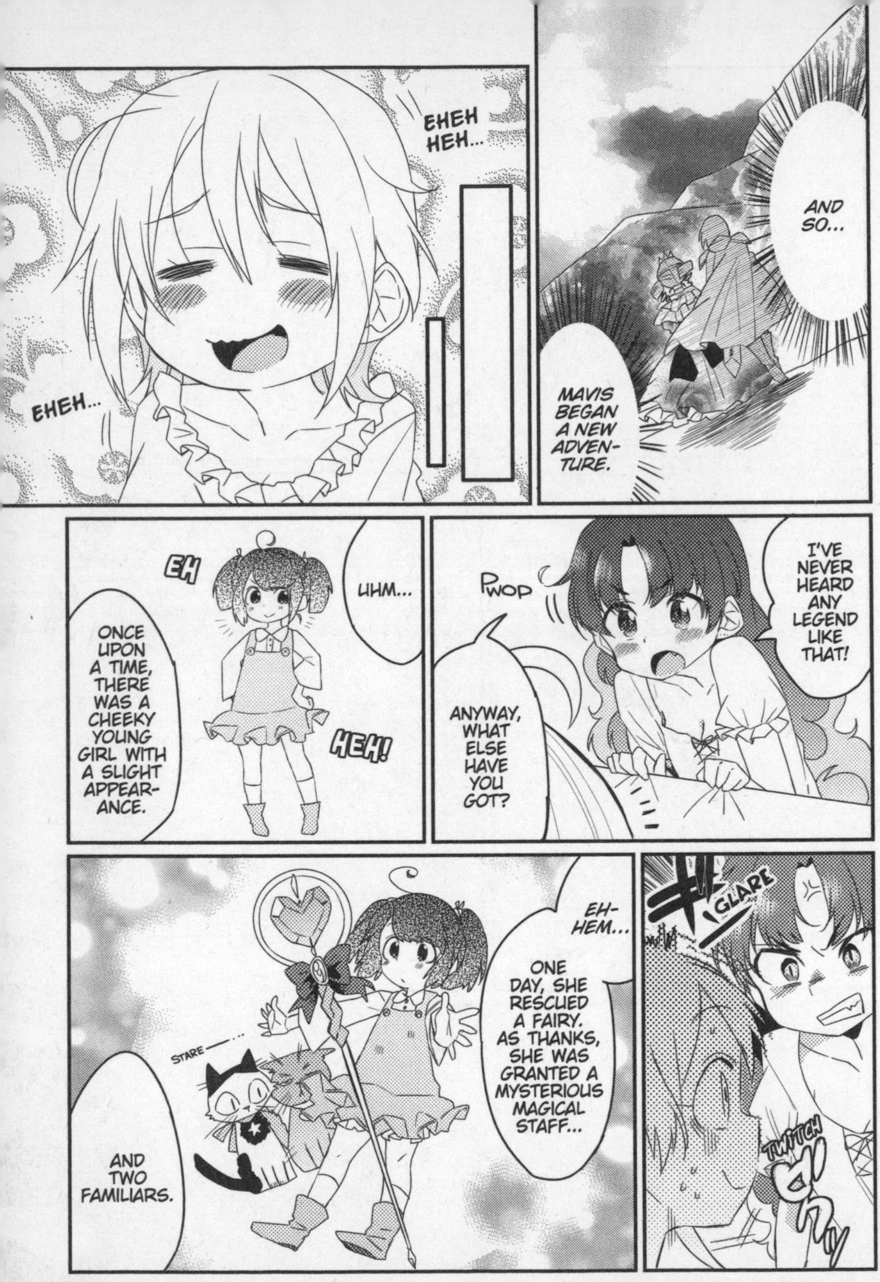
AND SO...
MAVIS BEGAN A NEW ADVENTURE.
EHEH HEH...
EHEH...
PWOP
I'VE NEVER HEARD ANY LEGEND LIKE THAT!
ANYWAY, WHAT ELSE HAVE YOU GOT?
UHM...
EH
HEH!
ONCE UPON A TIME, THERE WAS A CHEEKY YOUNG GIRL WITH A SLIGHT APPEARANCE.
GLARE
TWITCH
EH-HEM...
ONE DAY, SHE RESCUED A FAIRY. AS THANKS, SHE WAS GRANTED A MYSTERIOUS MAGICAL STAFF...
STARE
AND TWO FAMILIARS.

THE GIRL USED THE STAFF'S POWER TO TAKE AN ADULT FORM. SHE WENT WALKING THROUGH TOWN, AND THAT WAS WHEN...
"YOU THERE, BEAUTIFUL YOUNG WOMAN! WON'T YOU BECOME THE OFFICIAL SONGSTRESS OF THE CAPITAL?"
Twing
Twing
I'VE NEVER HEARD OF A MAGIC THAT CAN MAKE YOU GROW!
THAT'S THE POWER OF THE MYSTERIOUS STAFF, I BET!
HA HA HA HA HA!
WELL... I HAVE NO NEED FOR SUCH MAGIC.
PFFT!
FuMe
FuMe
BUT...
IF I DID HAVE A STAFF LIKE THAT...
GRIN GRIN
KICK KICK
FWAAAH

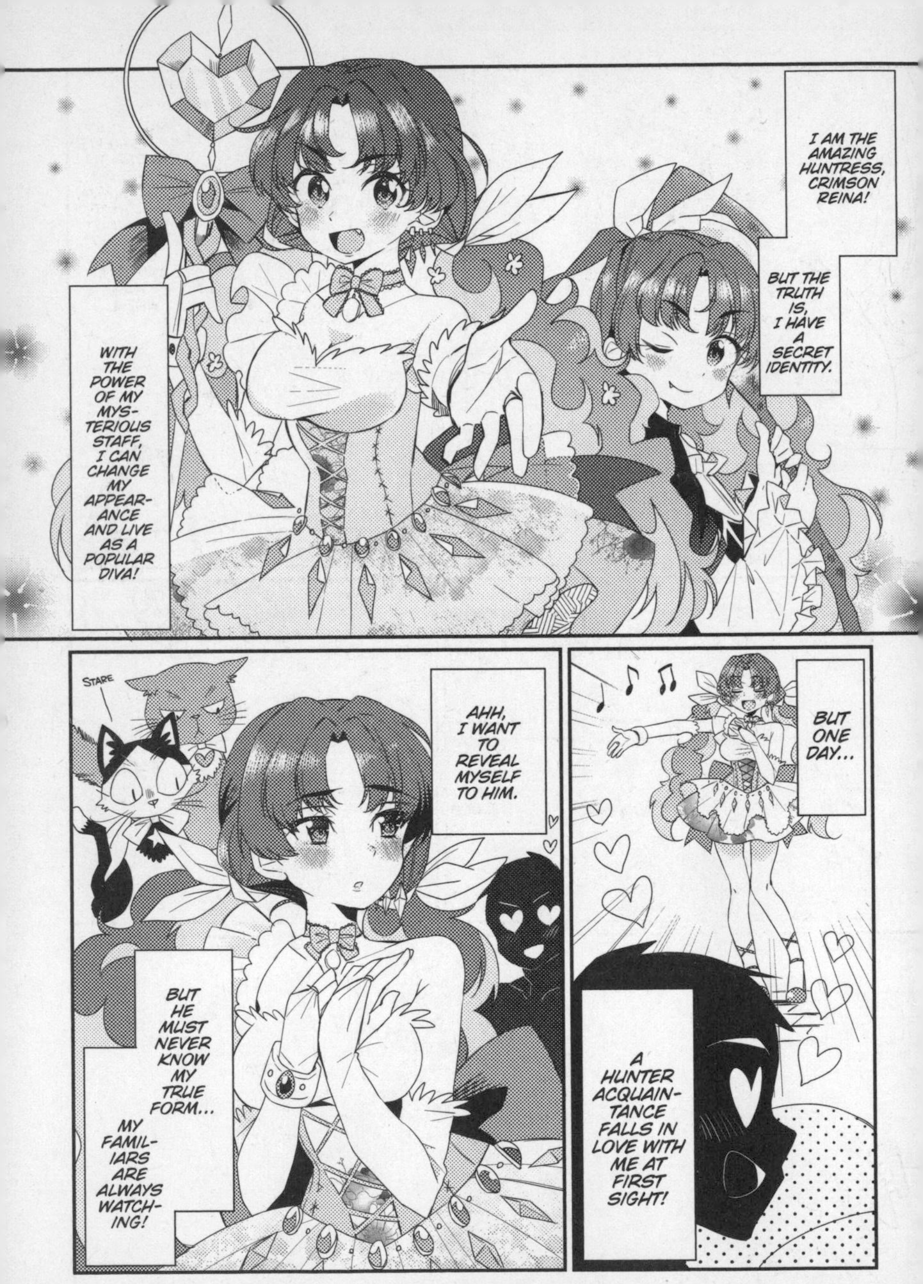
I AM THE AMAZING HUNTRESS, CRIMSON REINA!
BUT THE TRUTH IS, I HAVE A SECRET IDENTITY.
WITH THE POWER OF MY MYSTERIOUS STAFF, I CAN CHANGE MY APPEARANCE AND LIVE AS A POPULAR DIVA!
BUT ONE DAY...
A HUNTER ACQUAINTANCE FALLS IN LOVE WITH ME AT FIRST SIGHT!
AHH, I WANT TO REVEAL MYSELF TO HIM.
STARE
BUT HE MUST NEVER KNOW MY TRUE FORM...
MY FAMILIARS ARE ALWAYS WATCHING!

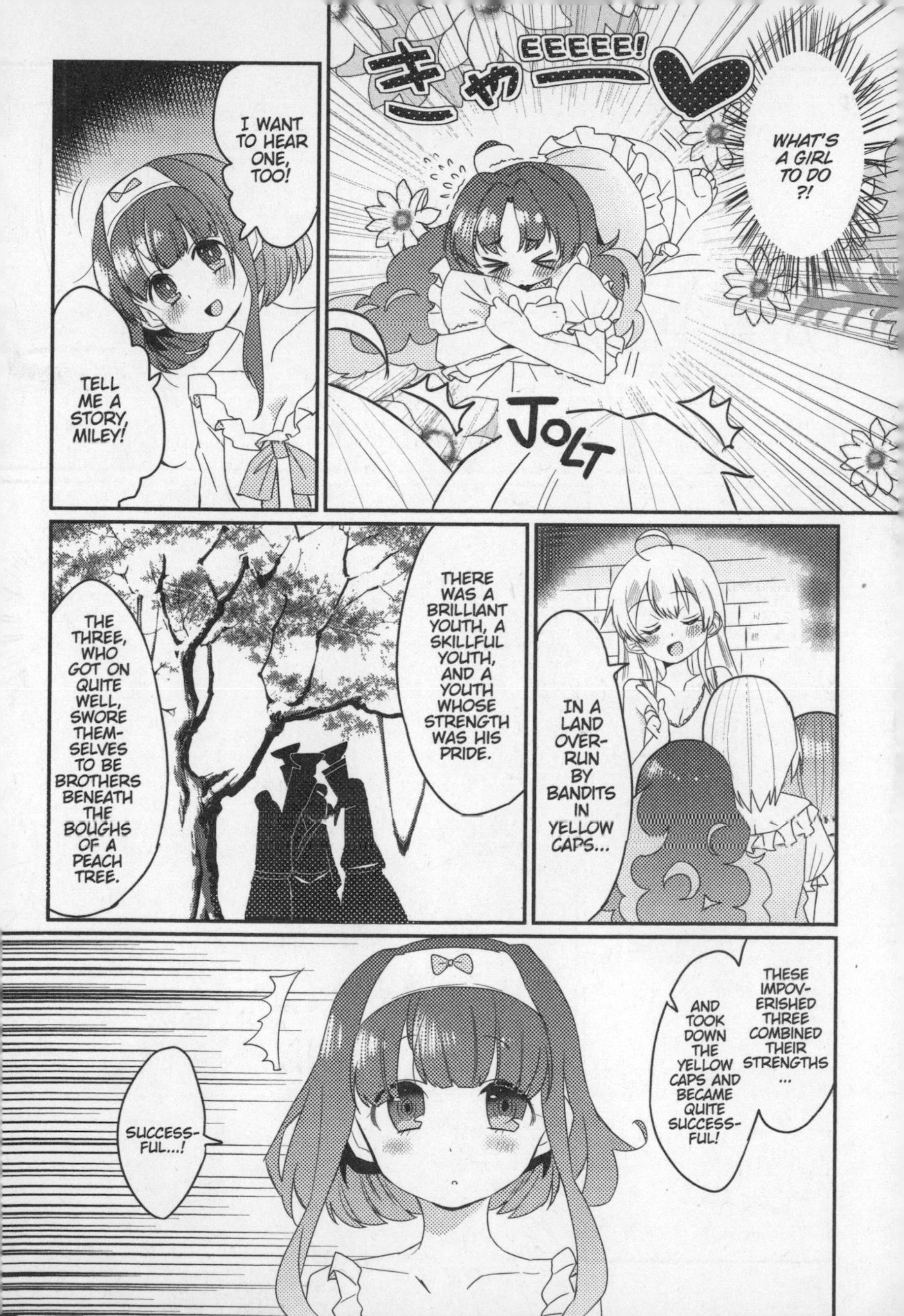
きゃーーー EEEEEE!
WHAT'S A GIRL TO DO ?!
JOLT
I WANT TO HEAR ONE, TOO!
TELL ME A STORY, MILEY!
IN A LAND OVER-RUN BY BANDITS IN YELLOW CAPS...
THERE WAS A BRILLIANT YOUTH, A SKILLFUL YOUTH, AND A YOUTH WHOSE STRENGTH WAS HIS PRIDE.
THE THREE, WHO GOT ON QUITE WELL, SWORE THEM-SELVES TO BE BROTHERS BENEATH THE BOUGHS OF A PEACH TREE.
THESE IMPOV-ERISHED THREE COMBINED THEIR STRENGTHS ...
AND TOOK DOWN THE YELLOW CAPS AND BECAME QUITE SUCCESS-FUL!
SUCCESS-FUL...!

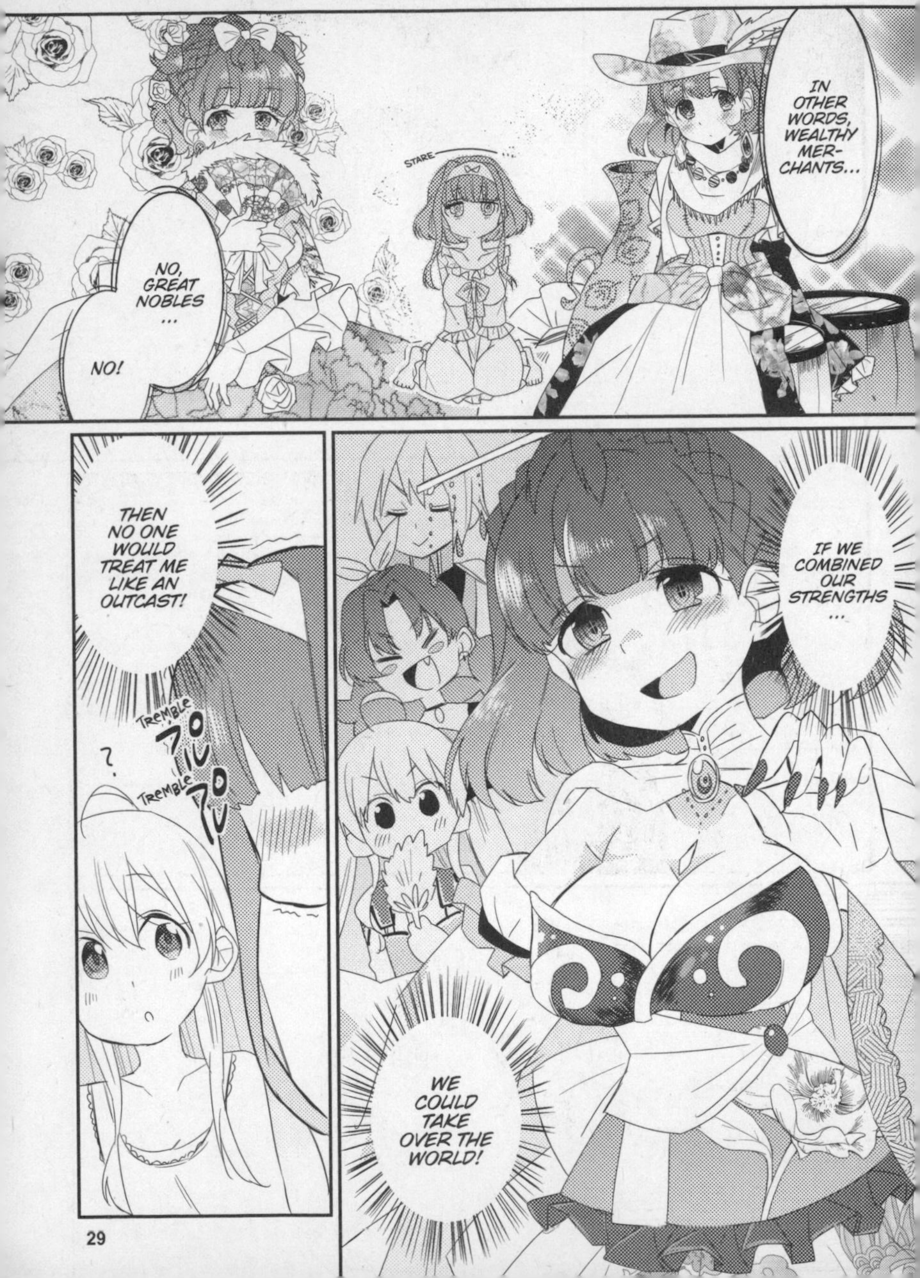
IN OTHER WORDS, WEALTHY MER-CHANTS...
STARE
NO, GREAT NOBLES ...
NO!
IF WE COMBINED OUR STRENGTHS ...
WE COULD TAKE OVER THE WORLD!
THEN NO ONE WOULD TREAT ME LIKE AN OUTCAST!
プルプル
TREMBLE TREMBLE
?

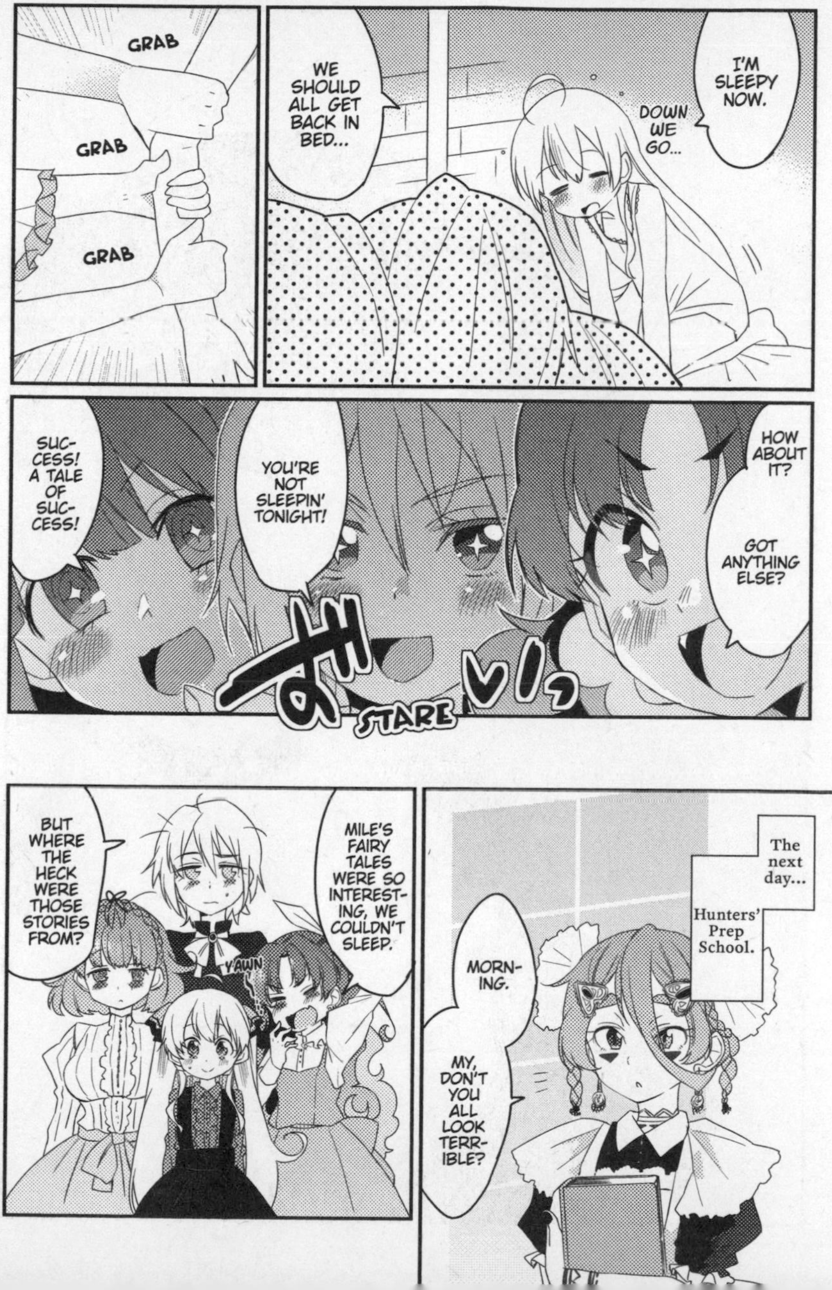
I'M SLEEPY NOW.
DOWN WE GO...
WE SHOULD ALL GET BACK IN BED...
GRAB
GRAB
GRAB
HOW ABOUT IT?
GOT ANYTHING ELSE?
YOU'RE NOT SLEEPIN' TONIGHT!
SUC-CESS! A TALE OF SUC-CESS!
STARE
The next day...
Hunters' Prep School.
MORNING.
MY, DON'T YOU ALL LOOK TERRIBLE?
MILE'S FAIRY TALES WERE SO INTEREST-ING, WE COULDN'T SLEEP.
YAWN
BUT WHERE THE HECK WERE THOSE STORIES FROM?

Chapter 8: The Orphan Boy

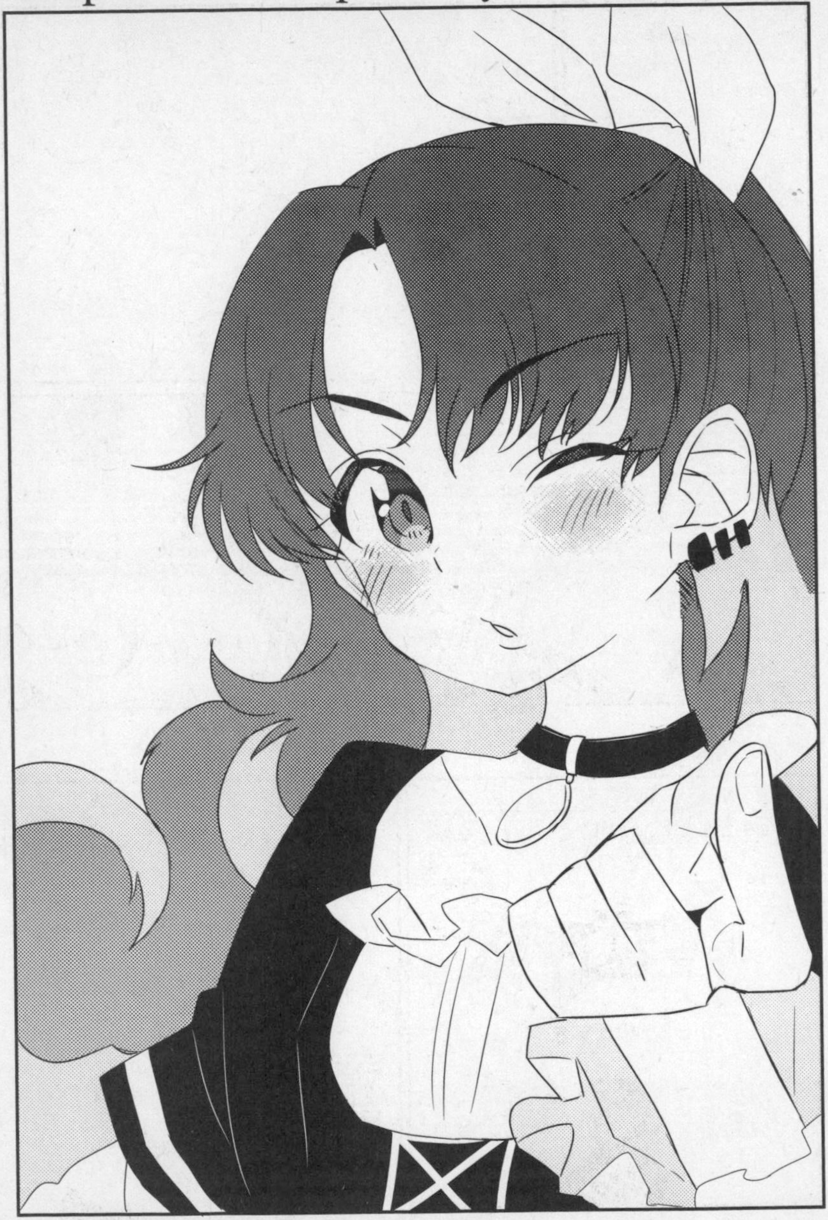

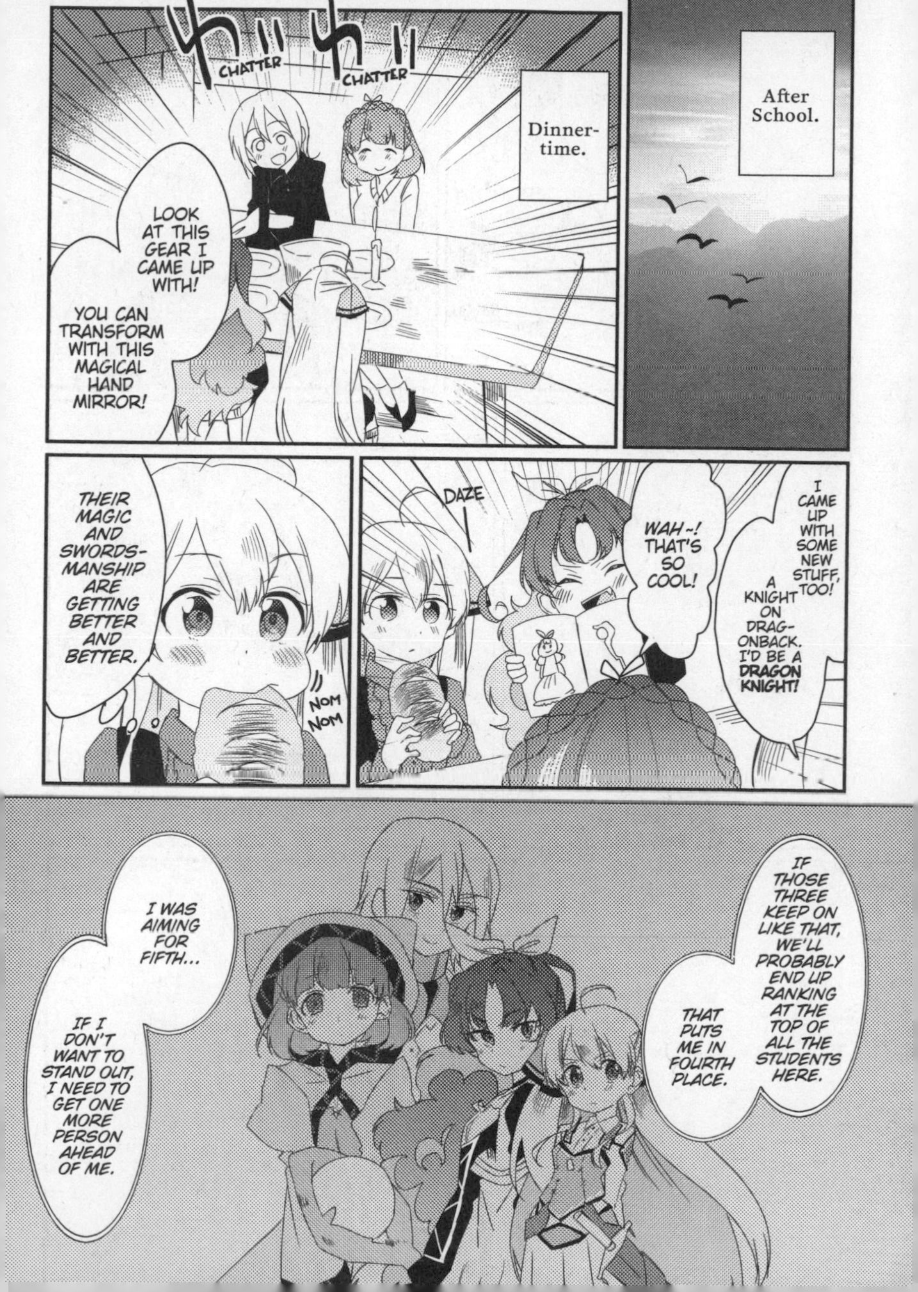
After School.
Dinner-time.
CHATTER CHATTER
LOOK AT THIS GEAR I CAME UP WITH!
YOU CAN TRANSFORM WITH THIS MAGICAL HAND MIRROR!
I CAME UP WITH SOME NEW STUFF, TOO!
A KNIGHT ON DRAGONBACK. I'D BE A DRAGON KNIGHT!
WAH~! THAT'S SO COOL!
DAZE
THEIR MAGIC AND SWORDSMANSHIP ARE GETTING BETTER AND BETTER.
NOM NOM
IF THOSE THREE KEEP ON LIKE THAT, WE'LL PROBABLY END UP RANKING AT THE TOP OF ALL THE STUDENTS HERE.
THAT PUTS ME IN FOURTH PLACE.
I WAS AIMING FOR FIFTH...
IF I DON'T WANT TO STAND OUT, I NEED TO GET ONE MORE PERSON AHEAD OF ME.

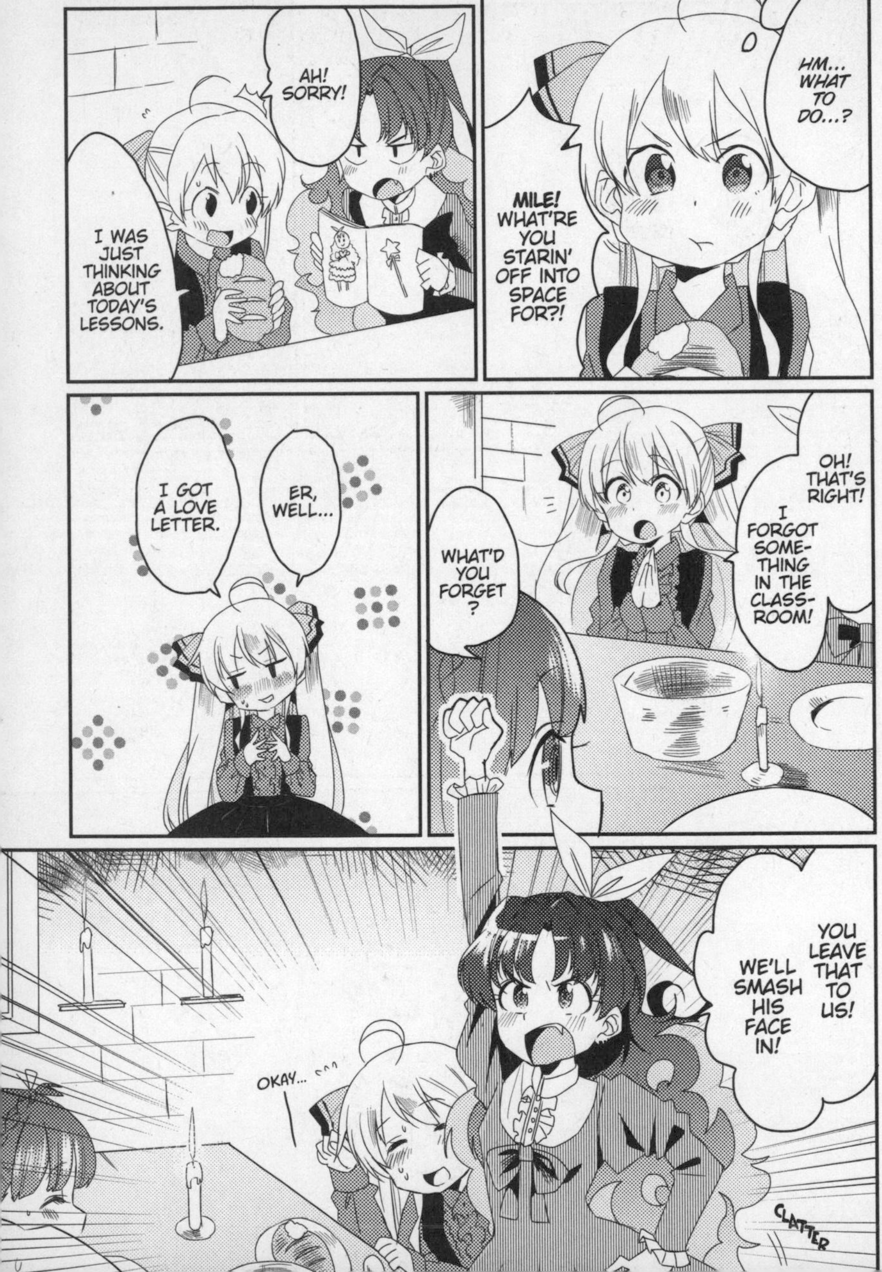
HM... WHAT TO DO...?
MILE! WHAT'RE YOU STARIN' OFF INTO SPACE FOR?!
AH! SORRY!
I WAS JUST THINKING ABOUT TODAY'S LESSONS.
OH! THAT'S RIGHT! I FORGOT SOME-THING IN THE CLASS-ROOM!
WHAT'D YOU FORGET?
ER, WELL...
I GOT A LOVE LETTER.
YOU LEAVE THAT TO US!
WE'LL SMASH HIS FACE IN!
CLATTER
OKAY...

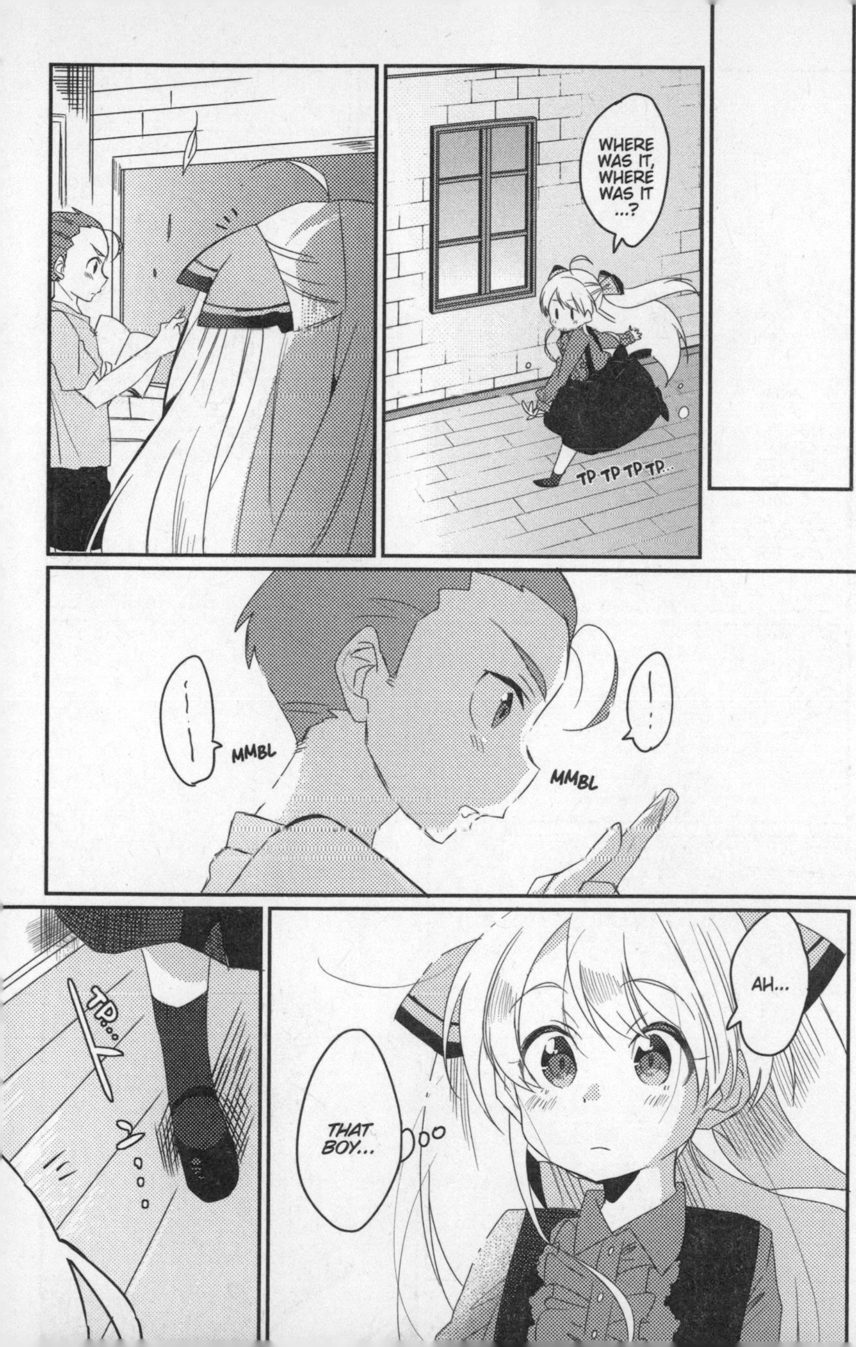
WHERE WAS IT, WHERE WAS IT ...?
TP TP TP TP...
!
MMBL
!
MMBL
AH...
THAT BOY...
TP...

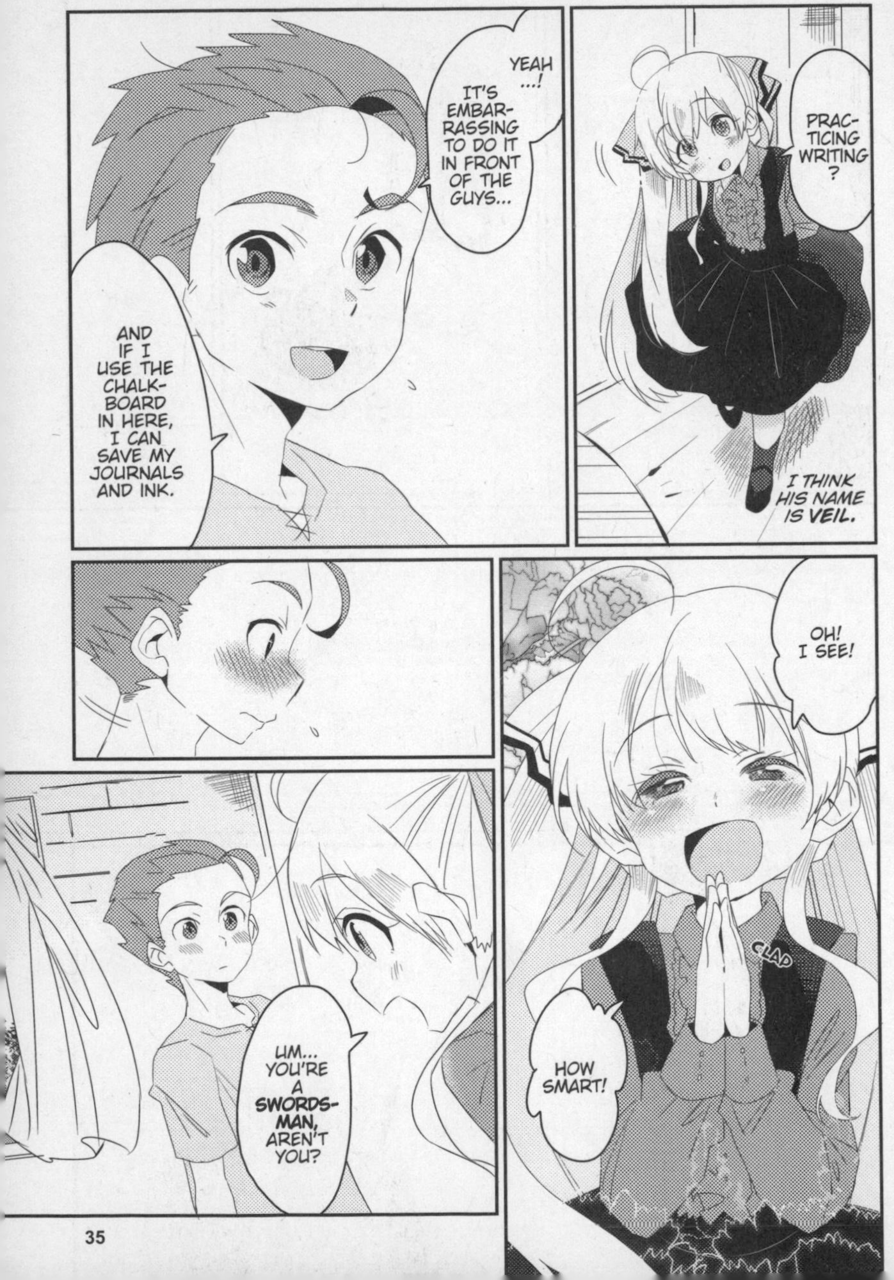
PRACTICING WRITING?
I THINK HIS NAME IS VEIL.
YEAH...! IT'S EMBARRASSING TO DO IT IN FRONT OF THE GUYS...
AND IF I USE THE CHALKBOARD IN HERE, I CAN SAVE MY JOURNALS AND INK.
OH! I SEE!
CLAP
HOW SMART!
UM... YOU'RE A SWORDSMAN, AREN'T YOU?

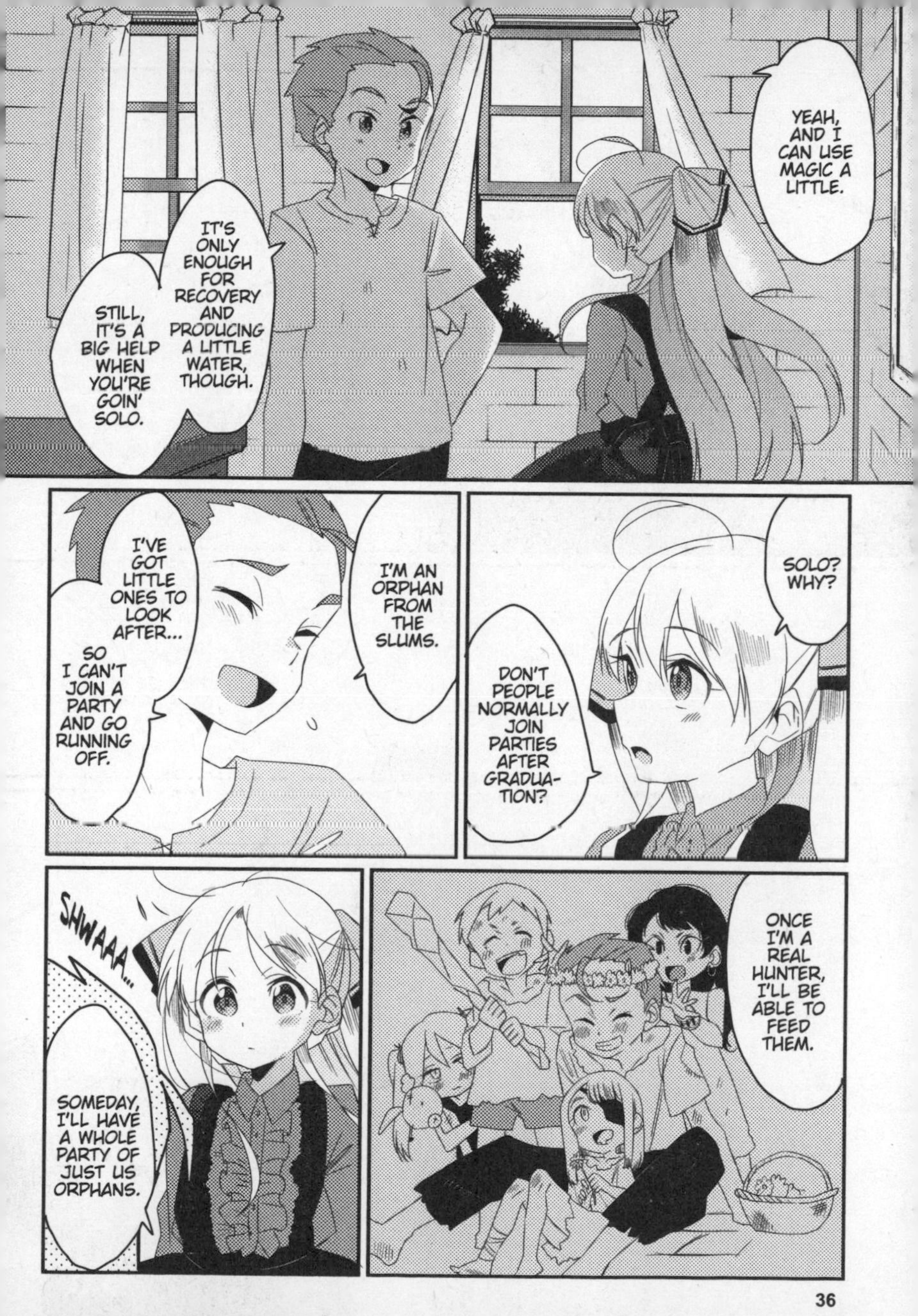
YEAH, AND I CAN USE MAGIC A LITTLE.
IT'S ONLY ENOUGH FOR RECOVERY AND PRODUCING A LITTLE WATER, THOUGH.
STILL, IT'S A BIG HELP WHEN YOU'RE GOIN' SOLO.
SOLO? WHY?
DON'T PEOPLE NORMALLY JOIN PARTIES AFTER GRADUATION?
I'M AN ORPHAN FROM THE SLUMS.
I'VE GOT LITTLE ONES TO LOOK AFTER...
SO I CAN'T JOIN A PARTY AND GO RUNNING OFF.
ONCE I'M A REAL HUNTER, I'LL BE ABLE TO FEED THEM.
SHWAAA...
SOMEDAY, I'LL HAVE A WHOLE PARTY OF JUST US ORPHANS.

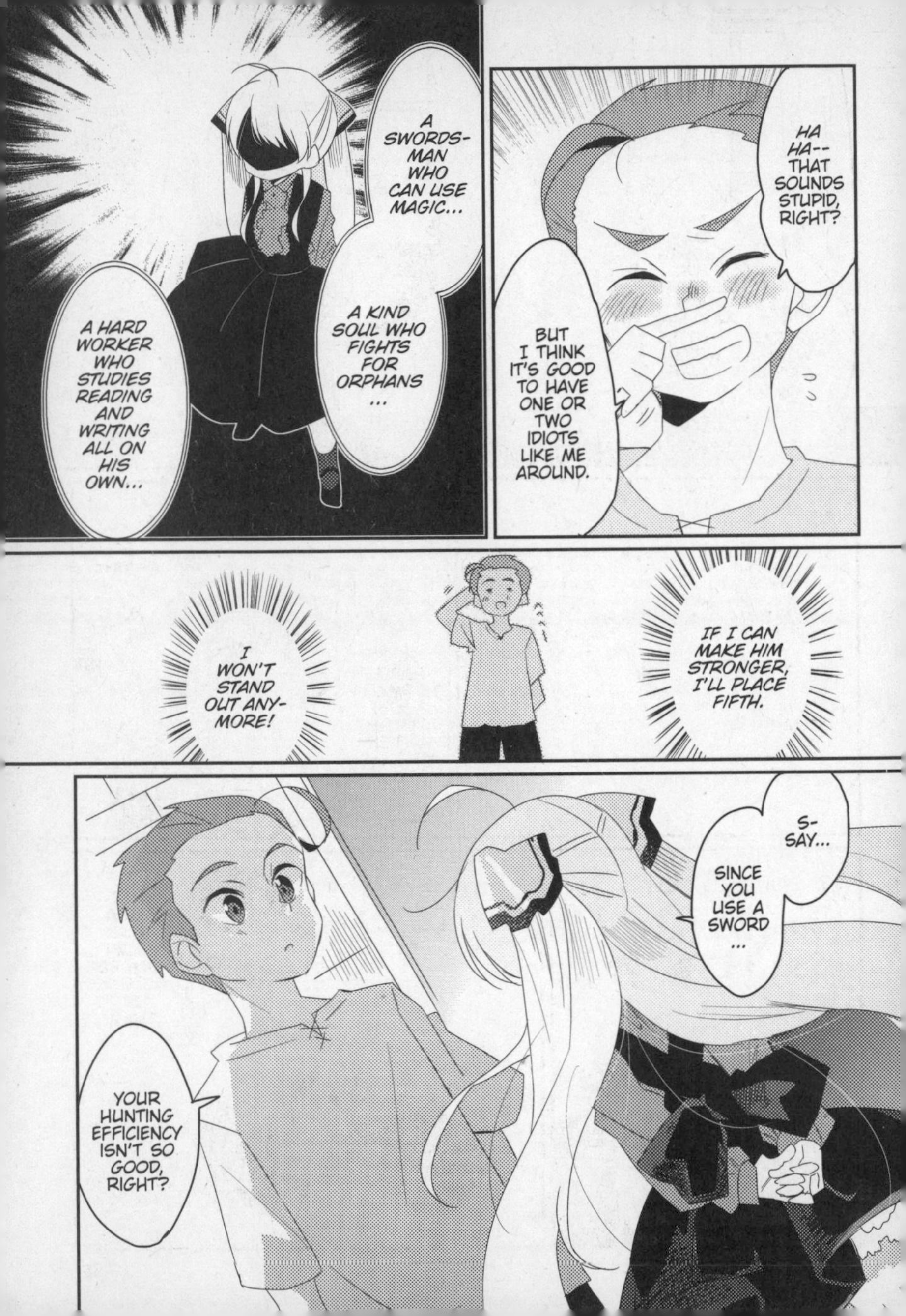
HA HA-- THAT SOUNDS STUPID, RIGHT?
BUT I THINK IT'S GOOD TO HAVE ONE OR TWO IDIOTS LIKE ME AROUND.
A SWORDS-MAN WHO CAN USE MAGIC...
A KIND SOUL WHO FIGHTS FOR ORPHANS...
A HARD WORKER WHO STUDIES READING AND WRITING ALL ON HIS OWN...
IF I CAN MAKE HIM STRONGER, I'LL PLACE FIFTH.
I WON'T STAND OUT ANY-MORE!
S-SAY...
SINCE YOU USE A SWORD...
YOUR HUNTING EFFICIENCY ISN'T SO GOOD, RIGHT?

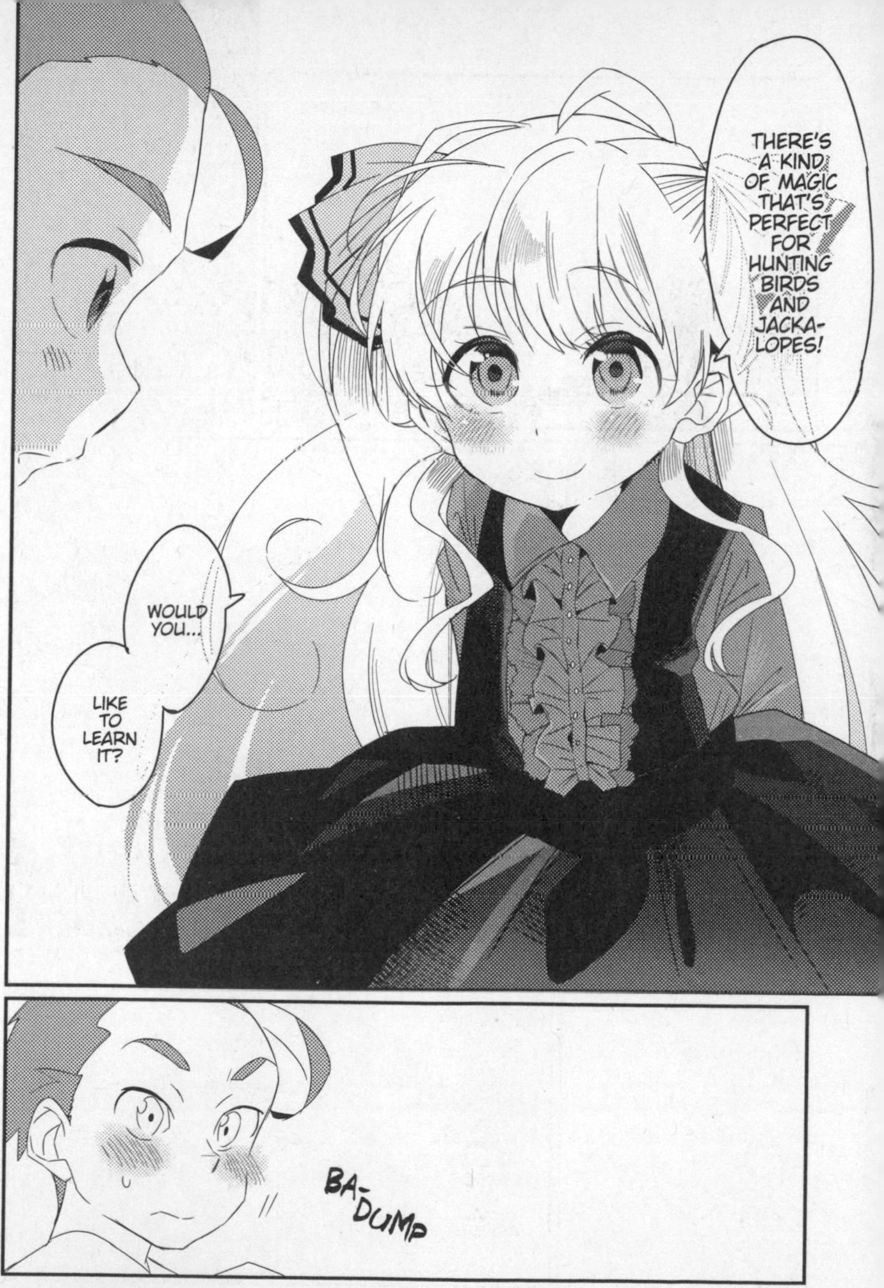
THERE'S A KIND OF MAGIC THAT'S PERFECT FOR HUNTING BIRDS AND JACKA-LOPES!
WOULD YOU...
LIKE TO LEARN IT?
BA-DUMP

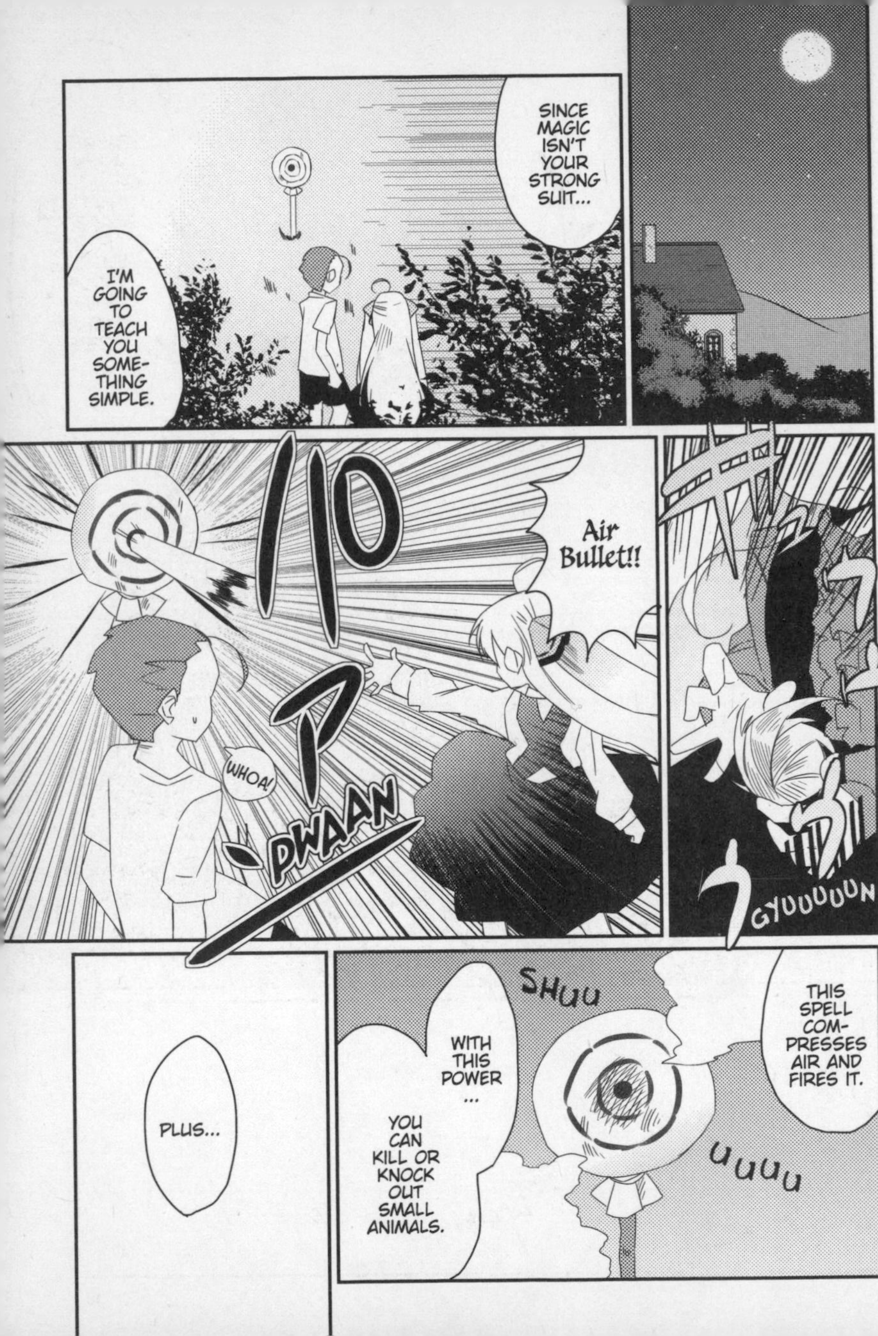
SINCE MAGIC ISN'T YOUR STRONG SUIT...
I'M GOING TO TEACH YOU SOME-THING SIMPLE.
GYUUUUUN
Air Bullet!!
WHOA!
PWAAN
THIS SPELL COM-PRESSES AIR AND FIRES IT.
SHUU
UUUU
WITH THIS POWER...
YOU CAN KILL OR KNOCK OUT SMALL ANIMALS.
PLUS...

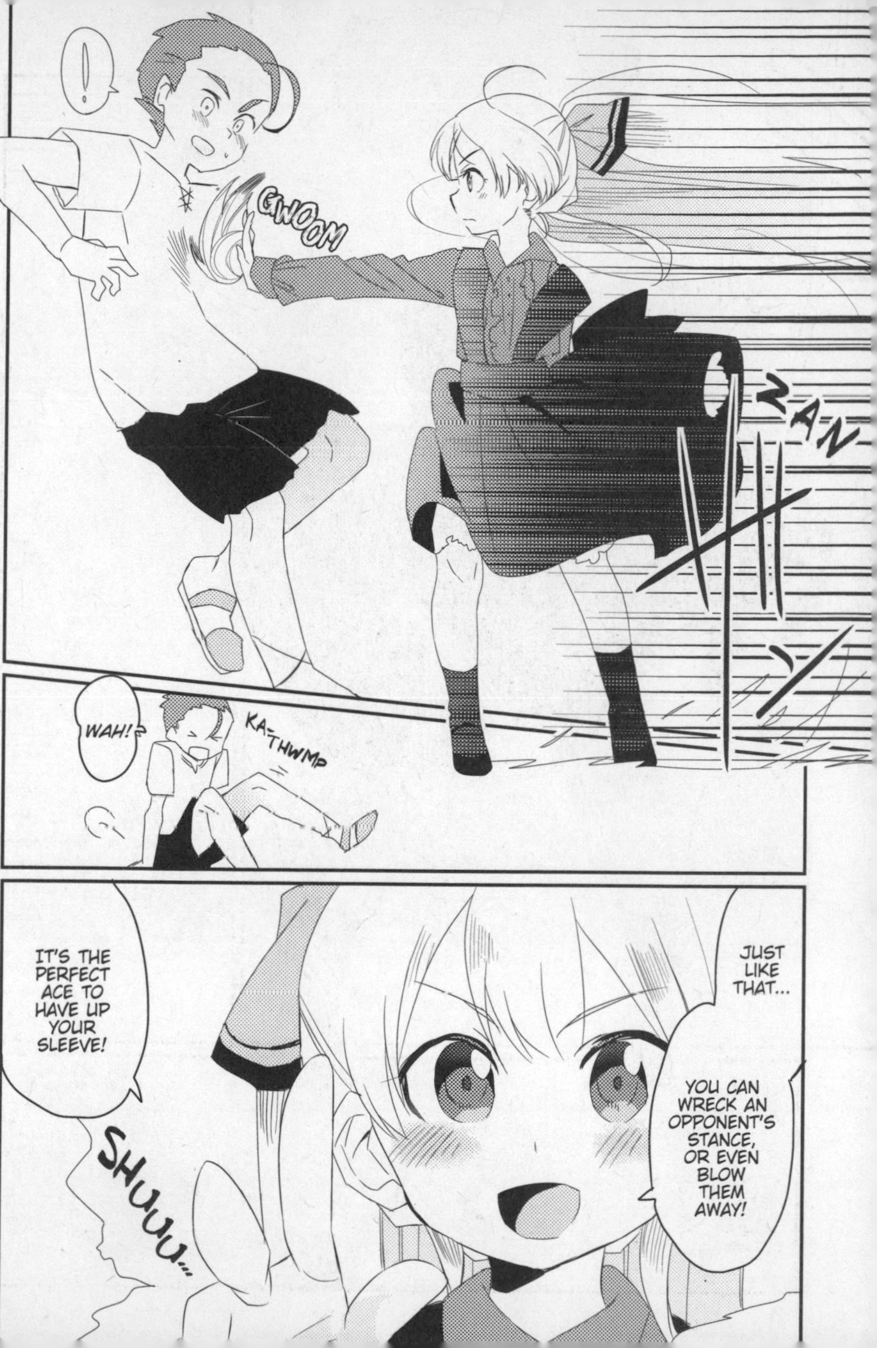
!
GWOOM
ZAN
KA-THWMP
WAH!
JUST LIKE THAT...
YOU CAN WRECK AN OPPONENT'S STANCE, OR EVEN BLOW THEM AWAY!
IT'S THE PERFECT ACE TO HAVE UP YOUR SLEEVE!
SHUUU...

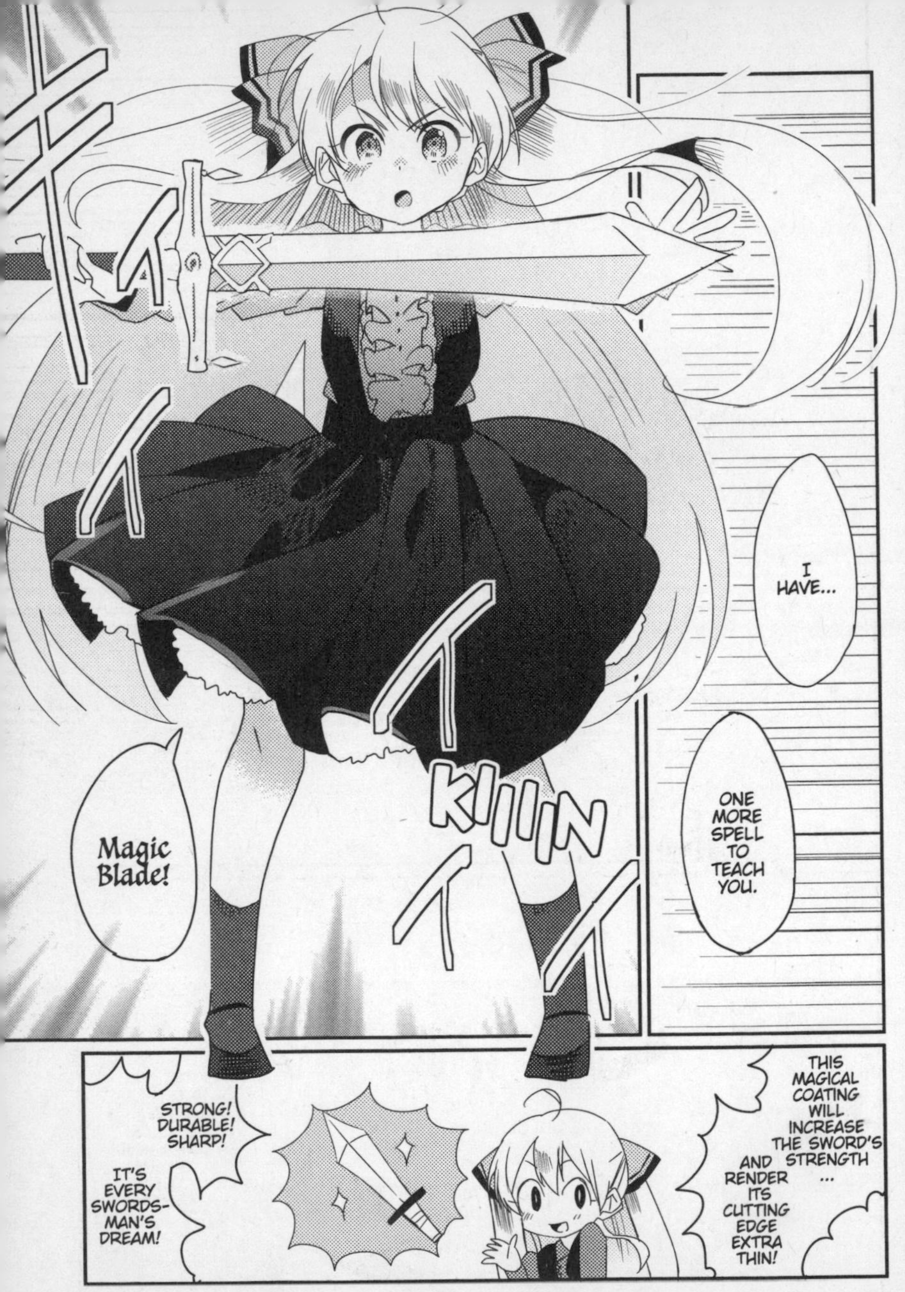
I HAVE...
ONE MORE SPELL TO TEACH YOU.
Magic Blade!
KIIIN
THIS MAGICAL COATING WILL INCREASE THE SWORD'S STRENGTH ...
AND RENDER ITS CUTTING EDGE EXTRA THIN!
STRONG! DURABLE! SHARP!
IT'S EVERY SWORDS-MAN'S DREAM!

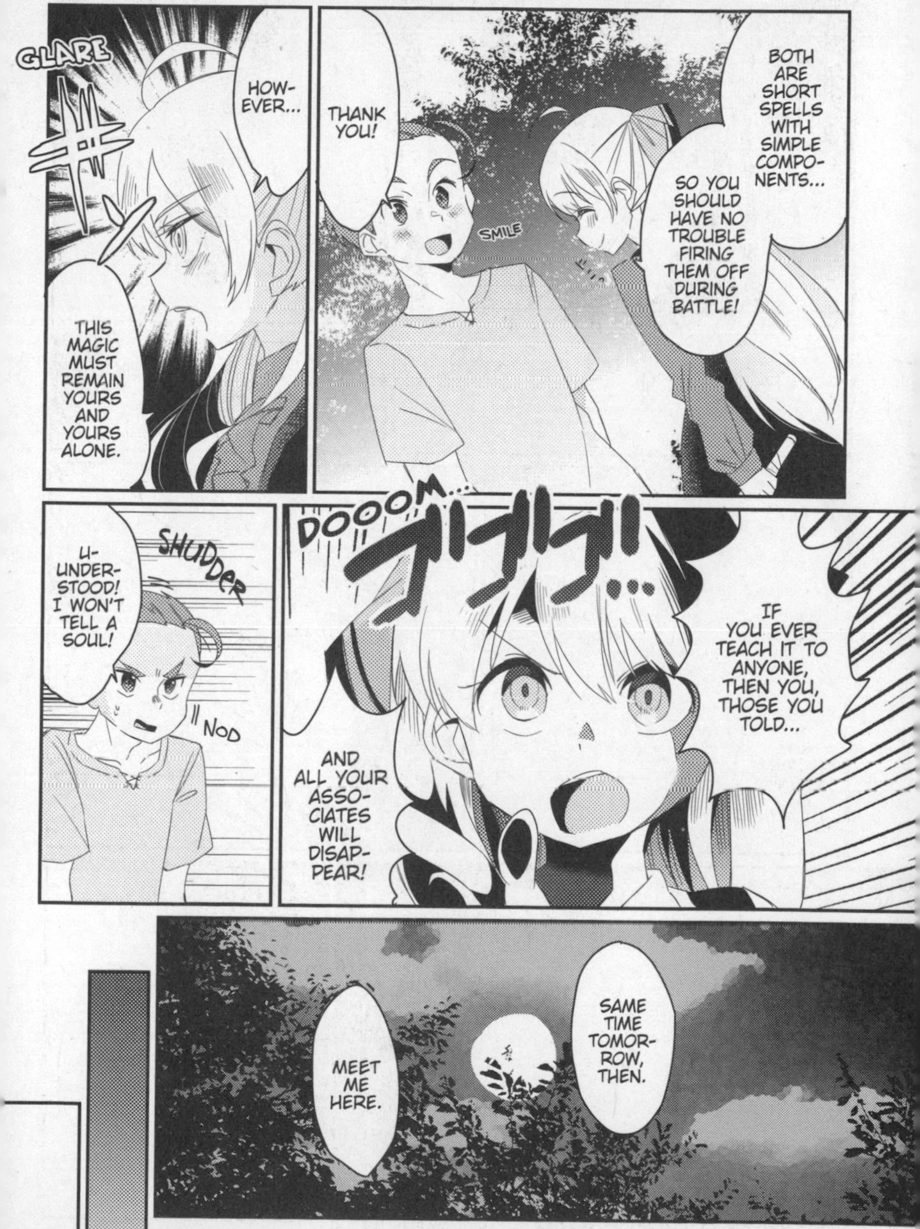
BOTH ARE SHORT SPELLS WITH SIMPLE COMPO-NENTS...
SO YOU SHOULD HAVE NO TROUBLE FIRING THEM OFF DURING BATTLE!
SMILE
THANK YOU!
GLARE
HOW-EVER...
THIS MAGIC MUST REMAIN YOURS AND YOURS ALONE.
DOOOM...
IF YOU EVER TEACH IT TO ANYONE, THEN YOU, THOSE YOU TOLD...
AND ALL YOUR ASSO-CIATES WILL DISAP-PEAR!
SHUDDER
U-UNDER-STOOD! I WON'T TELL A SOUL!
NOD
SAME TIME TOMOR-ROW, THEN.
MEET ME HERE.

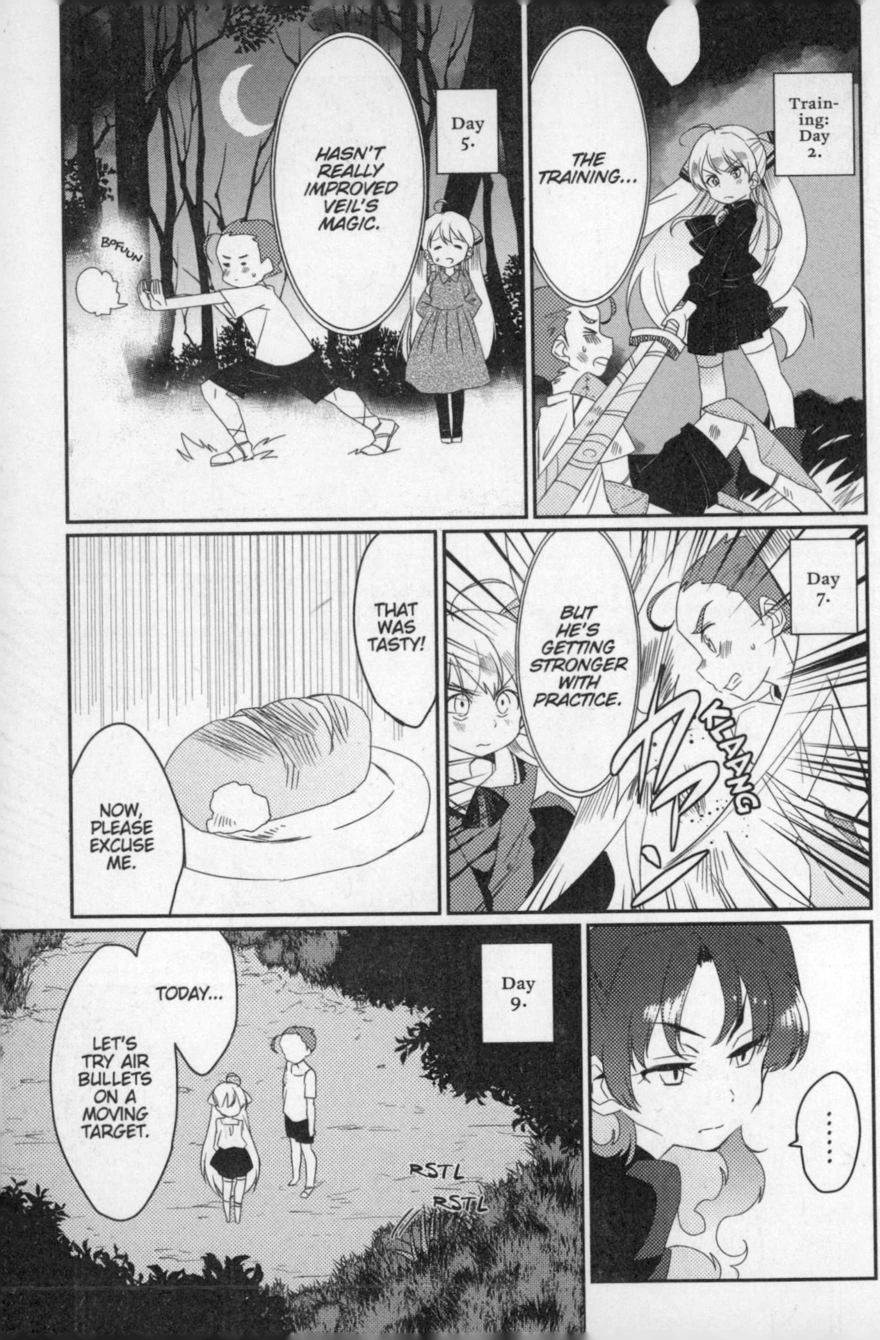
Training: Day 2.
THE TRAINING...
Day 5.
HASN'T REALLY IMPROVED VEIL'S MAGIC.
BOFUUN
Day 7.
BUT HE'S GETTING STRONGER WITH PRACTICE.
KLAANG
THAT WAS TASTY!
NOW, PLEASE EXCUSE ME.
......
Day 9.
TODAY...
LET'S TRY AIR BULLETS ON A MOVING TARGET.
RSTL
RSTL

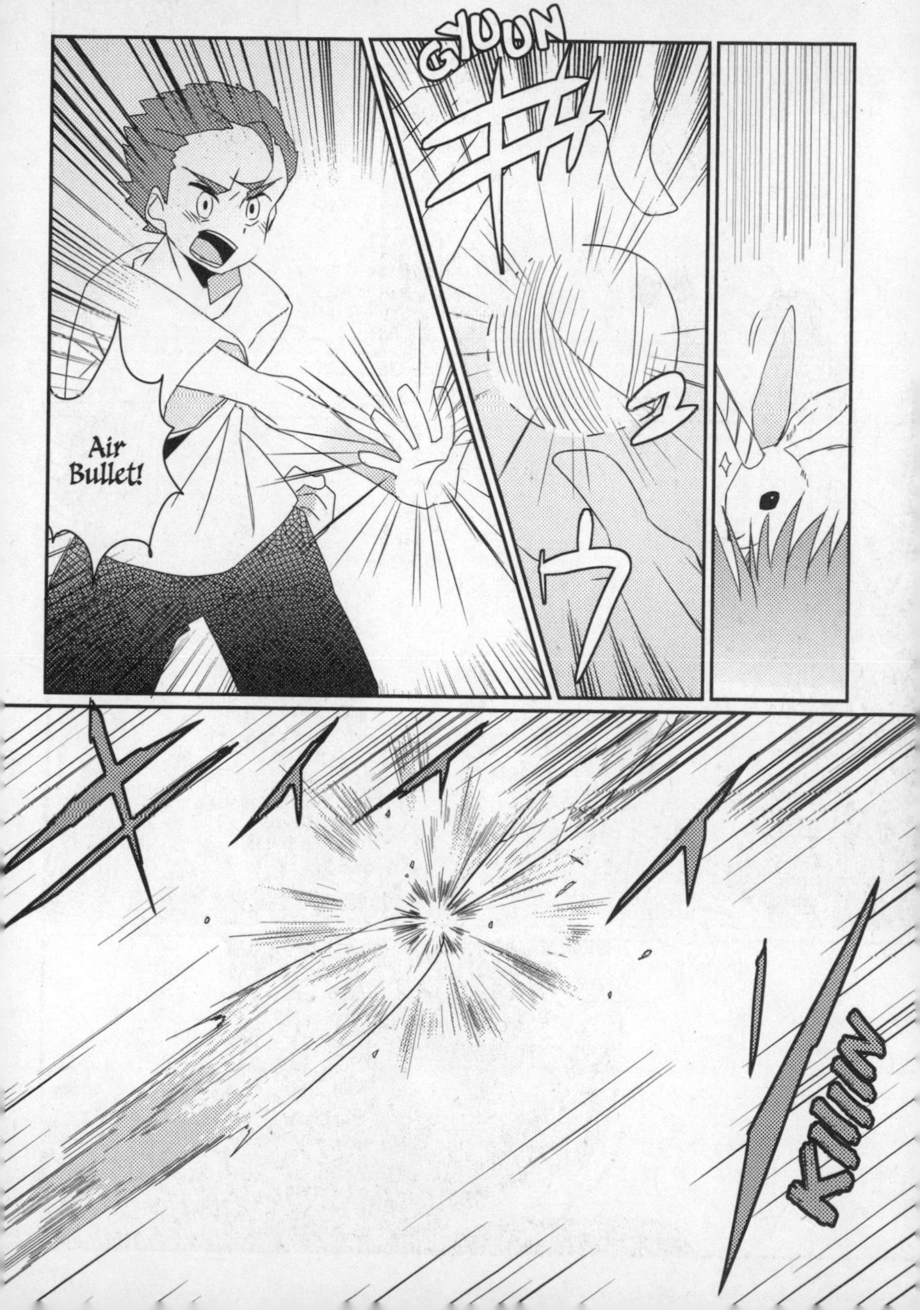
GYUUN
Air Bullet!
KIIIN

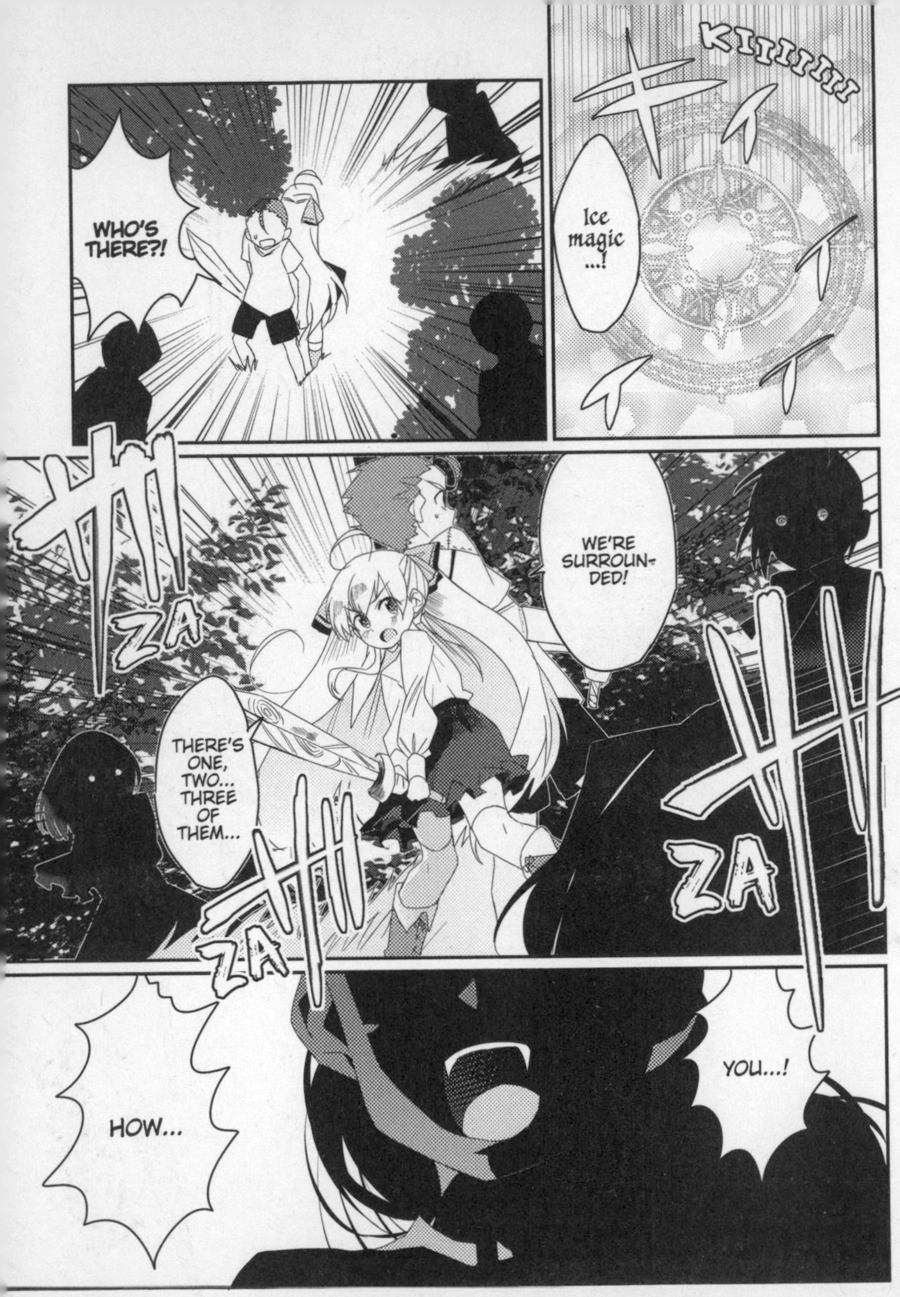
KIIIIIII
Ice magic ...!
WHO'S THERE?!
WE'RE SURROUN-DED!
ZA
ZA
THERE'S ONE, TWO... THREE OF THEM...
ZA
YOU...!
HOW...

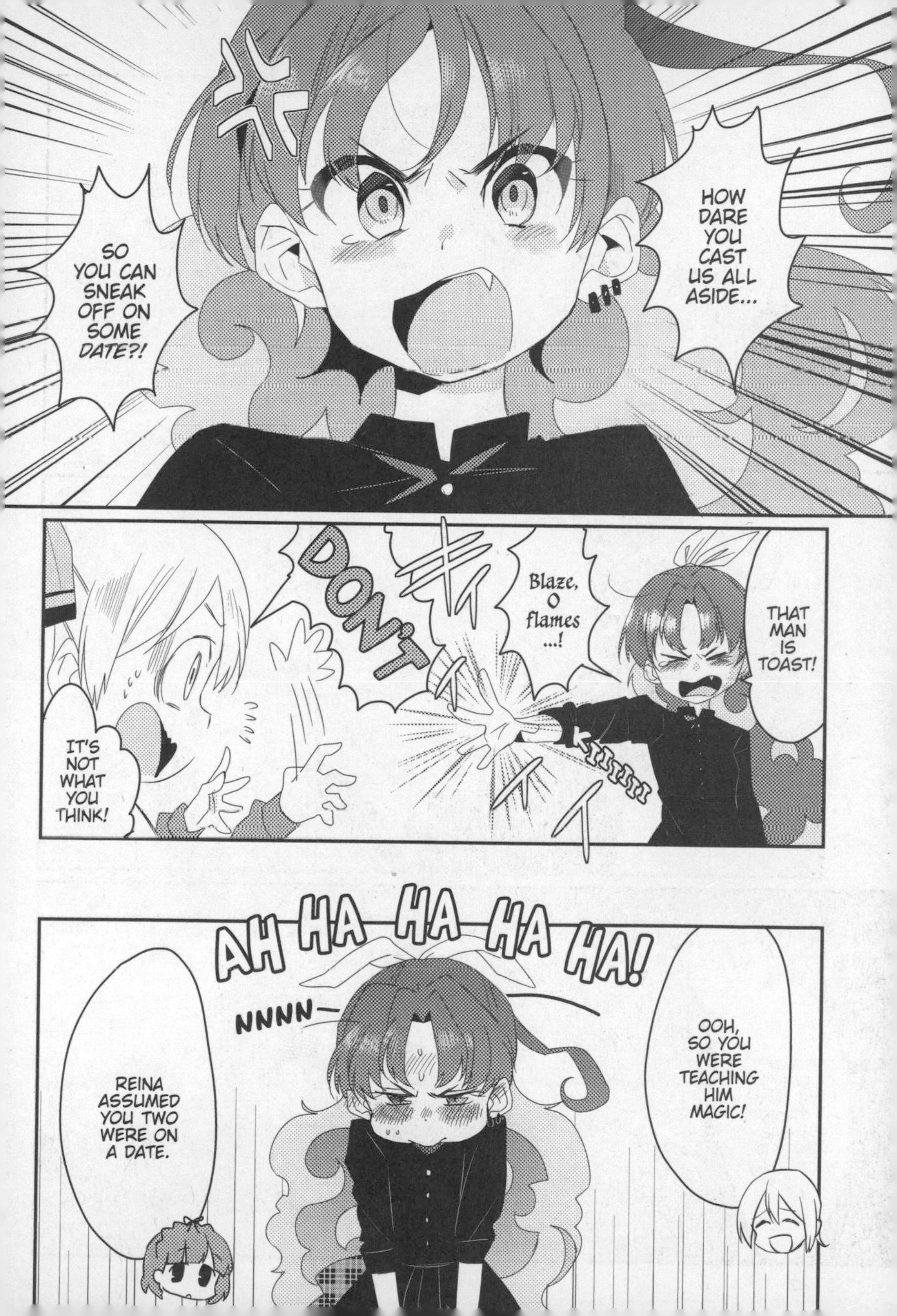
HOW DARE YOU CAST US ALL ASIDE...
SO YOU CAN SNEAK OFF ON SOME DATE?!
THAT MAN IS TOAST!
Blaze, O flames ...!
DON'T
KIIIIII
IT'S NOT WHAT YOU THINK!
AH HA HA HA HA HA!
OOH, SO YOU WERE TEACHING HIM MAGIC!
NNNN—
REINA ASSUMED YOU TWO WERE ON A DATE.

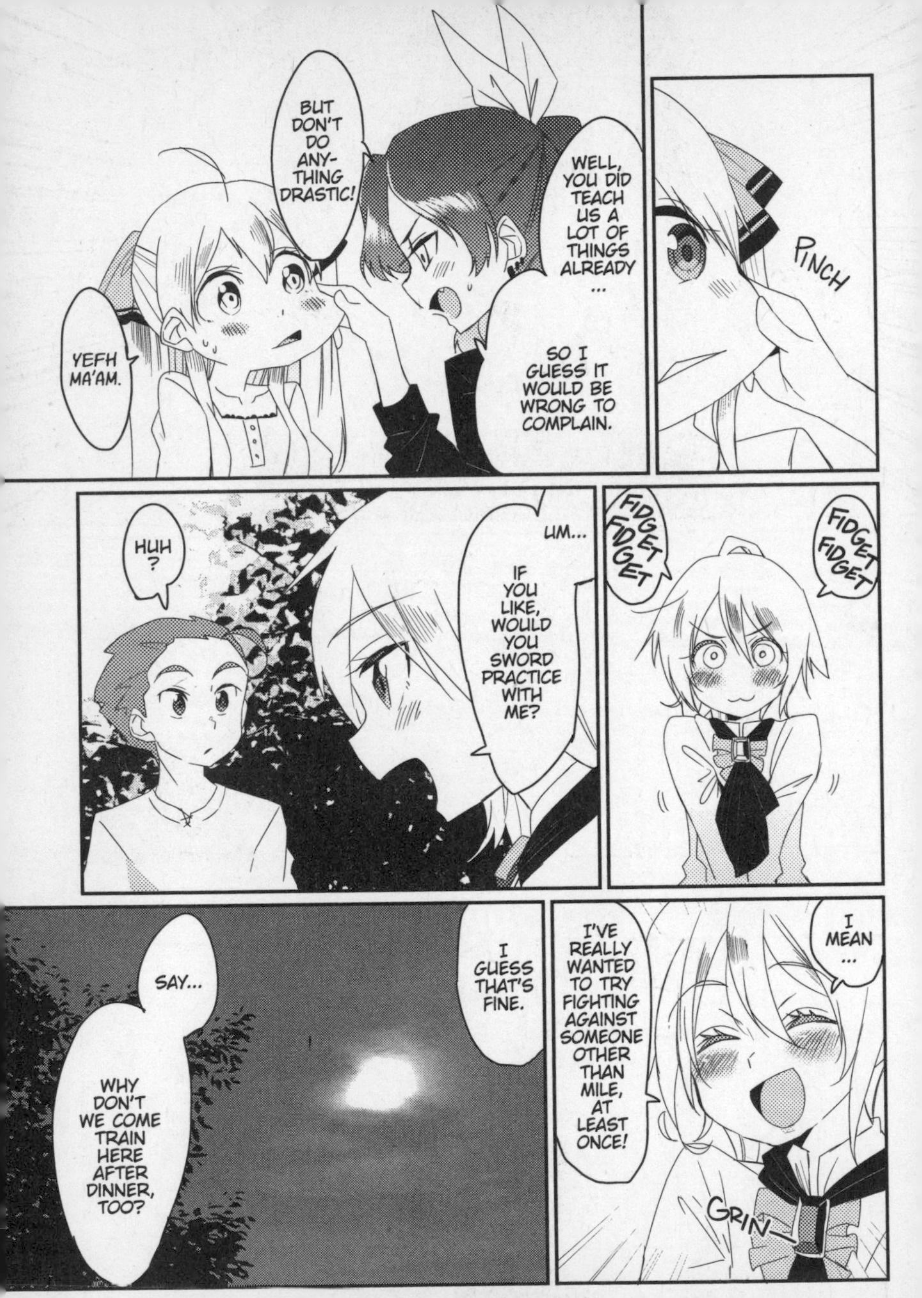
PINCH
WELL, YOU DID TEACH US A LOT OF THINGS ALREADY...
SO I GUESS IT WOULD BE WRONG TO COMPLAIN.
BUT DON'T DO ANY-THING DRASTIC!
YEFH MA'AM.
FIDGET FIDGET
FIDGET FIDGET
UM...
IF YOU LIKE, WOULD YOU SWORD PRACTICE WITH ME?
HUH?
I MEAN...
I'VE REALLY WANTED TO TRY FIGHTING AGAINST SOMEONE OTHER THAN MILE, AT LEAST ONCE!
GRIN—
I GUESS THAT'S FINE.
SAY...
WHY DON'T WE COME TRAIN HERE AFTER DINNER, TOO?

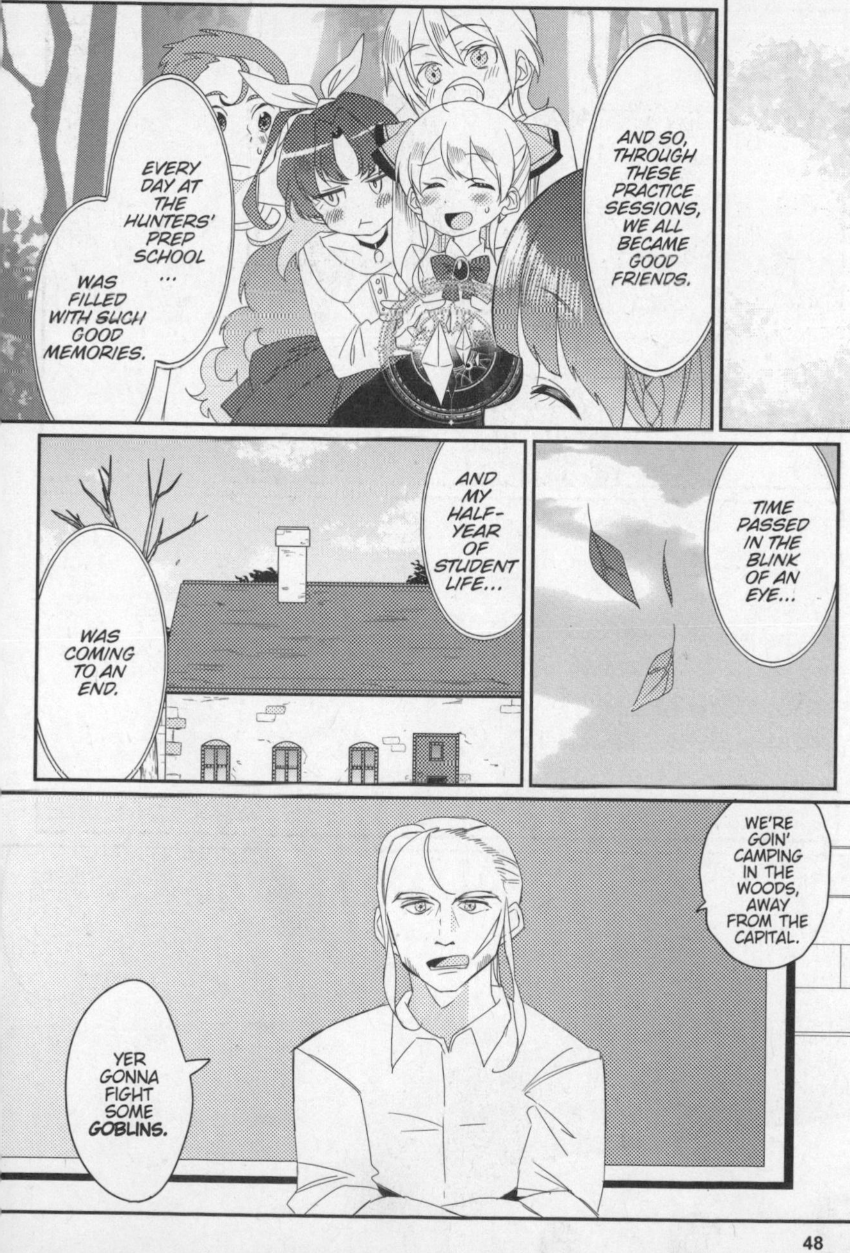
AND SO, THROUGH THESE PRACTICE SESSIONS, WE ALL BECAME GOOD FRIENDS.
EVERY DAY AT THE HUNTERS' PREP SCHOOL ...
WAS FILLED WITH SUCH GOOD MEMORIES.
TIME PASSED IN THE BLINK OF AN EYE...
AND MY HALF-YEAR OF STUDENT LIFE...
WAS COMING TO AN END.
WE'RE GOIN' CAMPING IN THE WOODS, AWAY FROM THE CAPITAL.
YER GONNA FIGHT SOME GOBLINS.

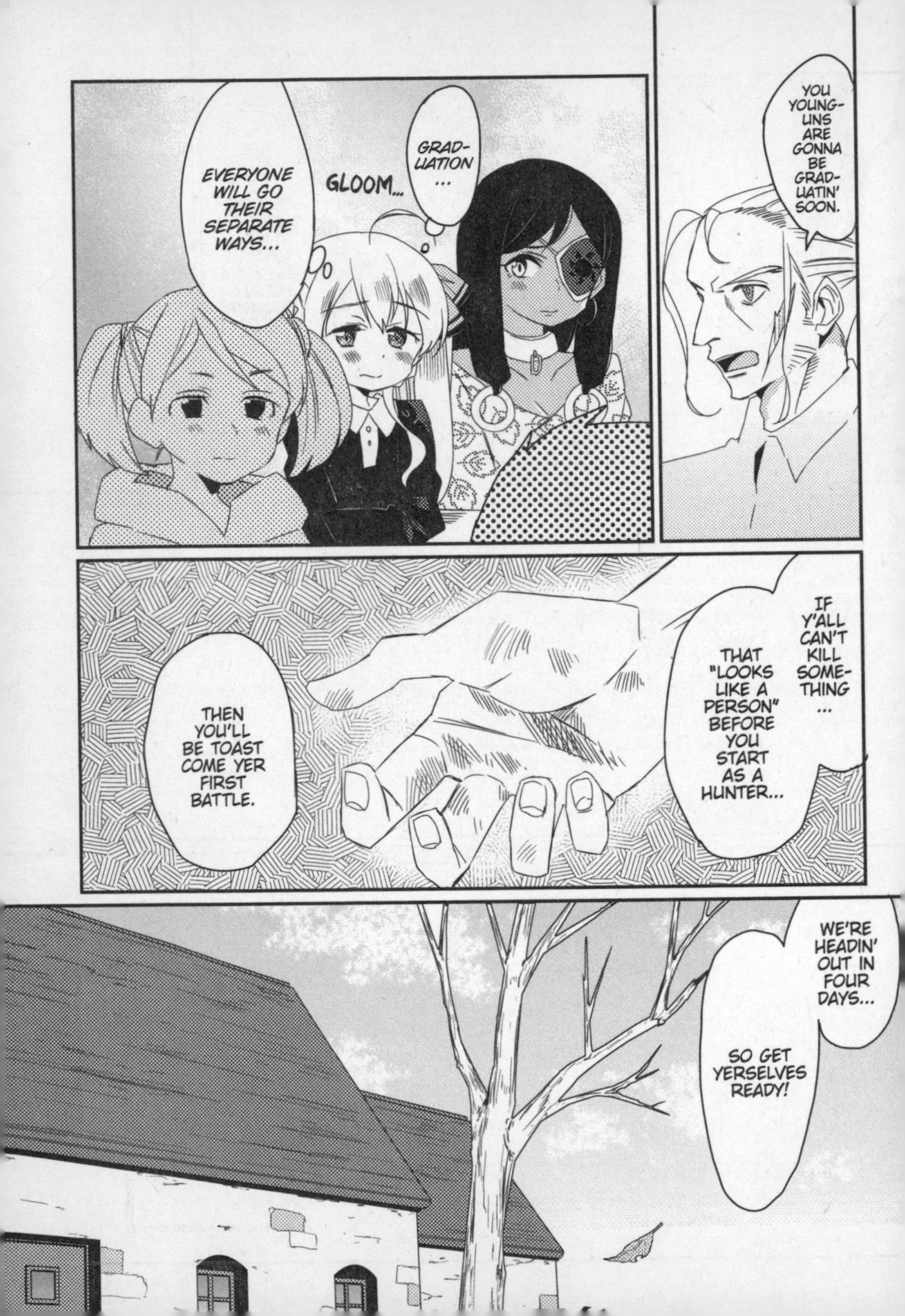
YOU YOUNG-UNS ARE GONNA BE GRAD-UATIN' SOON.
GRAD-UATION...
GLOOM...
EVERYONE WILL GO THEIR SEPARATE WAYS...
IF Y'ALL CAN'T KILL SOME-THING...
THAT "LOOKS LIKE A PERSON" BEFORE YOU START AS A HUNTER...
THEN YOU'LL BE TOAST COME YER FIRST BATTLE.
WE'RE HEADIN' OUT IN FOUR DAYS...
SO GET YERSELVES READY!

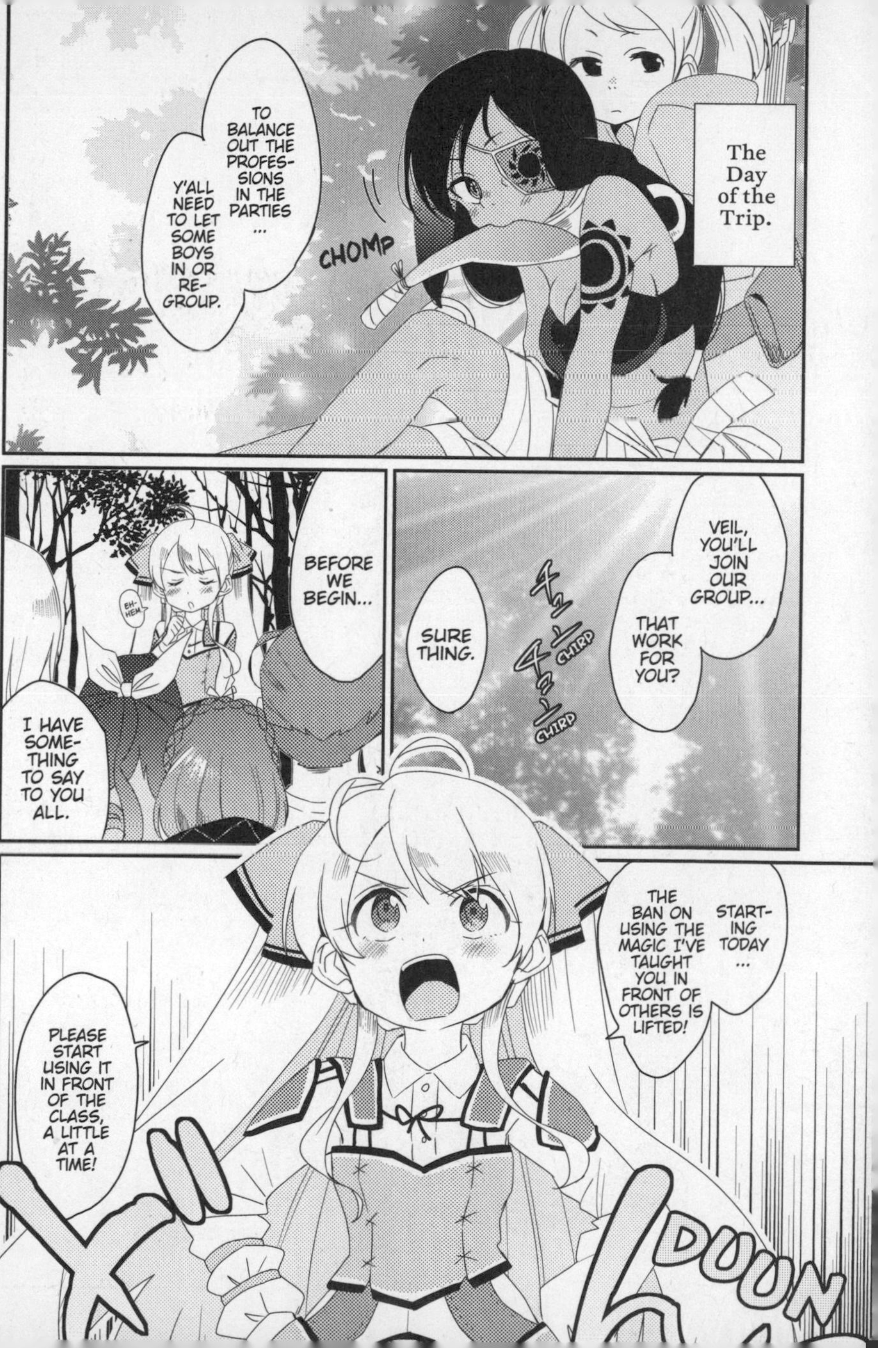
The Day of the Trip.
CHOMP
TO BALANCE OUT THE PROFESSIONS IN THE PARTIES ... Y'ALL NEED TO LET SOME BOYS IN OR REGROUP.
VEIL, YOU'LL JOIN OUR GROUP... THAT WORK FOR YOU?
CHIRP
CHIRP
SURE THING.
BEFORE WE BEGIN...
EH-HEM.
I HAVE SOMETHING TO SAY TO YOU ALL.
STARTING TODAY ...
THE BAN ON USING THE MAGIC I'VE TAUGHT YOU IN FRONT OF OTHERS IS LIFTED!
PLEASE START USING IT IN FRONT OF THE CLASS, A LITTLE AT A TIME!
DUUN

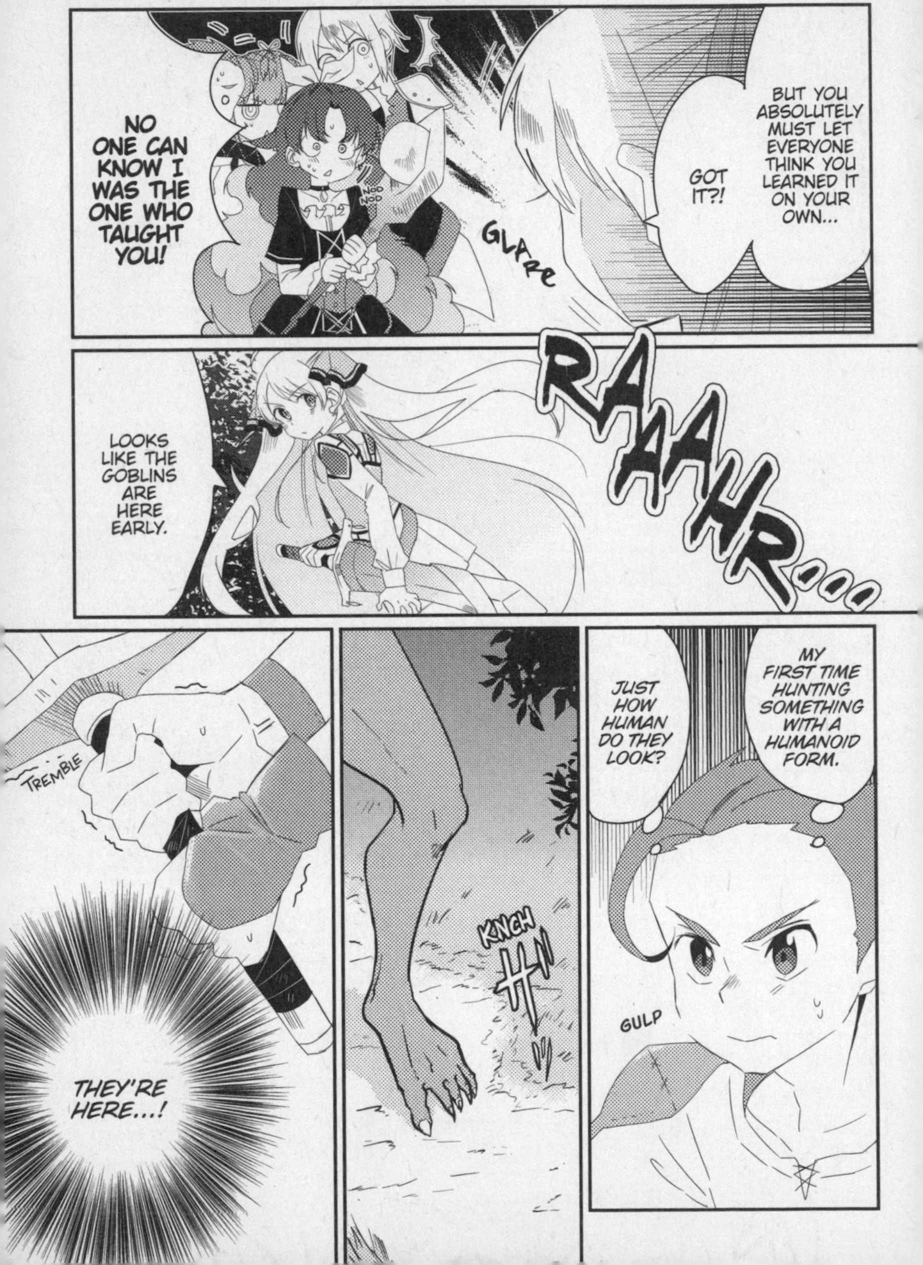
BUT YOU ABSOLUTELY MUST LET EVERYONE THINK YOU LEARNED IT ON YOUR OWN...
GOT IT?!
GLARE
NOD NOD
NO ONE CAN KNOW I WAS THE ONE WHO TAUGHT YOU!
RAAAHR...
LOOKS LIKE THE GOBLINS ARE HERE EARLY.
MY FIRST TIME HUNTING SOMETHING WITH A HUMANOID FORM.
JUST HOW HUMAN DO THEY LOOK?
GULP
KNCH
TREMBLE
THEY'RE HERE...!

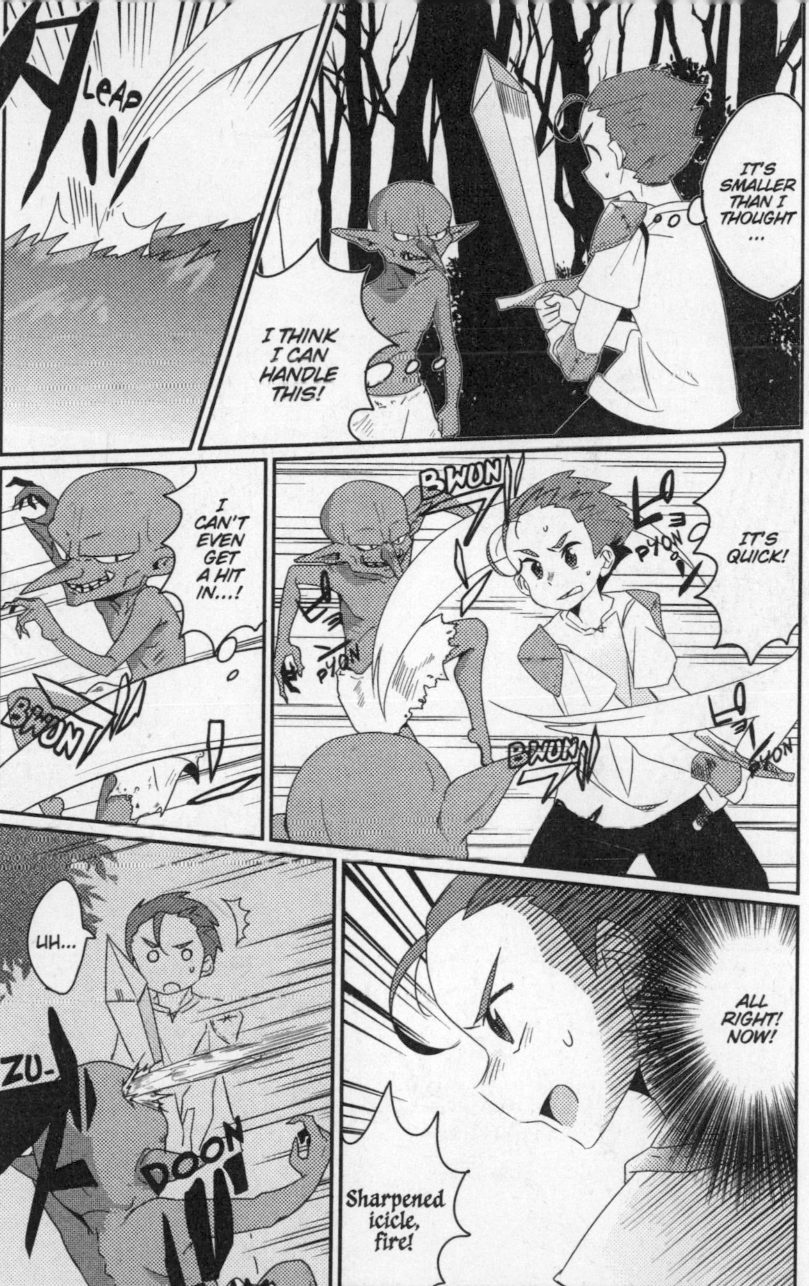
IT'S SMALLER THAN I THOUGHT ...
I THINK I CAN HANDLE THIS!
LEAP
BWUN
PYON
IT'S QUICK!
PYON
BWUN
PYON
I CAN'T EVEN GET A HIT IN...!
BWUN
ALL RIGHT! NOW!
Sharpened icicle, fire!
UH...
ZU-
DOON

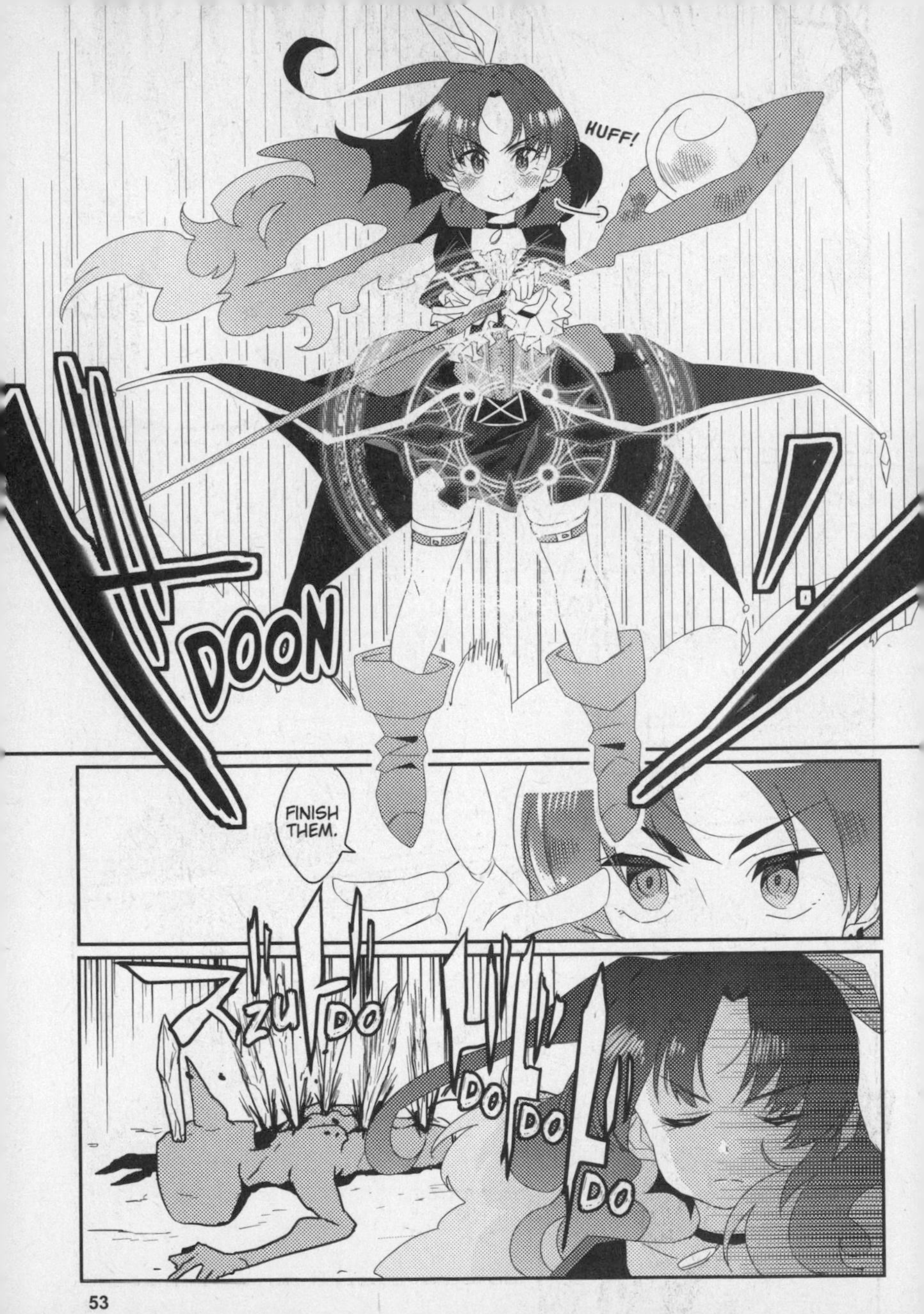
HUFF!
DOON
FINISH THEM.
ZU DO
DO DO DO

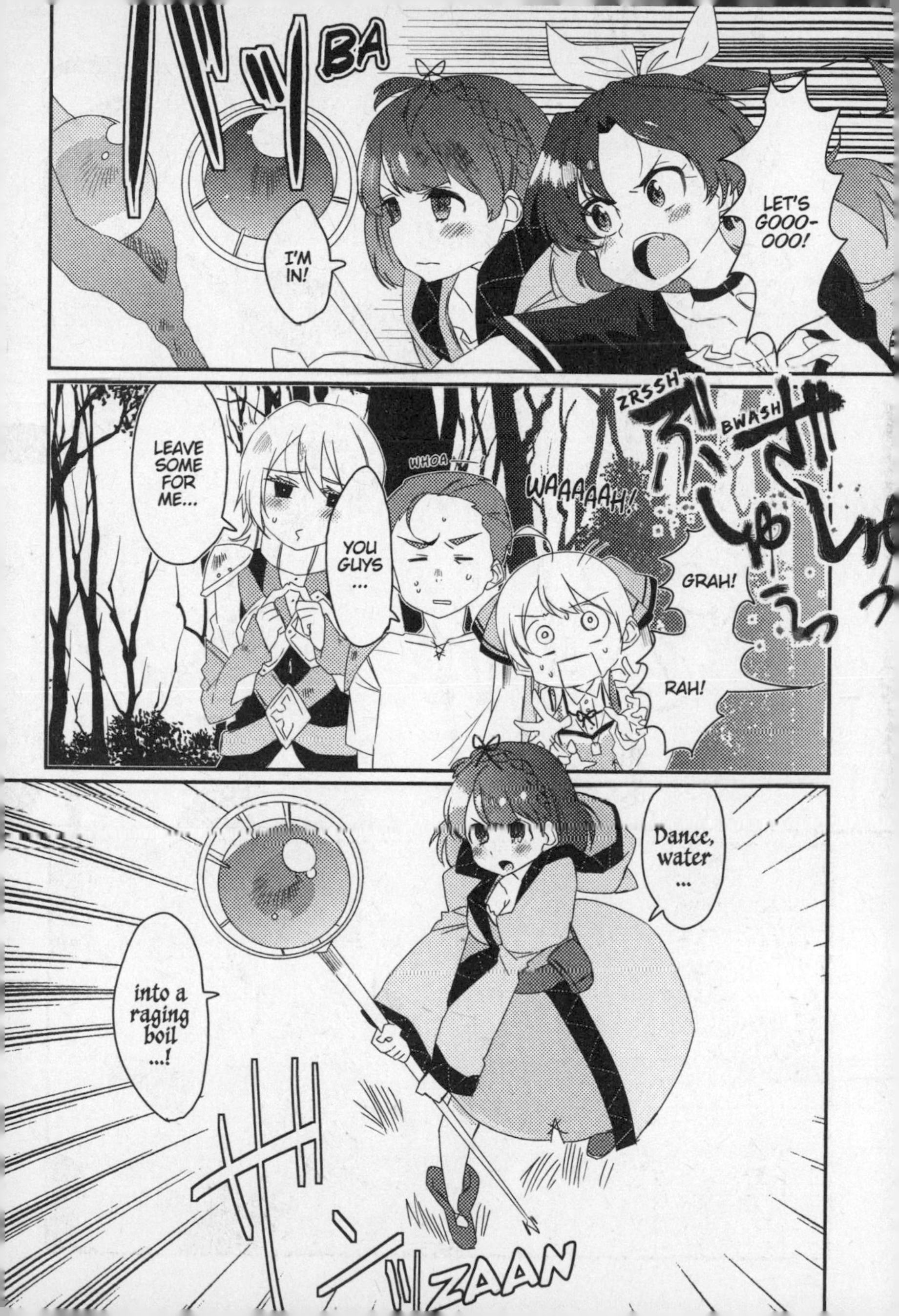
LET'S GOOOO-OOO!
BA
I'M IN!
ZRSSH
BWASH
GRAH!
RAH!
WAAAAAH!
WHOA
YOU GUYS ...
LEAVE SOME FOR ME...
Dance, water ...
into a raging boil ...!
ZAAN

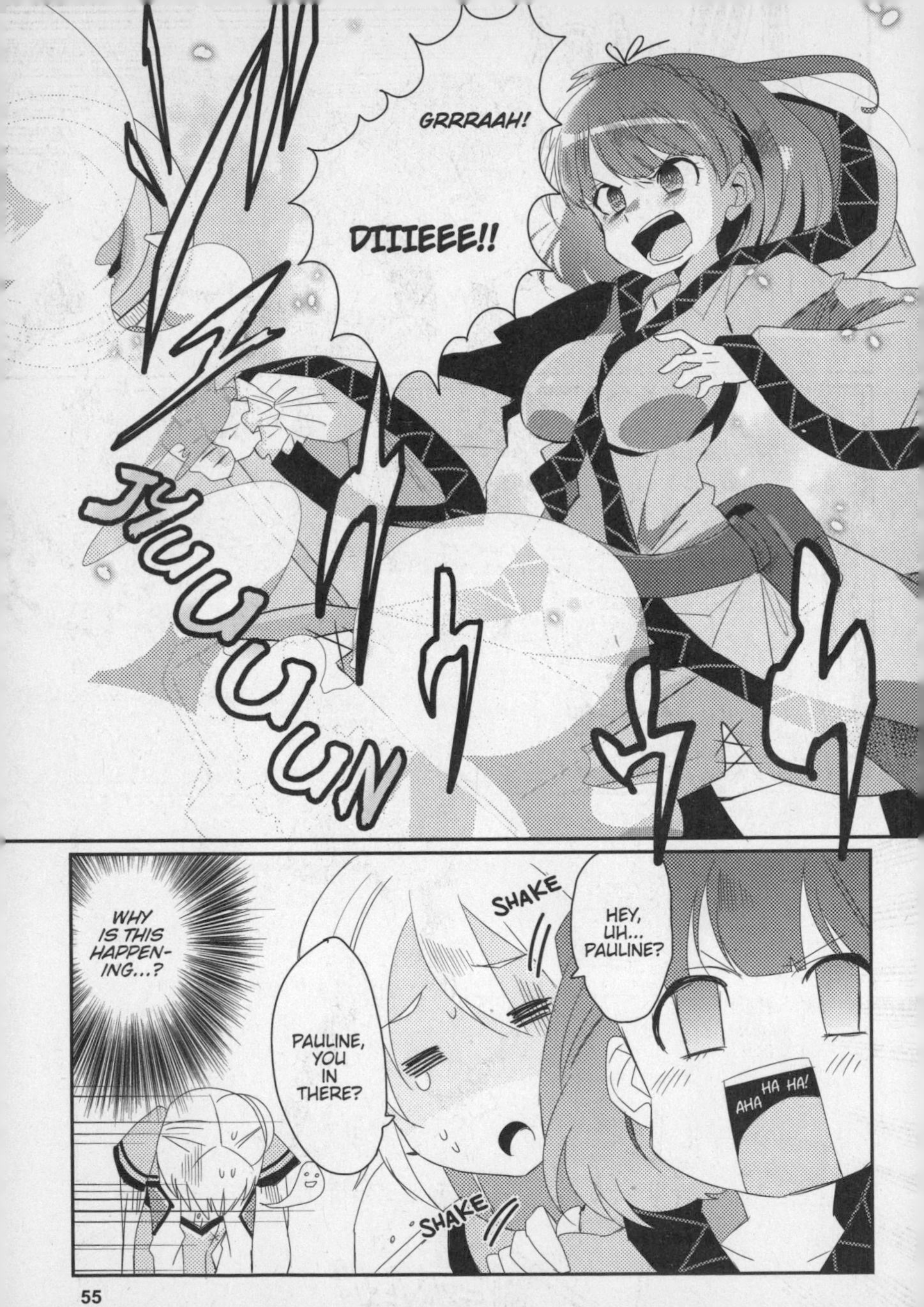
GRRRAAH!
DIIIEEE!!
JYUUUUN
HEY, UH... PAULINE?
AHA HA HA!
SHAKE
PAULINE, YOU IN THERE?
SHAKE
WHY IS THIS HAPPENING...?

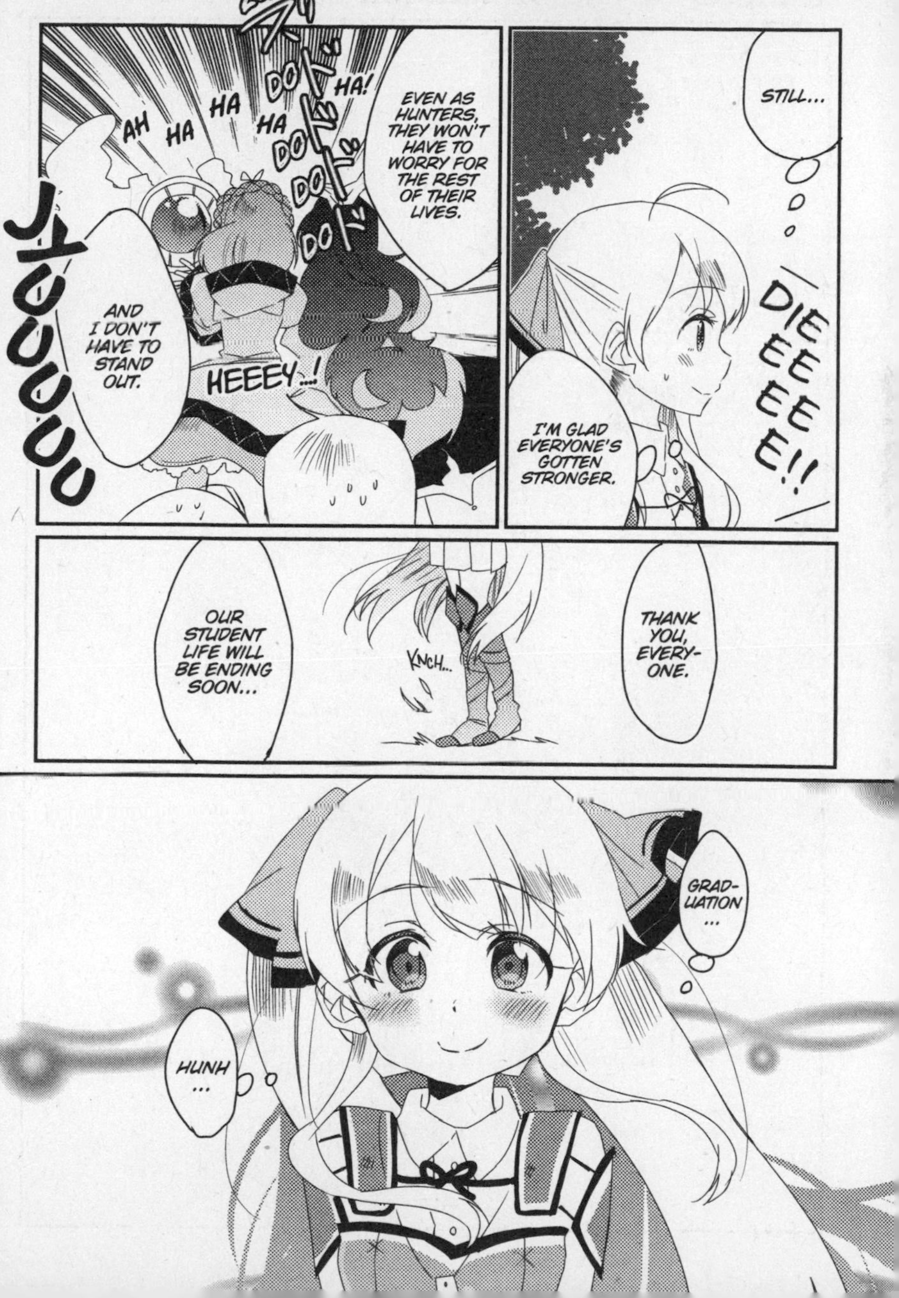
STILL...
DIEEEEEE!!
I'M GLAD EVERYONE'S GOTTEN STRONGER.
EVEN AS HUNTERS, THEY WON'T HAVE TO WORRY FOR THE REST OF THEIR LIVES.
ZU
HA!
HA
HA
HA
AH
DO DO DO DO DO
AND I DON'T HAVE TO STAND OUT.
YOUUUUU
HEEEY...!
THANK YOU, EVERY-ONE.
KNCH...
OUR STUDENT LIFE WILL BE ENDING SOON...
GRAD-UATION ...
HUNH ...

Chapter 9: The Graduation Exam Part 1

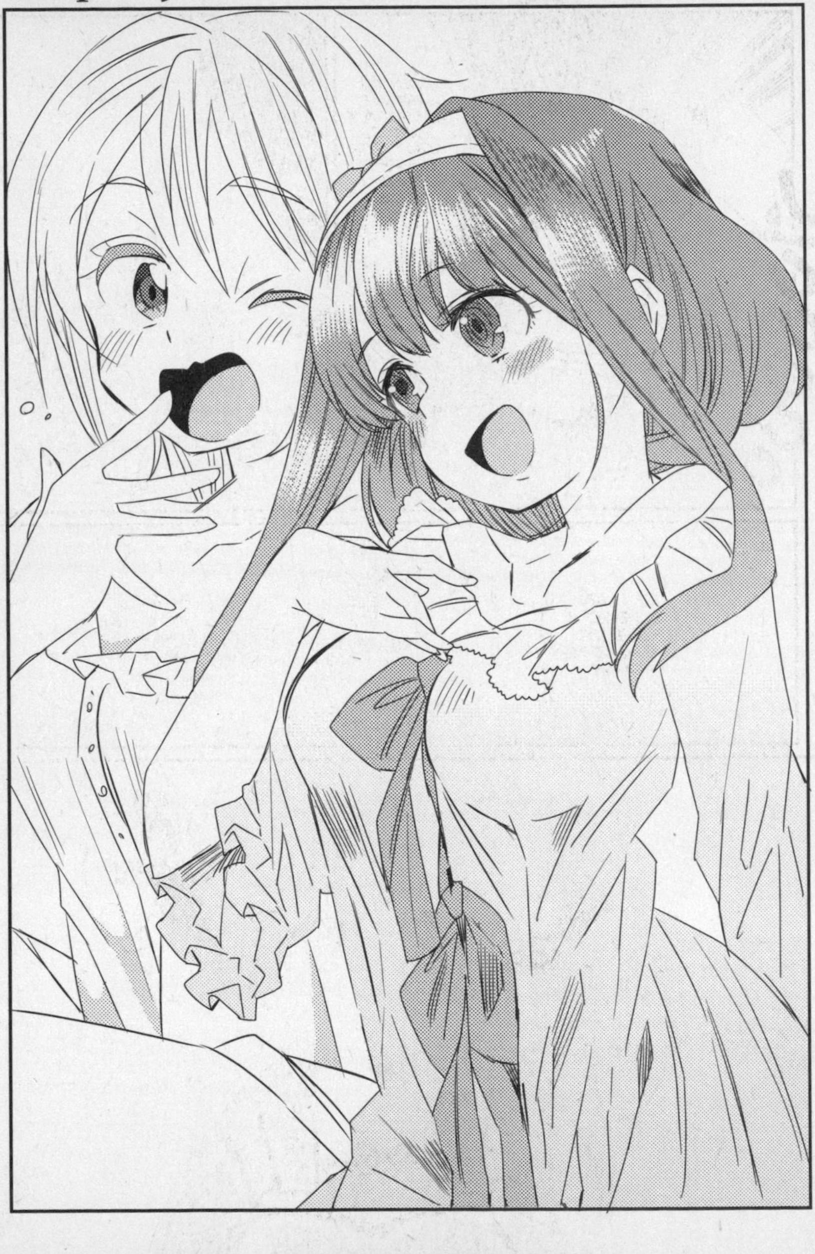

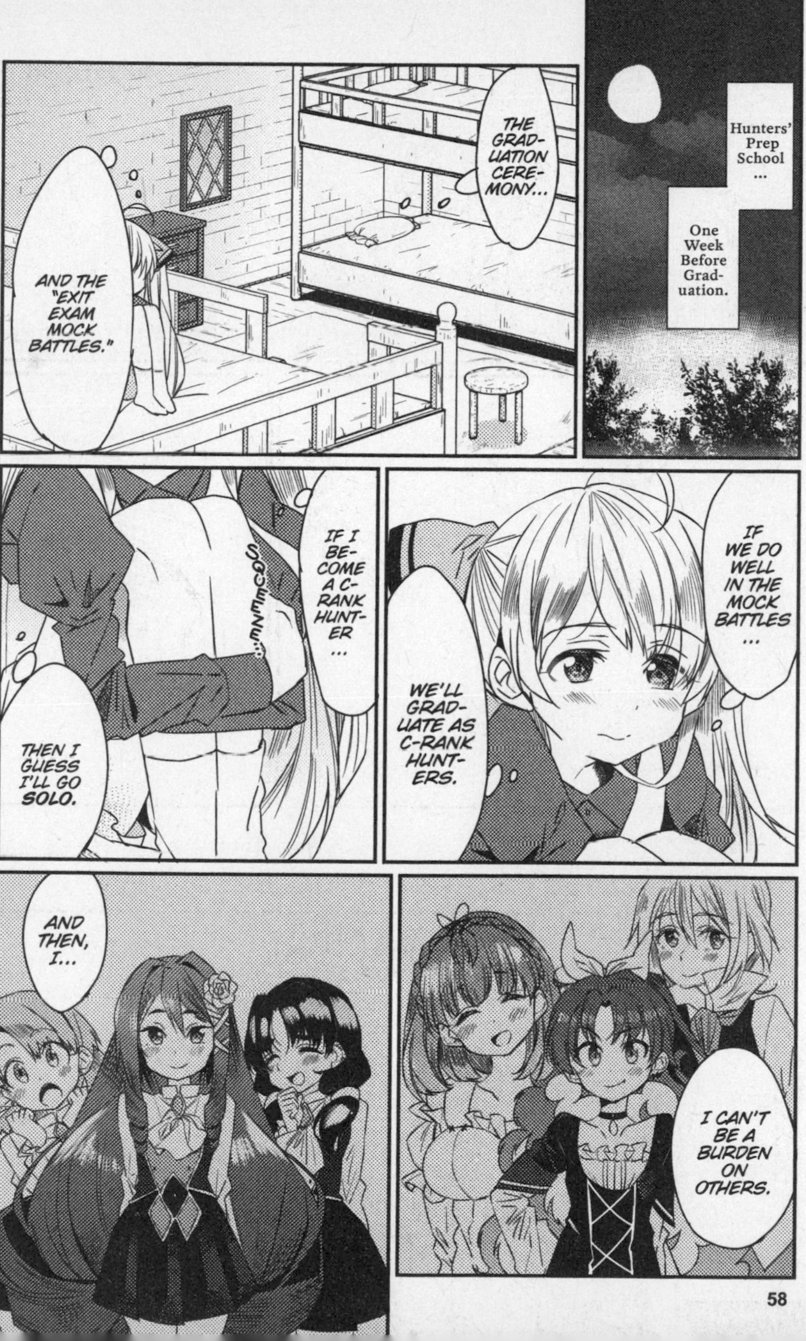
Hunters' Prep School ...
One Week Before Grad-uation.
THE GRAD-UATION CERE-MONY...
AND THE "EXIT EXAM MOCK BATTLES."
IF WE DO WELL IN THE MOCK BATTLES ...
WE'LL GRAD-UATE AS C-RANK HUNT-ERS.
IF I BE-COME A C-RANK HUNT-ER ...
SQUEEZE...
THEN I GUESS I'LL GO SOLO.
I CAN'T BE A BURDEN ON OTHERS.
AND THEN, I...

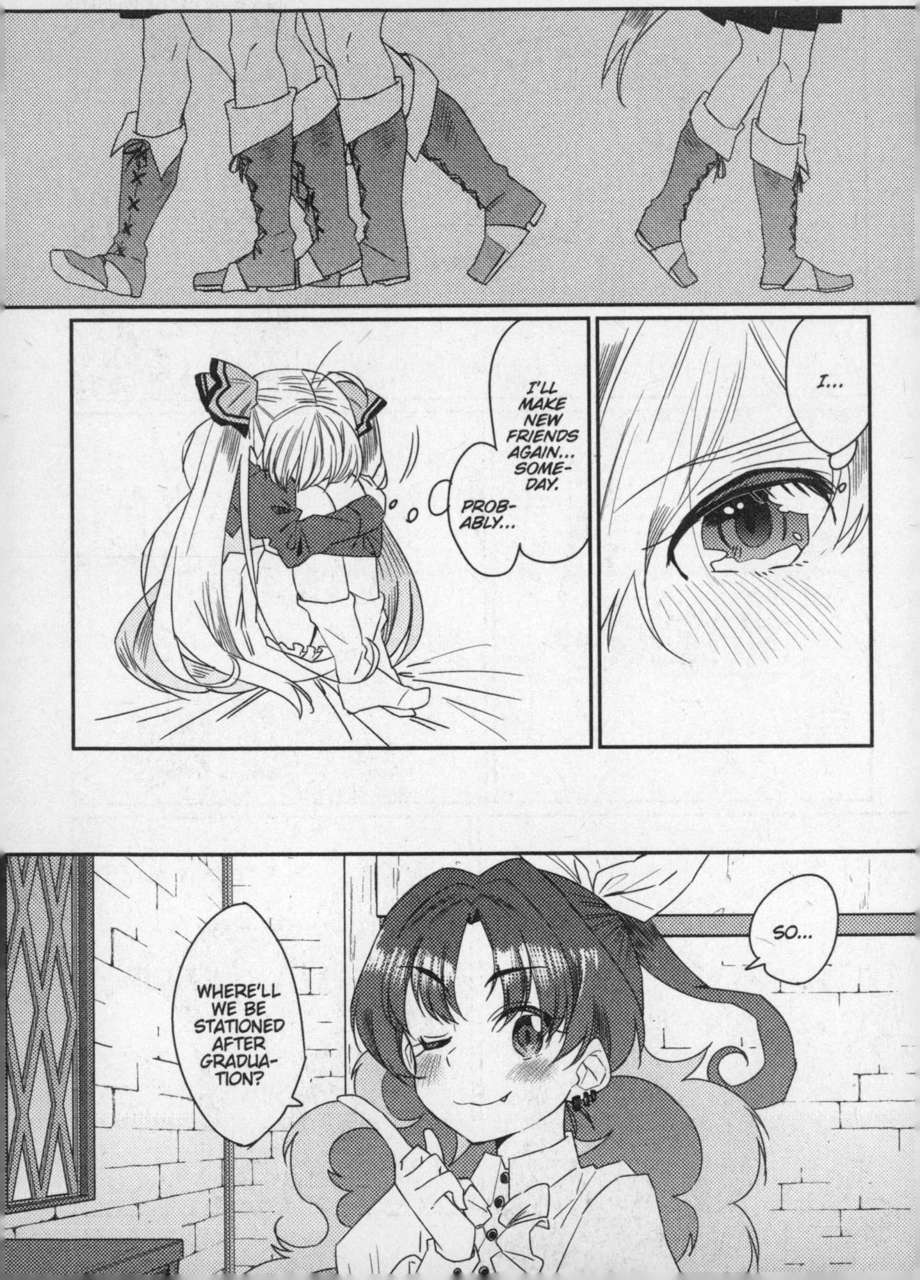
I...
I'LL MAKE NEW FRIENDS AGAIN... SOME-DAY.
PROB-ABLY...
SO...
WHERE'LL WE BE STATIONED AFTER GRADUA-TION?

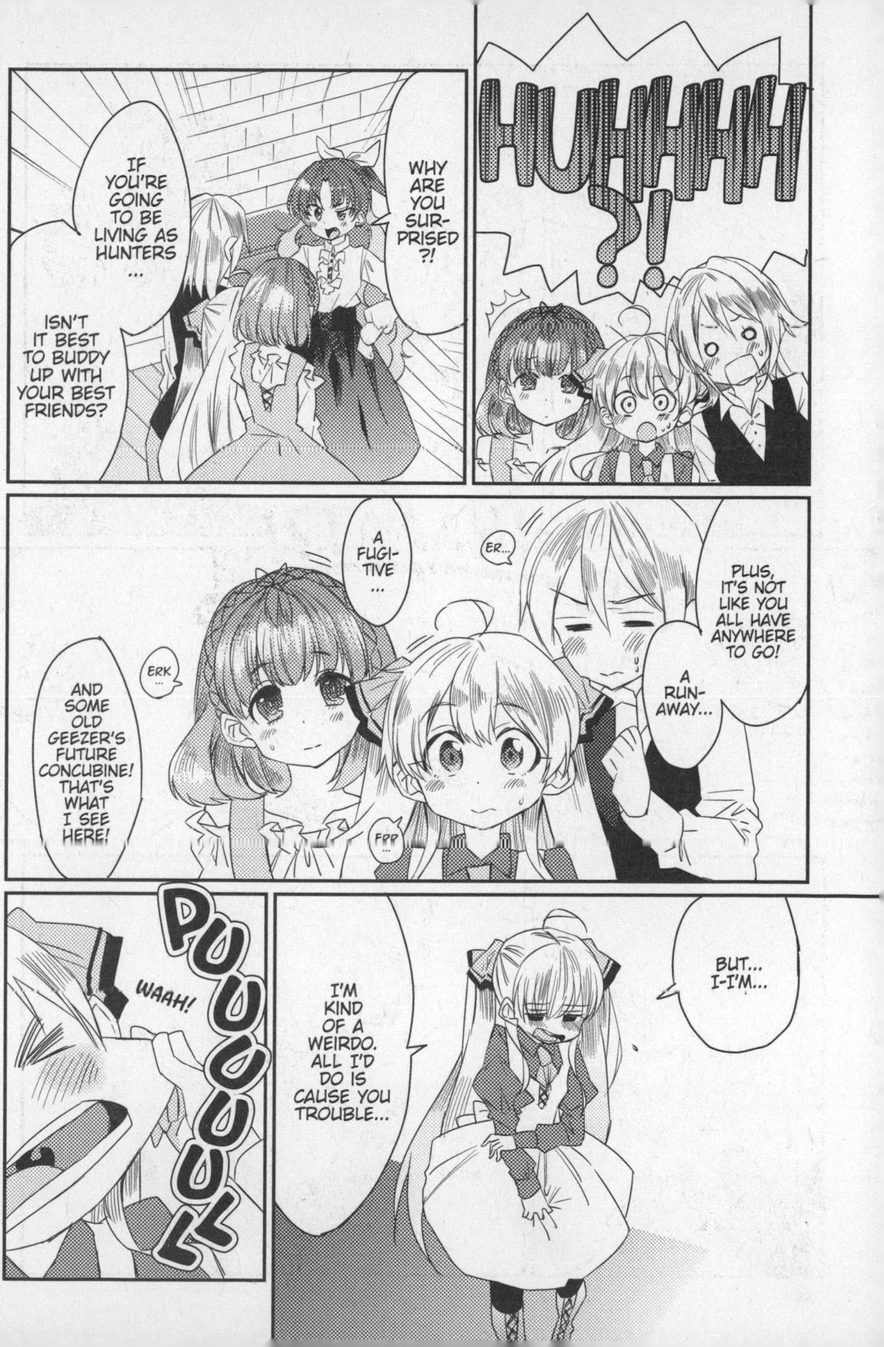

HUHHHHH
?!
WHY ARE YOU SURPRISED?!
IF YOU'RE GOING TO BE LIVING AS HUNTERS...
ISN'T IT BEST TO BUDDY UP WITH YOUR BEST FRIENDS?
PLUS, IT'S NOT LIKE YOU ALL HAVE ANYWHERE TO GO!
ER...
A FUGITIVE...
A RUNAWAY...
ERK...
AND SOME OLD GEEZER'S FUTURE CONCUBINE! THAT'S WHAT I SEE HERE!
FPP...
BUT... I-I'M...
I'M KIND OF A WEIRDO. ALL I'D DO IS CAUSE YOU TROUBLE...
PUUUUUL
WAAH!

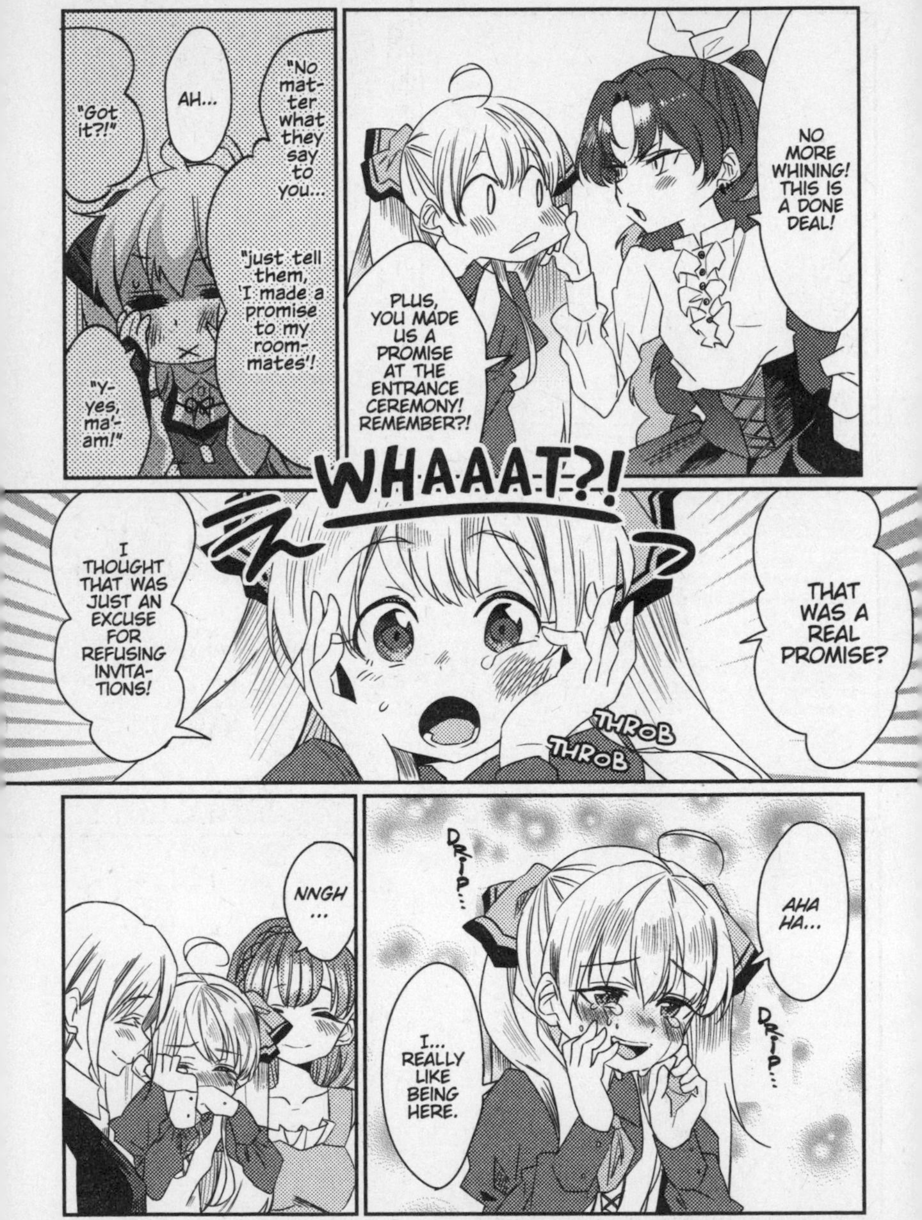
NO MORE WHINING! THIS IS A DONE DEAL!
PLUS, YOU MADE US A PROMISE AT THE ENTRANCE CEREMONY! REMEMBER?!
"No matter what they say to you...
AH...
"Got it?!"
"just tell them, 'I made a promise to my roommates'!
"y-yes, ma'am!"
WHAAAT?!
THAT WAS A REAL PROMISE?
THROB
THROB
I THOUGHT THAT WAS JUST AN EXCUSE FOR REFUSING INVITATIONS!
AHA HA...
DRIP...
I... REALLY LIKE BEING HERE.
DRIP...
NNGH...

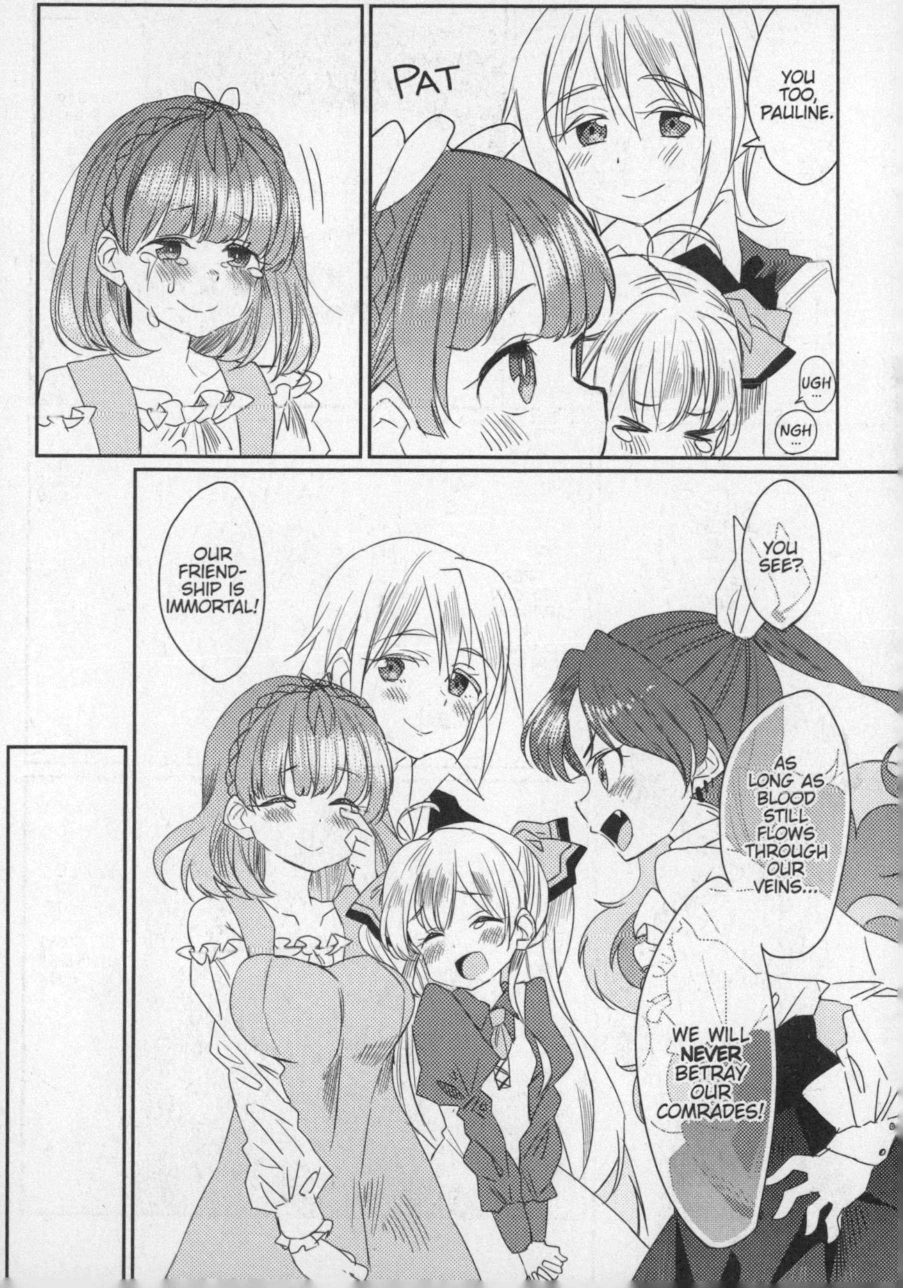
PAT
YOU TOO, PAULINE.
UGH...
NGH...
YOU SEE?
AS LONG AS BLOOD STILL FLOWS THROUGH OUR VEINS...
WE WILL NEVER BETRAY OUR COMRADES!
OUR FRIENDSHIP IS IMMORTAL!

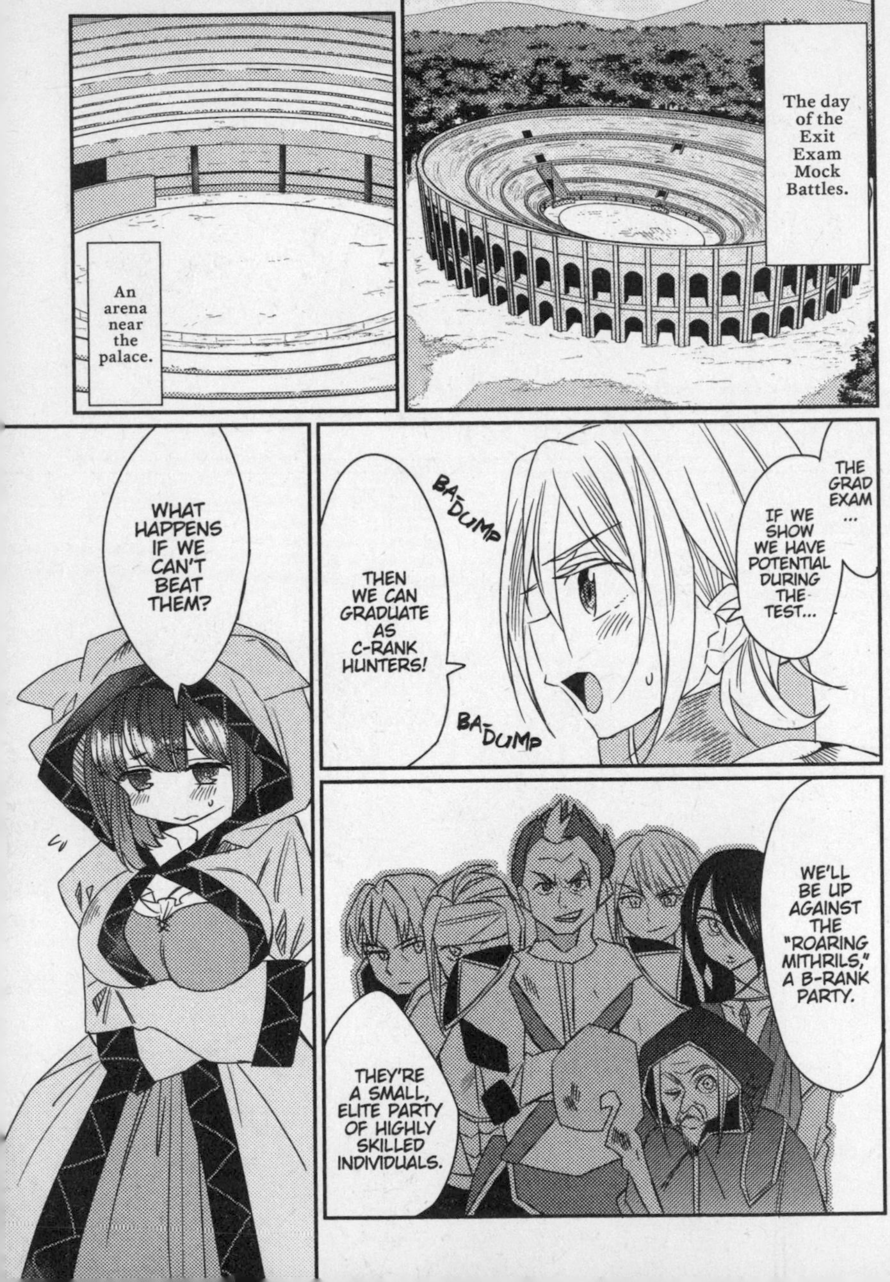
The day of the Exit Exam Mock Battles.
An arena near the palace.
THE GRAD EXAM...
IF WE SHOW WE HAVE POTENTIAL DURING THE TEST...
BA-DUMP
THEN WE CAN GRADUATE AS C-RANK HUNTERS!
BA-DUMP
WE'LL BE UP AGAINST THE "ROARING MITHRILS," A B-RANK PARTY.
THEY'RE A SMALL, ELITE PARTY OF HIGHLY SKILLED INDIVIDUALS.
WHAT HAPPENS IF WE CAN'T BEAT THEM?

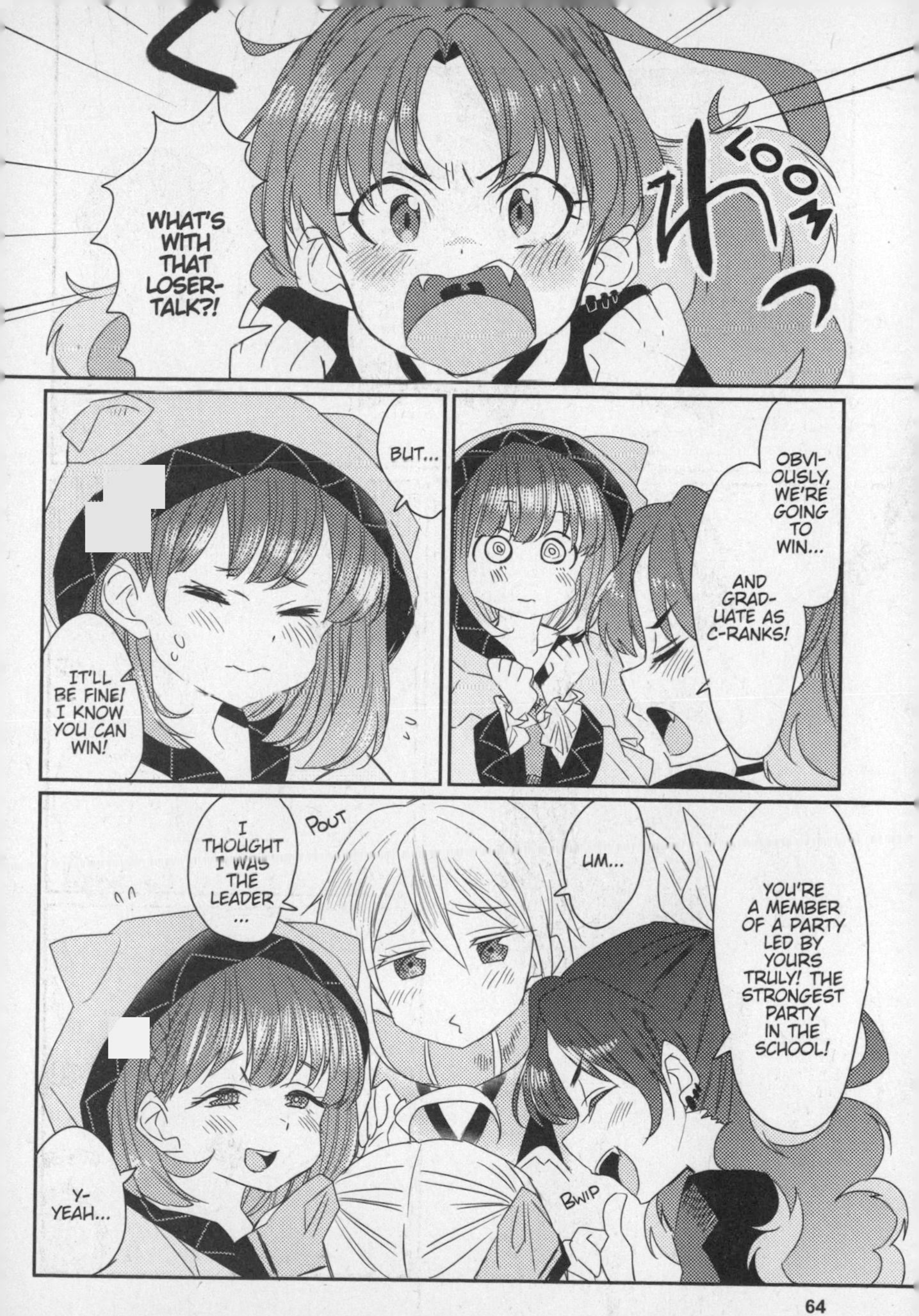
LOOM
WHAT'S WITH THAT LOSER-TALK?!
OBVI-OUSLY, WE'RE GOING TO WIN...
AND GRAD-UATE AS C-RANKS!
BUT...
IT'LL BE FINE! I KNOW YOU CAN WIN!
YOU'RE A MEMBER OF A PARTY LED BY YOURS TRULY! THE STRONGEST PARTY IN THE SCHOOL!
UM...
POUT
I THOUGHT I WAS THE LEADER...
BWIP
Y-YEAH...

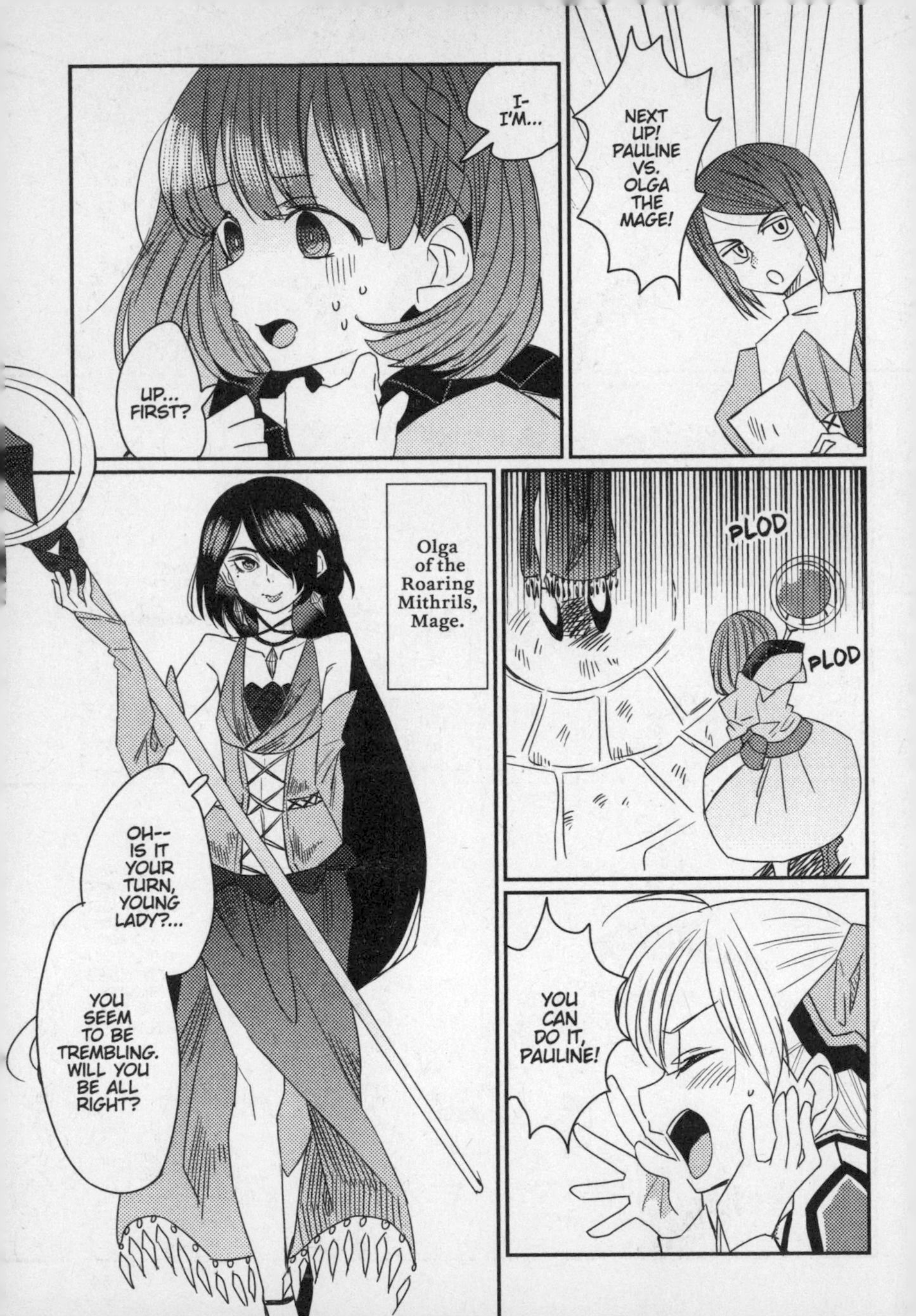
NEXT UP! PAULINE VS. OLGA THE MAGE!
I- I'M...
UP... FIRST?
PLOD
PLOD
YOU CAN DO IT, PAULINE!
Olga of the Roaring Mithrils, Mage.
OH-- IS IT YOUR TURN, YOUNG LADY?...
YOU SEEM TO BE TREMBLING. WILL YOU BE ALL RIGHT?

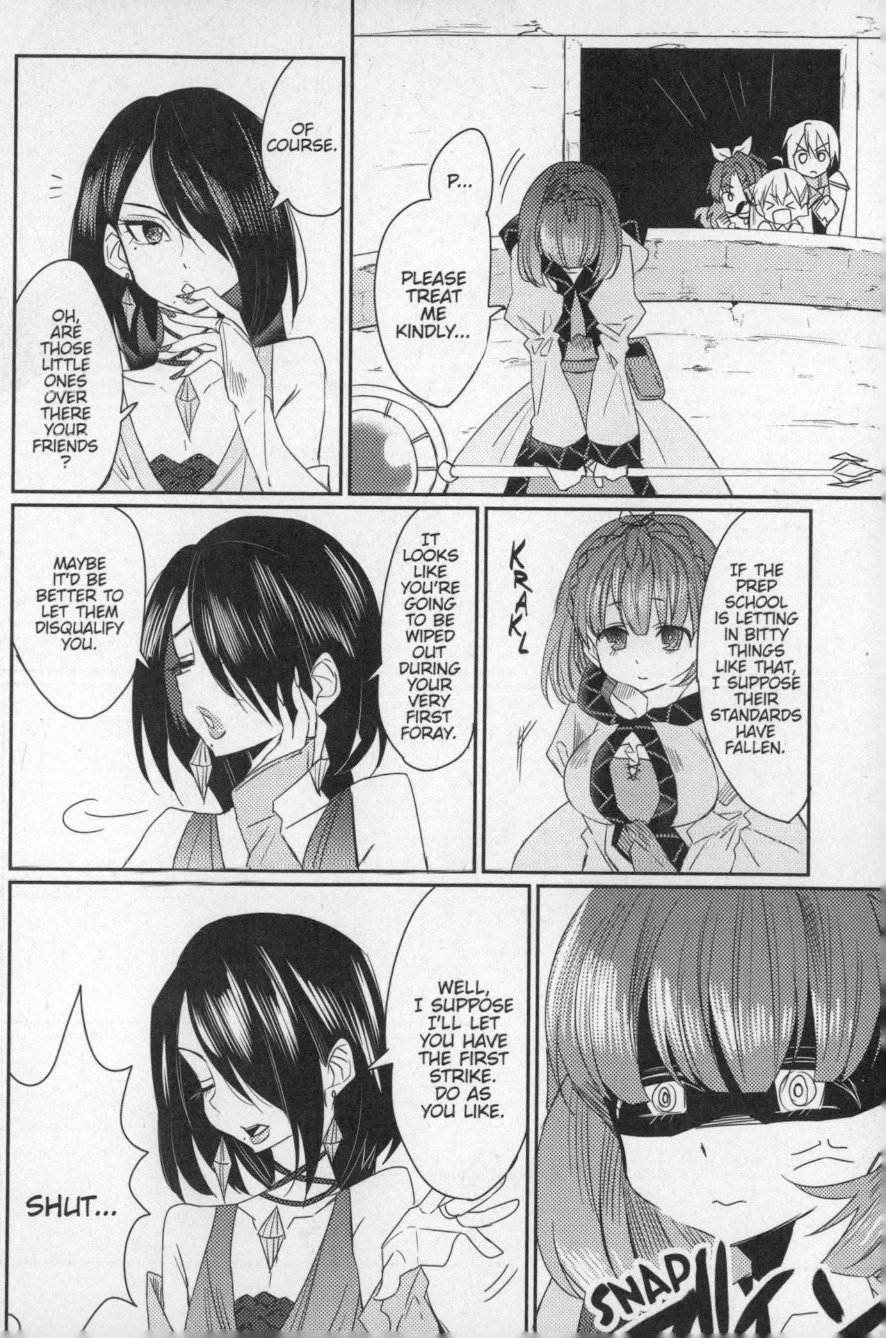
P...
PLEASE TREAT ME KINDLY...
OF COURSE.
OH, ARE THOSE LITTLE ONES OVER THERE YOUR FRIENDS?
KRAKL
IF THE PREP SCHOOL IS LETTING IN BITTY THINGS LIKE THAT, I SUPPOSE THEIR STANDARDS HAVE FALLEN.
IT LOOKS LIKE YOU'RE GOING TO BE WIPED OUT DURING YOUR VERY FIRST FORAY.
MAYBE IT'D BE BETTER TO LET THEM DISQUALIFY YOU.
SNAP
WELL, I SUPPOSE I'LL LET YOU HAVE THE FIRST STRIKE. DO AS YOU LIKE.
SHUT...

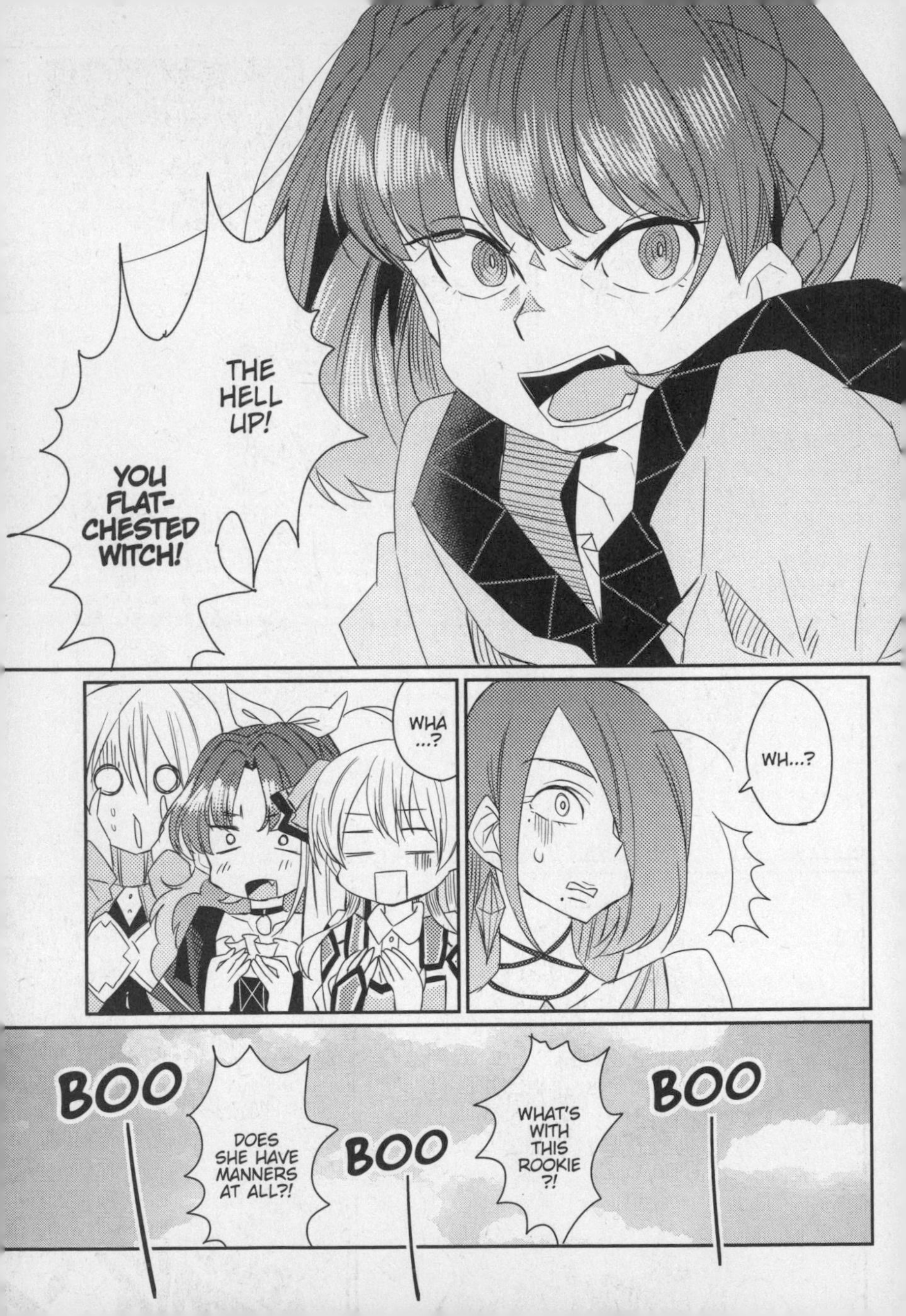
THE HELL UP!
YOU FLAT-CHESTED WITCH!
WH...?
WHA ...?
BOO
WHAT'S WITH THIS ROOKIE ?!
BOO
DOES SHE HAVE MANNERS AT ALL?!
BOO

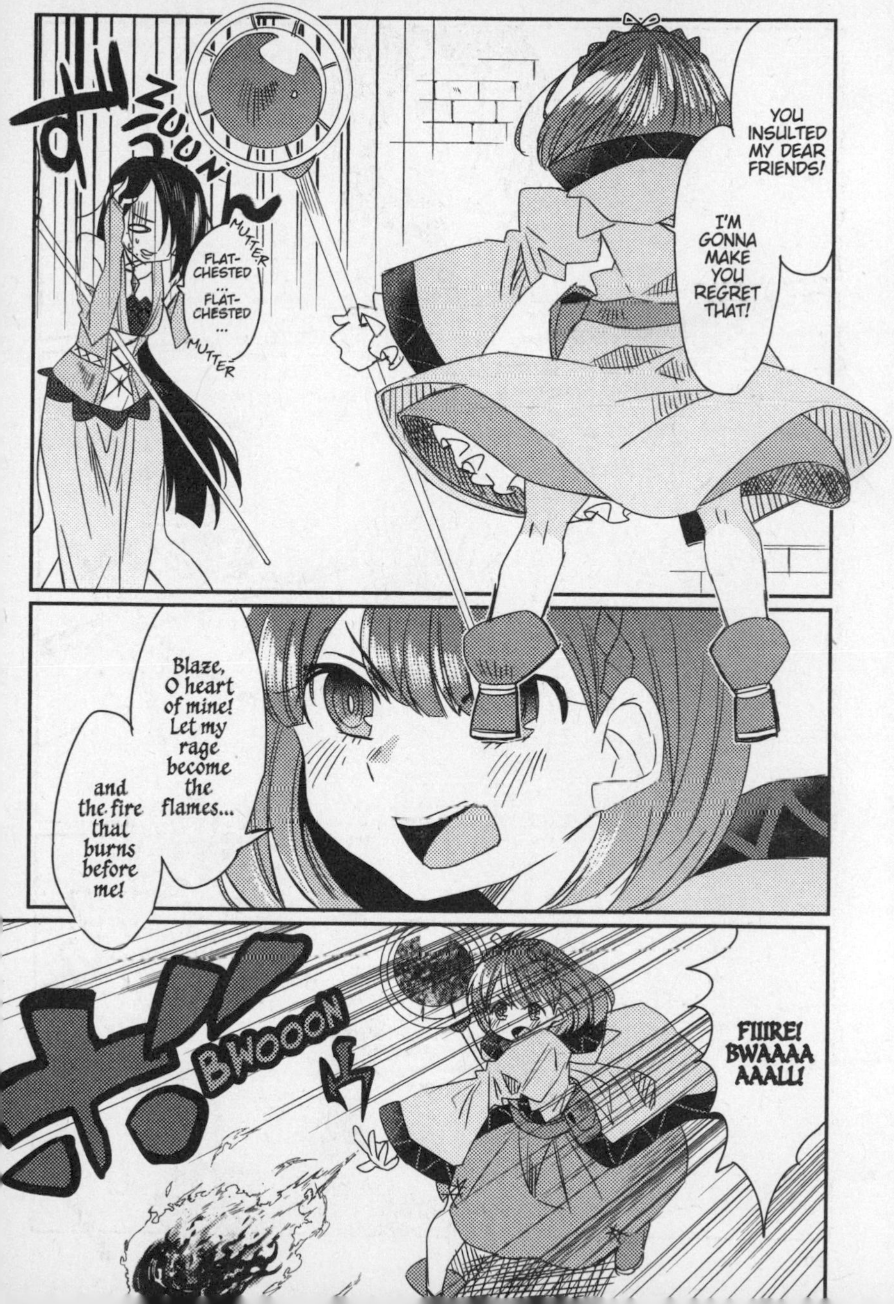
YOU INSULTED MY DEAR FRIENDS!
I'M GONNA MAKE YOU REGRET THAT!
ZUUUN
MUTTER
FLAT-CHESTED ... FLAT-CHESTED ...
MUTTER
Blaze, O heart of mine! Let my rage become the flames...
and the fire that burns before me!
FIIIRE! BWAAAAAAALL!
BWOOON

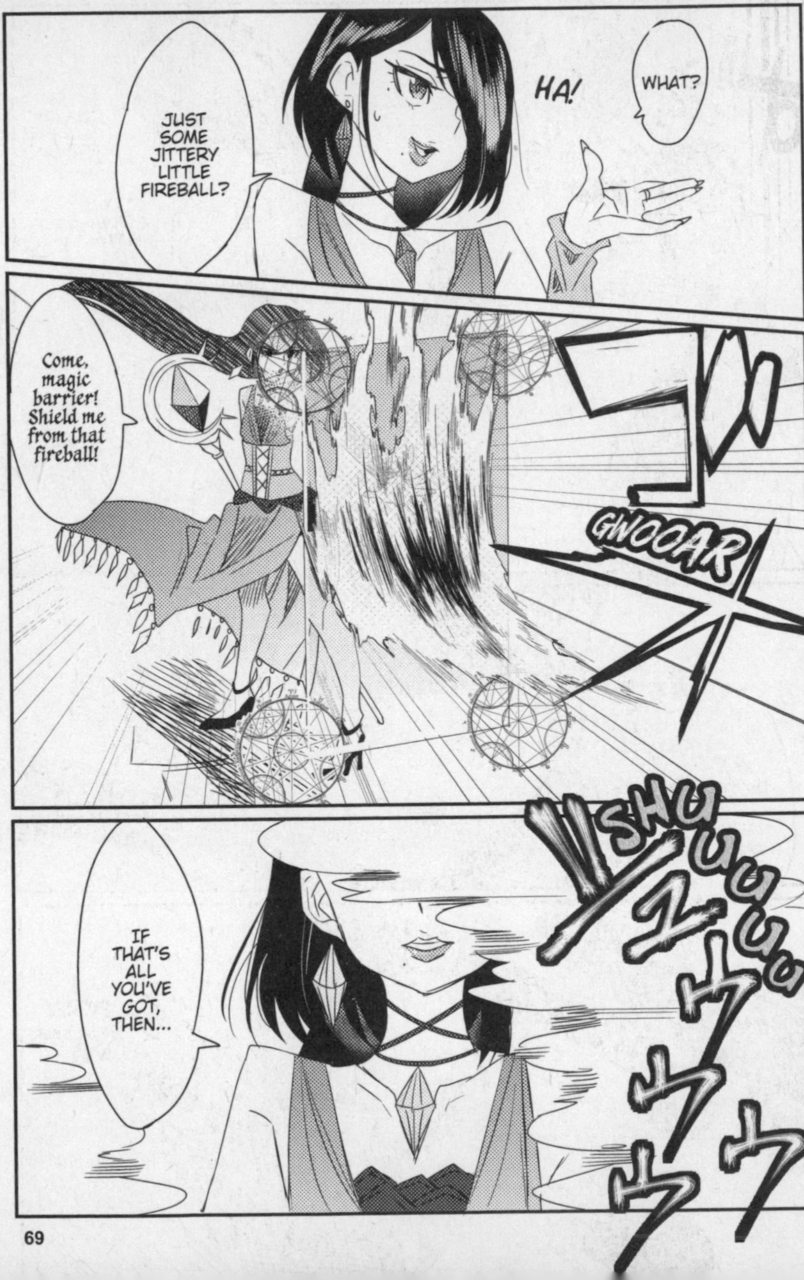
WHAT?
HA!
JUST SOME JITTERY LITTLE FIREBALL?
GWOOAR
Come, magic barrier! Shield me from that fireball!
SHUUUUUUUU
IF THAT'S ALL YOU'VE GOT, THEN...

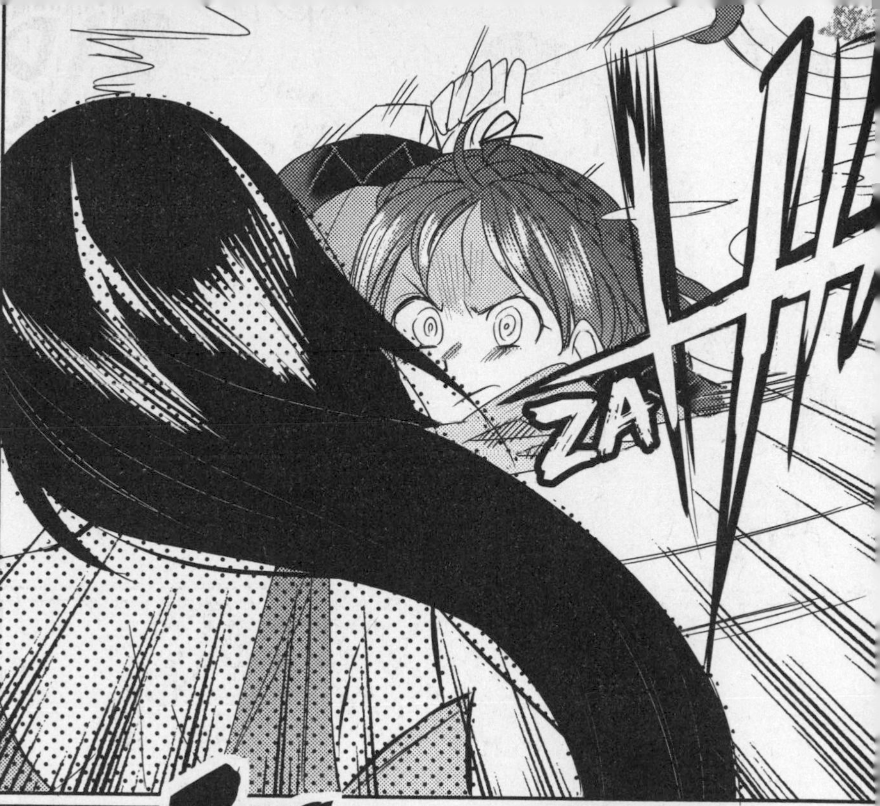
ZA
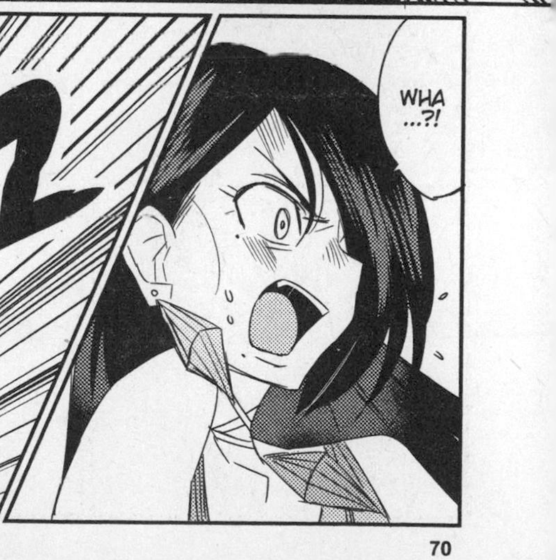
WHA ...?!
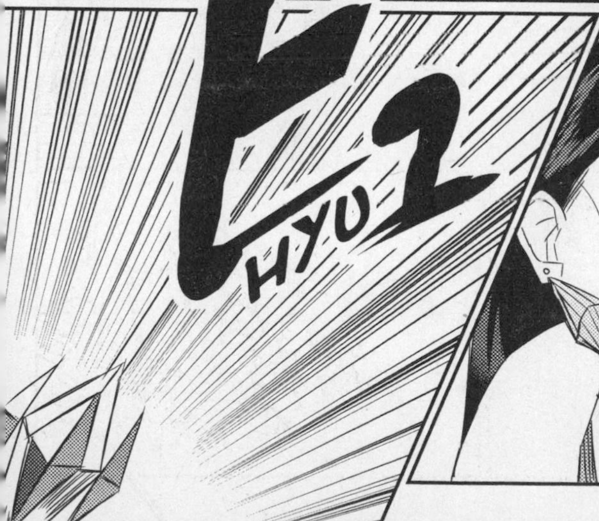
HYU

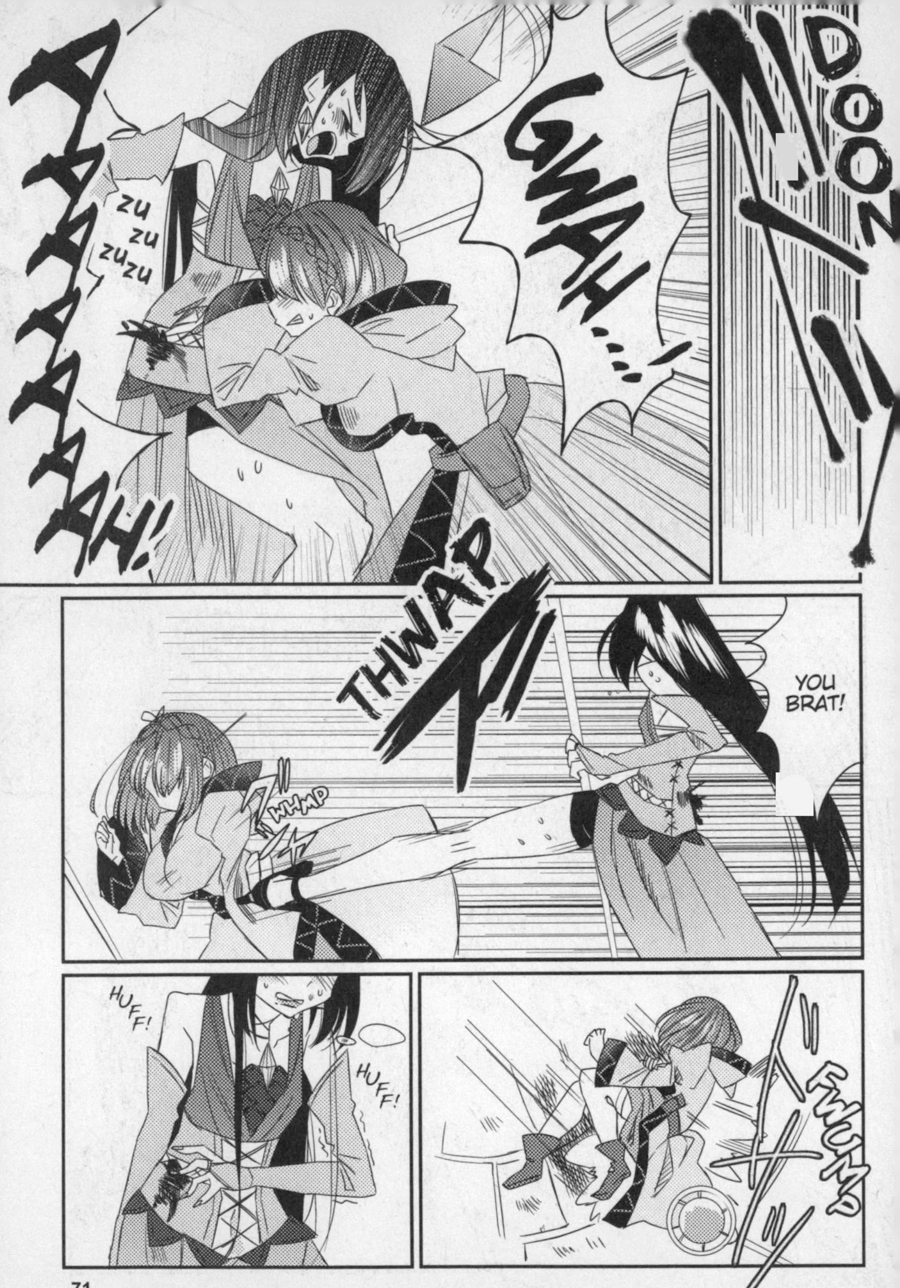
DOOON
GWAH...
ZU ZU ZUZU
AAAAAAAH!
THWAP
YOU BRAT!
WHMP
FWUMP
HUFF!
HUFF!

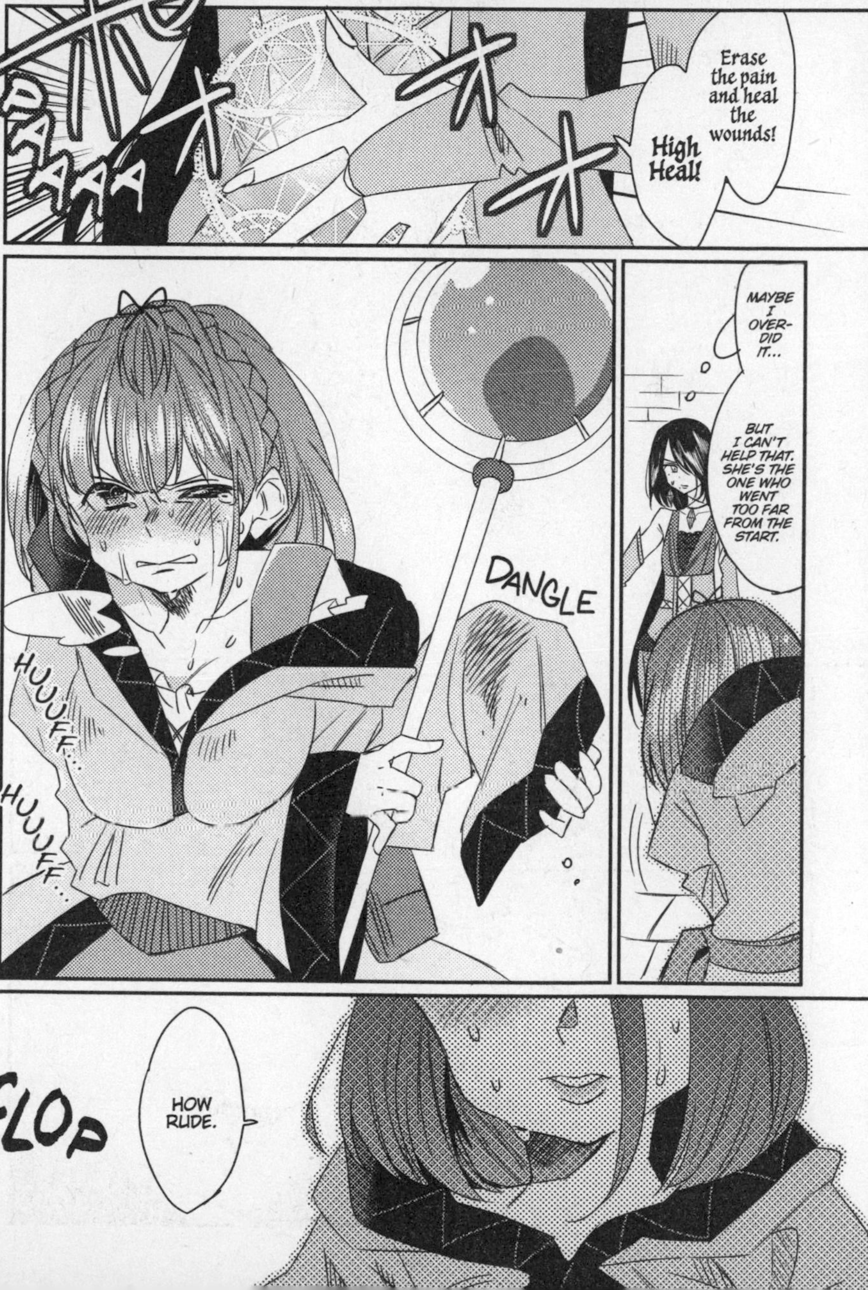
Erase the pain and heal the wounds!
High Heal!
PAAAAA
MAYBE I OVER-DID IT...
BUT I CAN'T HELP THAT. SHE'S THE ONE WHO WENT TOO FAR FROM THE START.
DANGLE
HUUUFF...
HUUUFF...
HOW RUDE.
CLOP

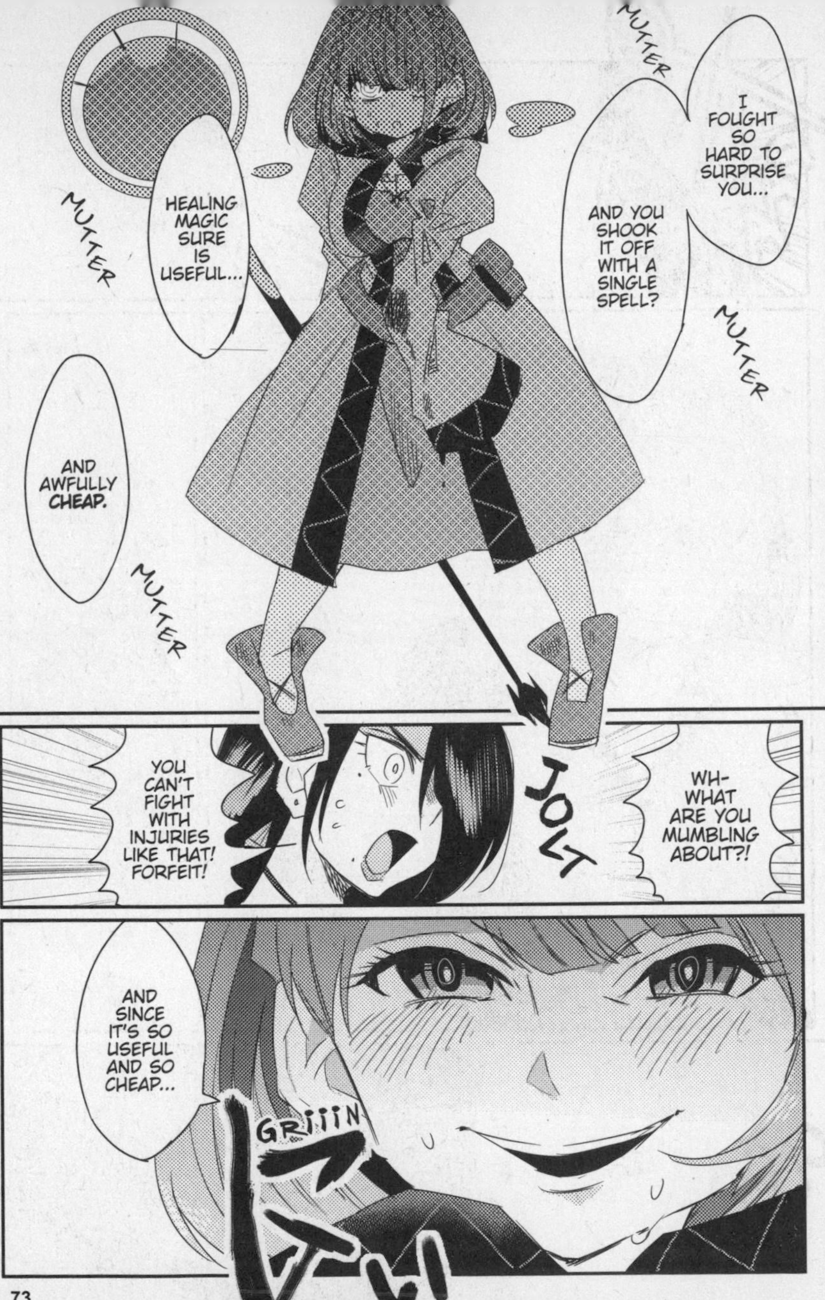
MUTTER
I FOUGHT SO HARD TO SURPRISE YOU...
AND YOU SHOOK IT OFF WITH A SINGLE SPELL?
MUTTER
HEALING MAGIC SURE IS USEFUL...
MUTTER
AND AWFULLY CHEAP.
MUTTER
WH-WHAT ARE YOU MUMBLING ABOUT?!
JOLT
YOU CAN'T FIGHT WITH INJURIES LIKE THAT! FORFEIT!
AND SINCE IT'S SO USEFUL AND SO CHEAP...
GRIIIN

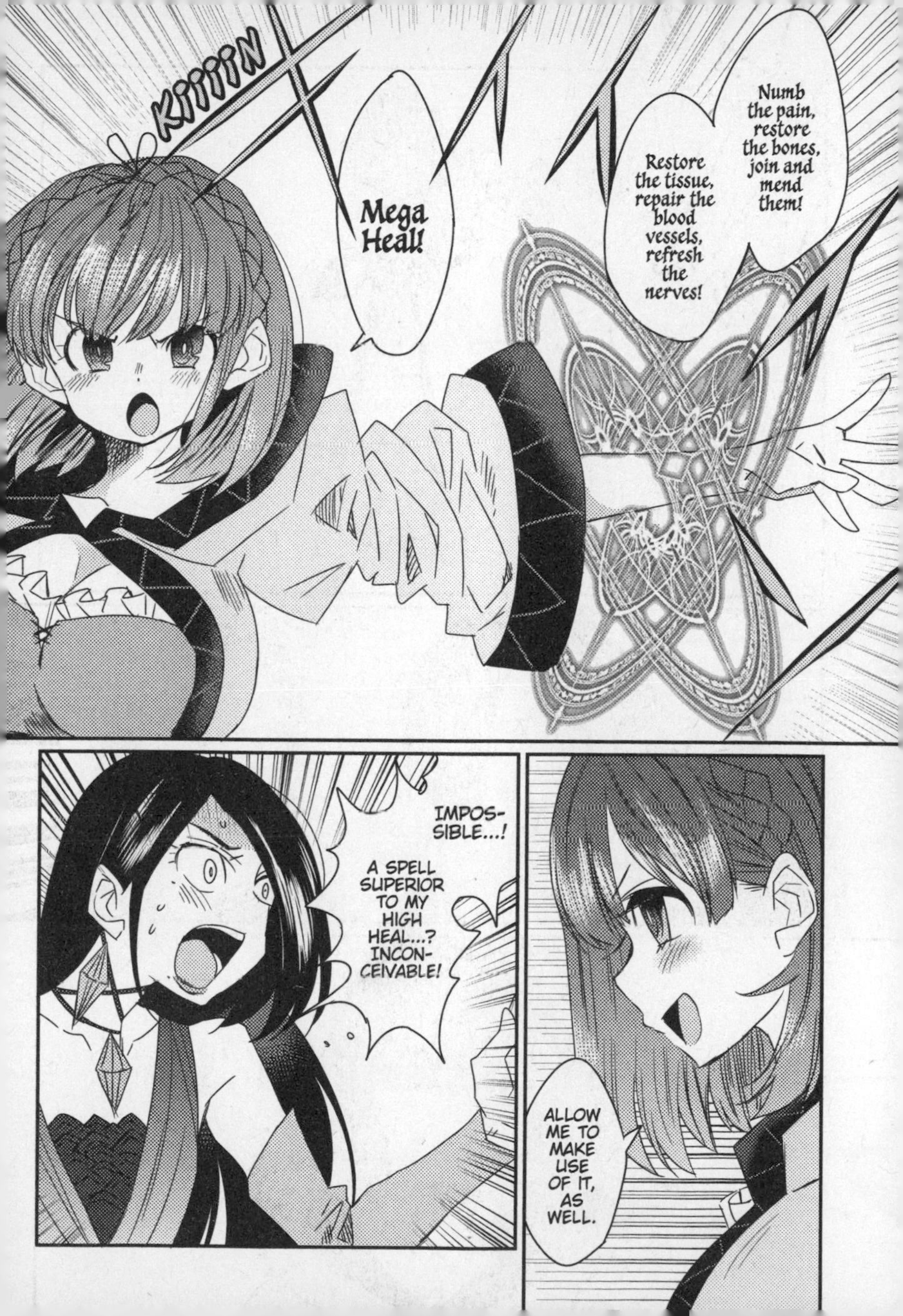
Numb the pain, restore the bones, join and mend them!
Restore the tissue, repair the blood vessels, refresh the nerves!
Mega Heal!
KIIIIN
ALLOW ME TO MAKE USE OF IT, AS WELL.
IMPOSSIBLE...!
A SPELL SUPERIOR TO MY HIGH HEAL...? INCONCEIVABLE!

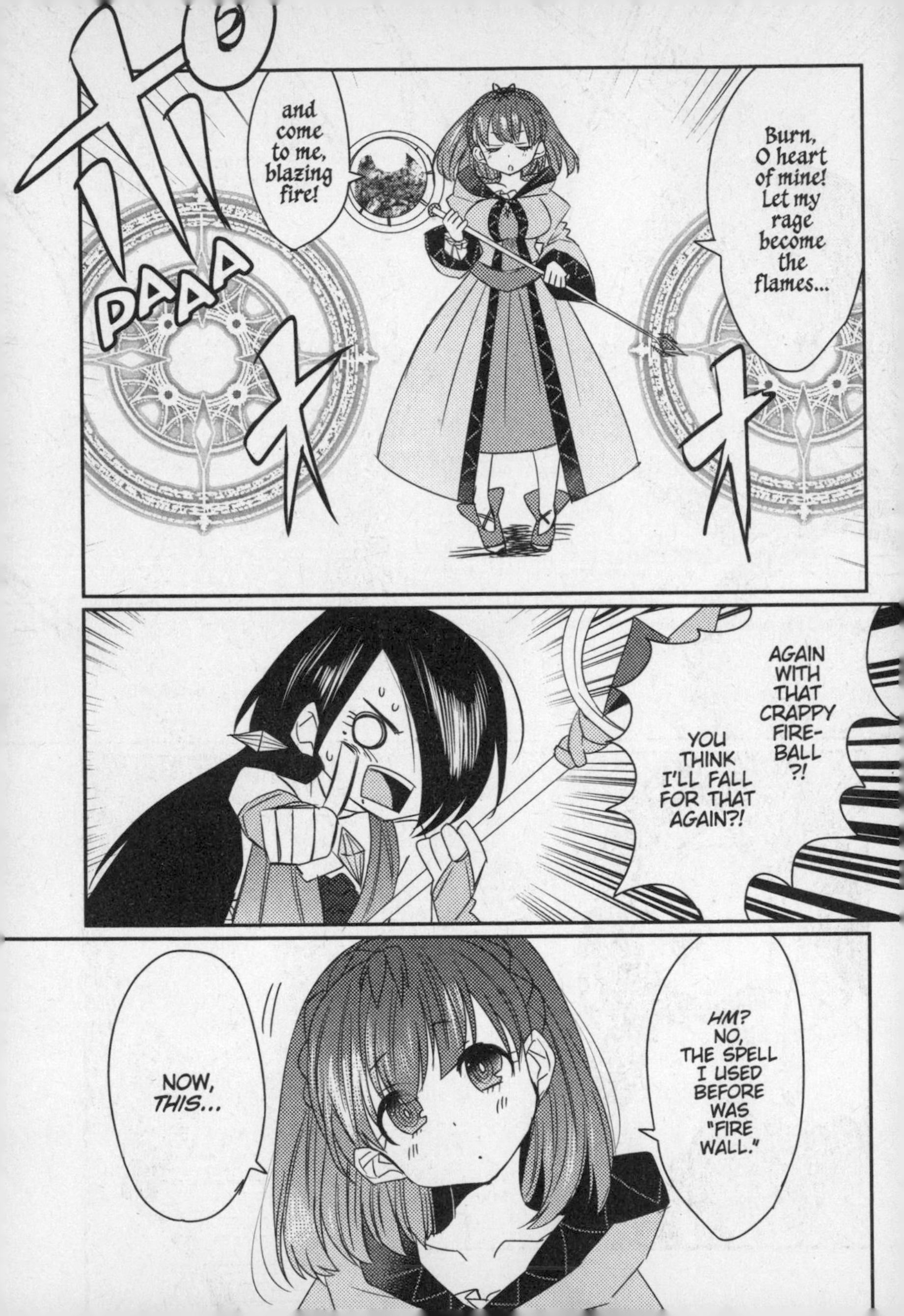
Burn, O heart of mine! Let my rage become the flames...
and come to me, blazing fire!
PAAA
AGAIN WITH THAT CRAPPY FIRE-BALL?!
YOU THINK I'LL FALL FOR THAT AGAIN?!
HM? NO, THE SPELL I USED BEFORE WAS "FIRE WALL."
NOW, THIS...

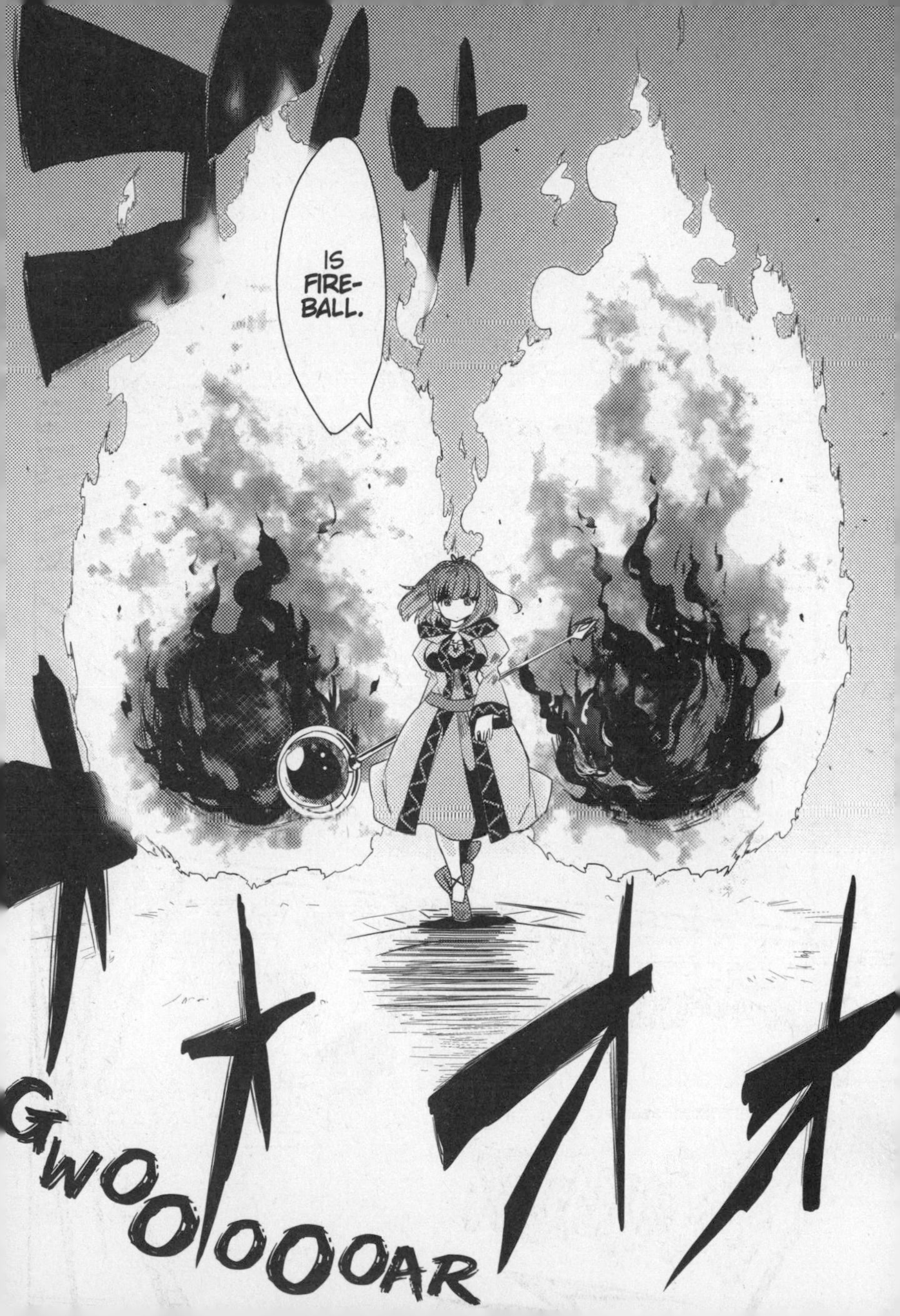
IS FIRE-BALL.
GWOOOOOOAR

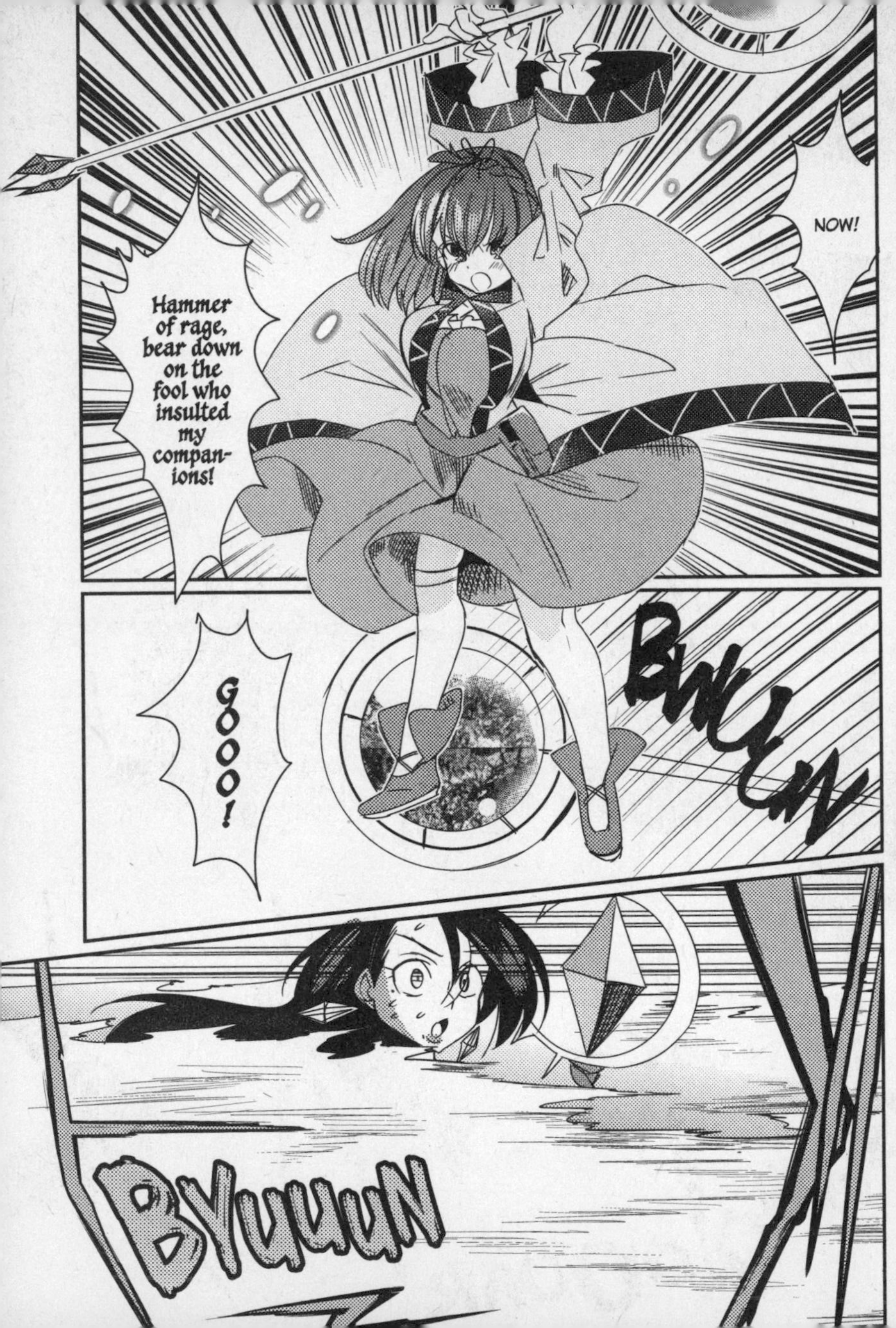
NOW!
Hammer of rage, bear down on the fool who insulted my compan-ions!
BWUUUN
GOOOO!
BYUUUN

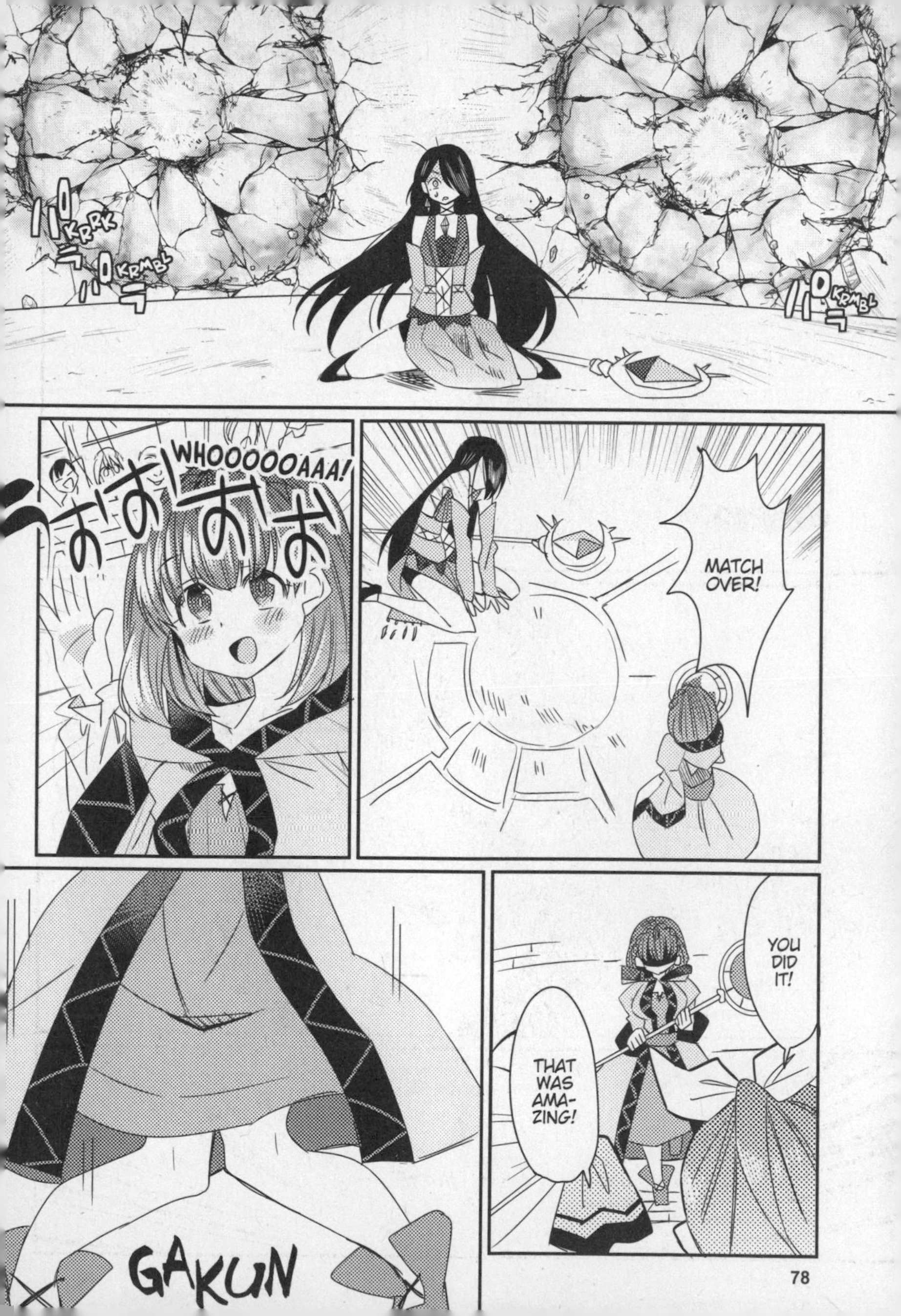
KRMBL
KRMBL
KRRK
MATCH OVER!
うおおお
WHOOOOOAAA!
YOU DID IT!
THAT WAS AMA-ZING!
GAKUN

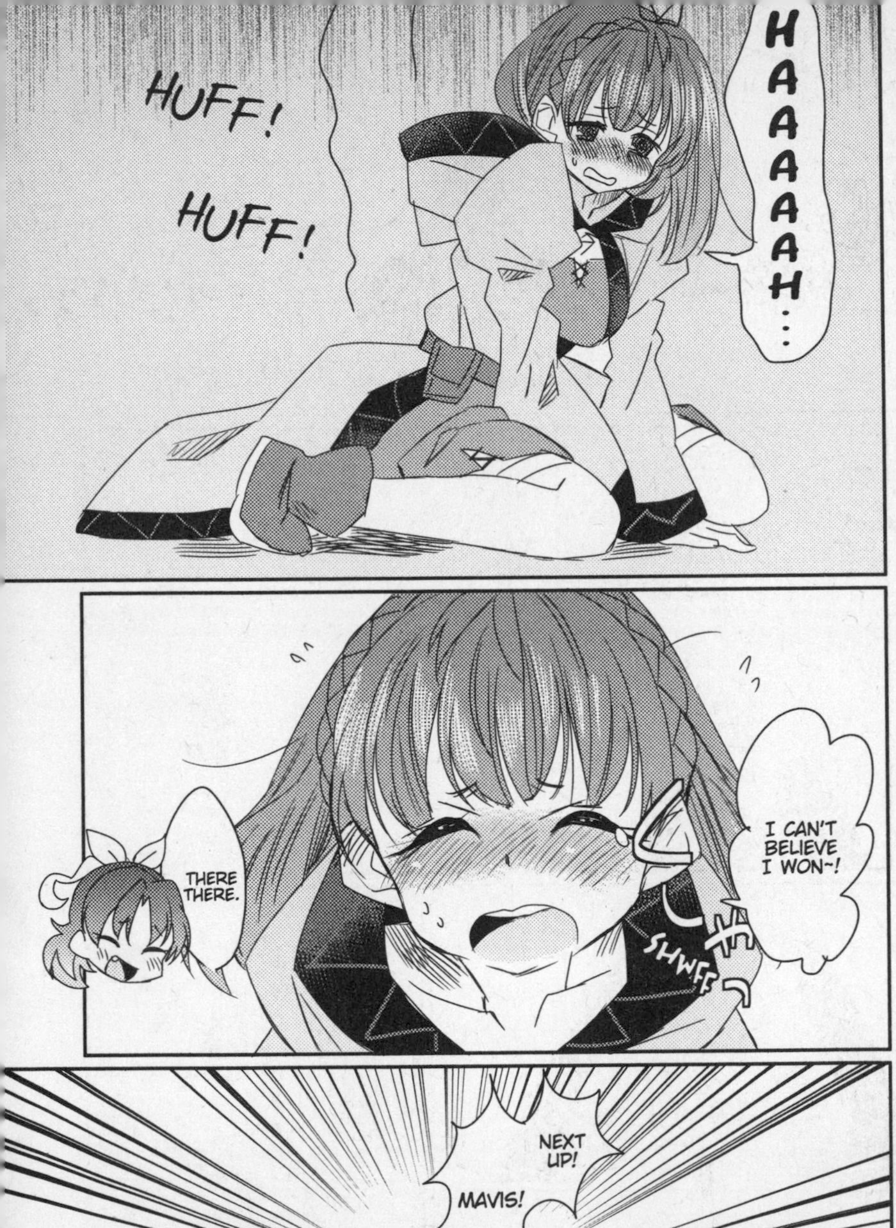
HAAAAAAH...
HUFF!
HUFF!
I CAN'T BELIEVE I WON~!
SHWFF
THERE THERE.
NEXT UP!
MAVIS!

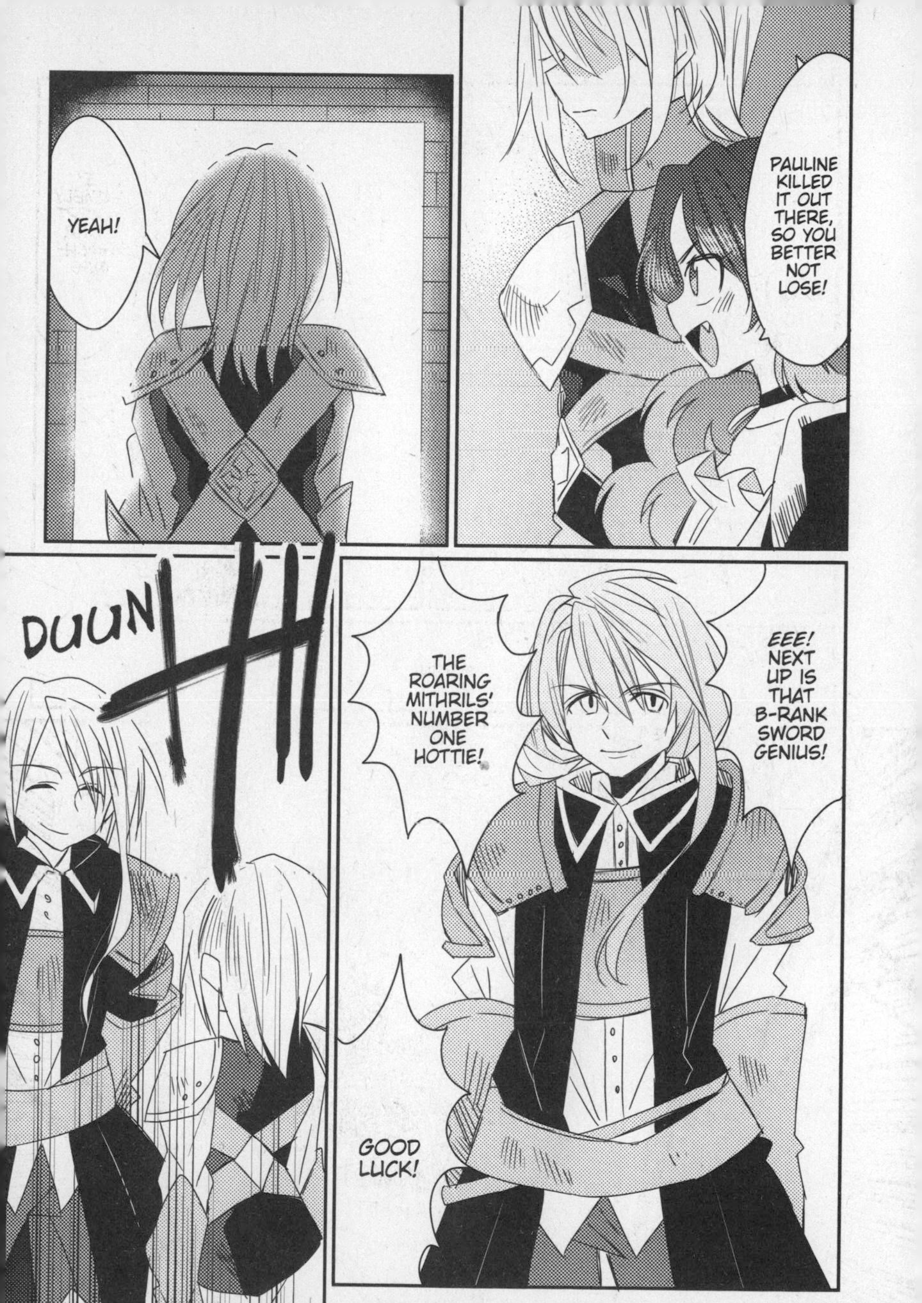
PAULINE KILLED IT OUT THERE, SO YOU BETTER NOT LOSE!
YEAH!
EEE! NEXT UP IS THAT B-RANK SWORD GENIUS!
THE ROARING MITHRILS' NUMBER ONE HOTTIE!
GOOD LUCK!
DUUN

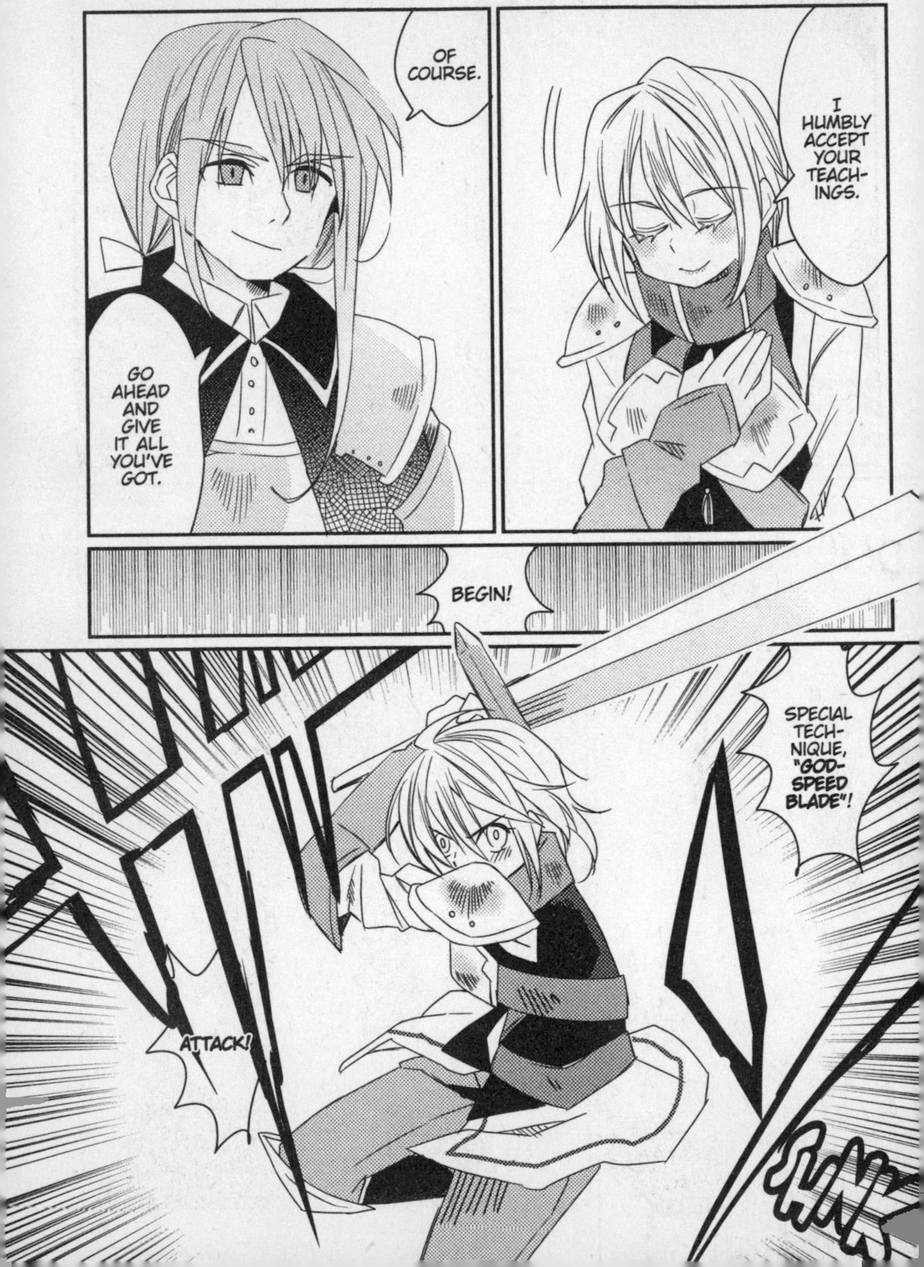
I HUMBLY ACCEPT YOUR TEACHINGS.
OF COURSE.
GO AHEAD AND GIVE IT ALL YOU'VE GOT.
BEGIN!
SPECIAL TECHNIQUE, "GOD-SPEED BLADE"!
ATTACK!

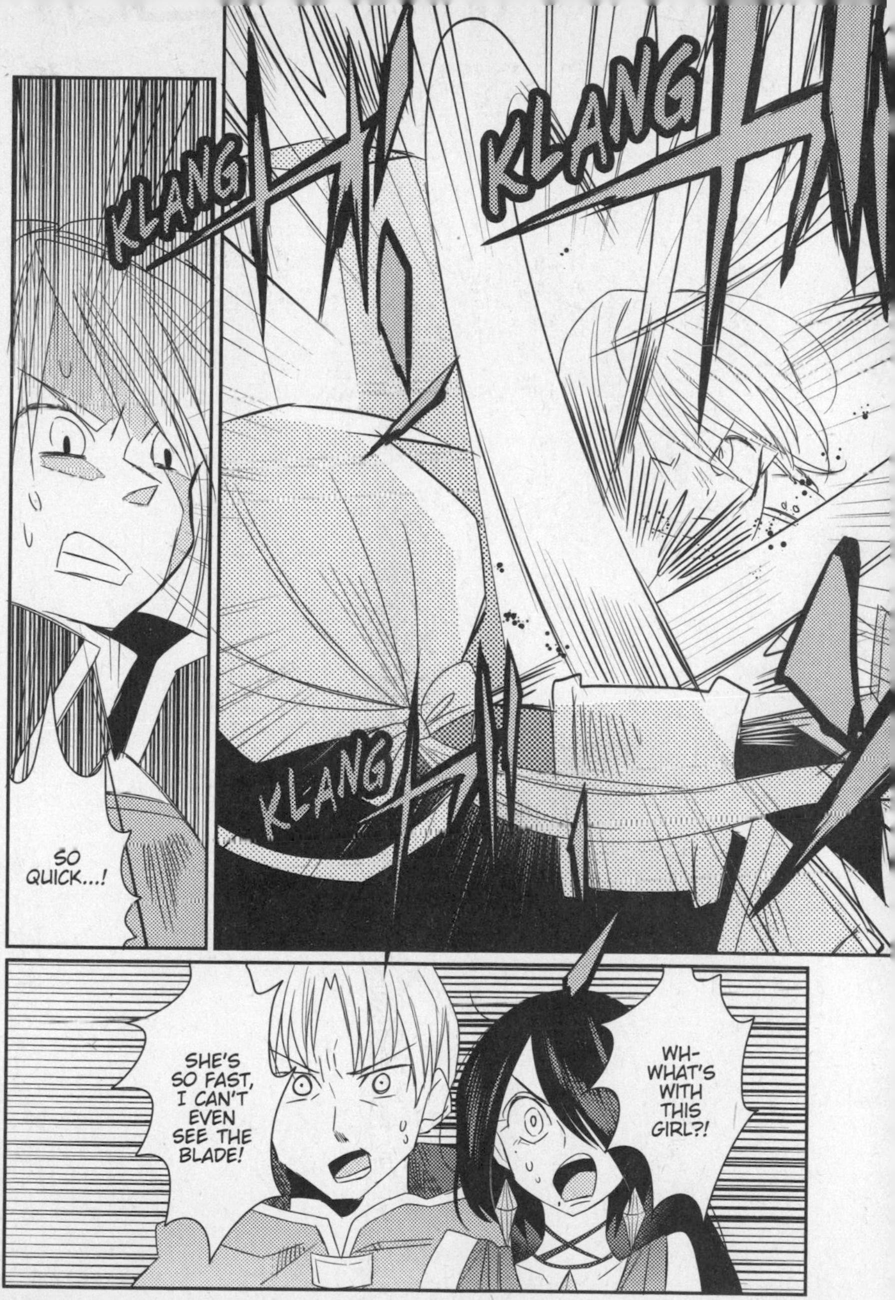
KLANG
KLANG
KLANG
SO QUICK...!
WH- WHAT'S WITH THIS GIRL?!
SHE'S SO FAST, I CAN'T EVEN SEE THE BLADE!

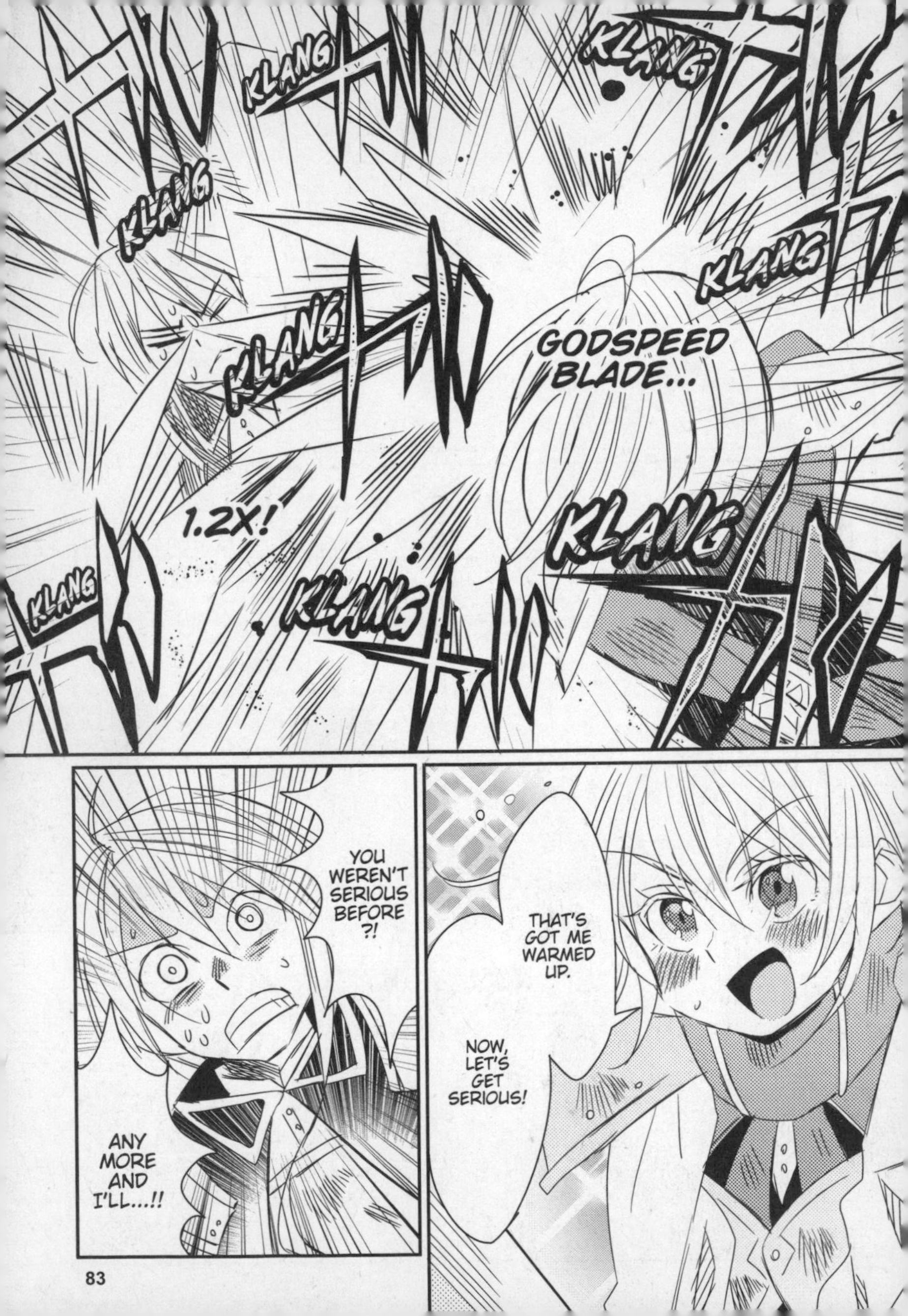
KLANG
KLANG
KLANG
KLANG
GODSPEED BLADE...
KLANG
KLANG
1.2X!
KLANG
KLANG
THAT'S GOT ME WARMED UP.
NOW, LET'S GET SERIOUS!
YOU WEREN'T SERIOUS BEFORE?!
ANY MORE AND I'LL...!!

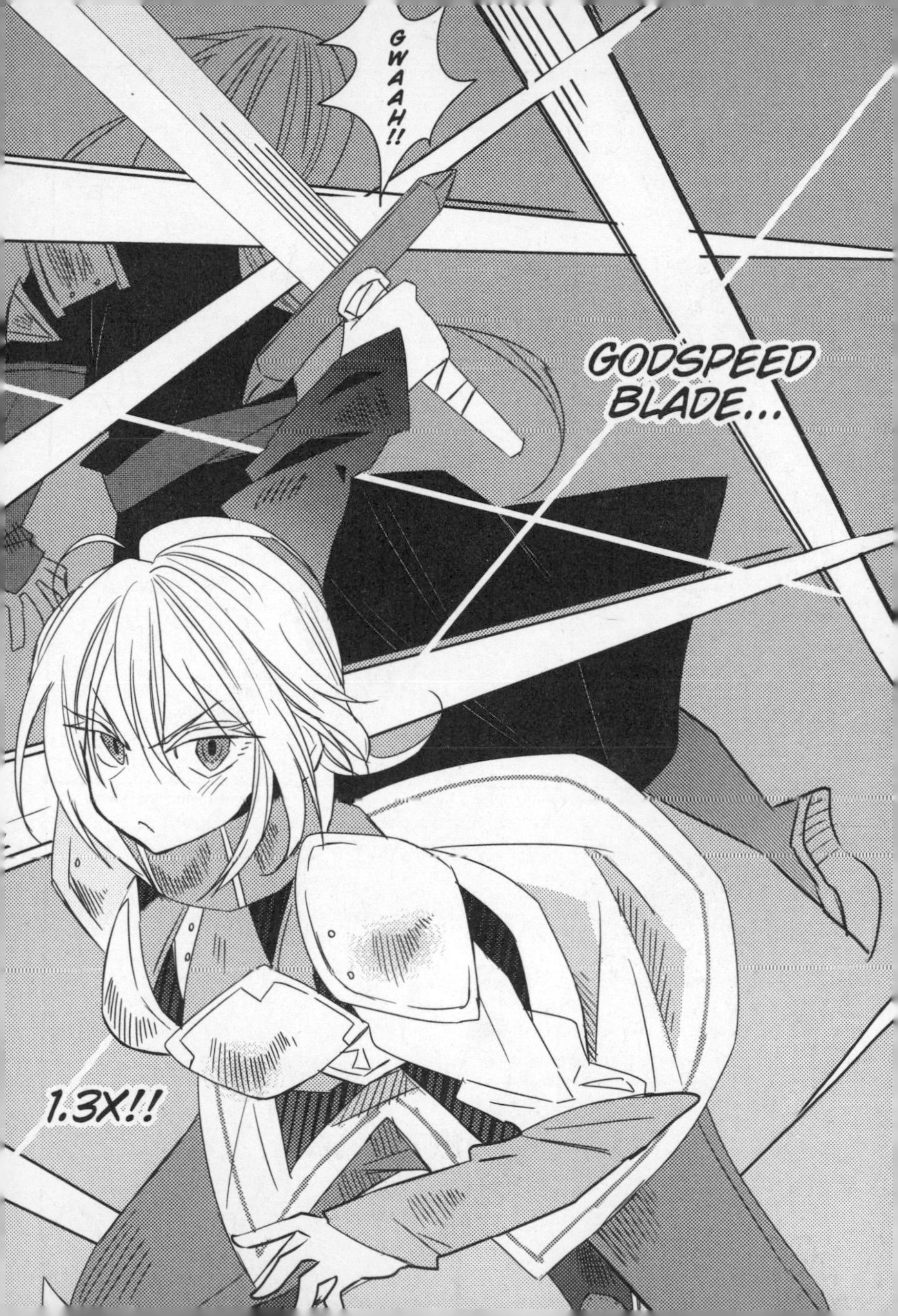
GWAAAH!!
GODSPEED BLADE...
1.3X!!

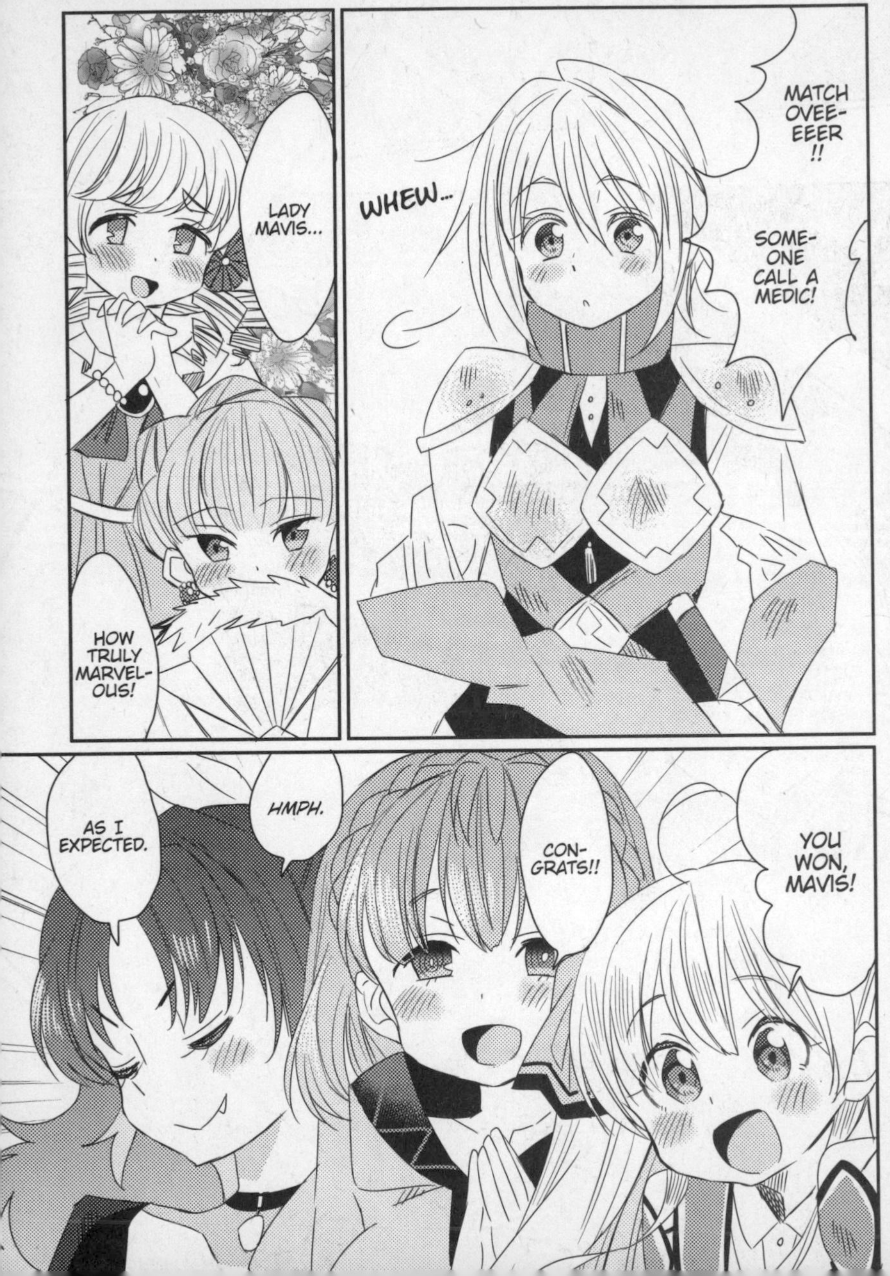
MATCH OVEEE-EEER!!
SOME-ONE CALL A MEDIC!
WHEW...
LADY MAVIS...
HOW TRULY MARVEL-OUS!
YOU WON, MAVIS!
CON-GRATS!!
HMPH.
AS I EXPECTED.

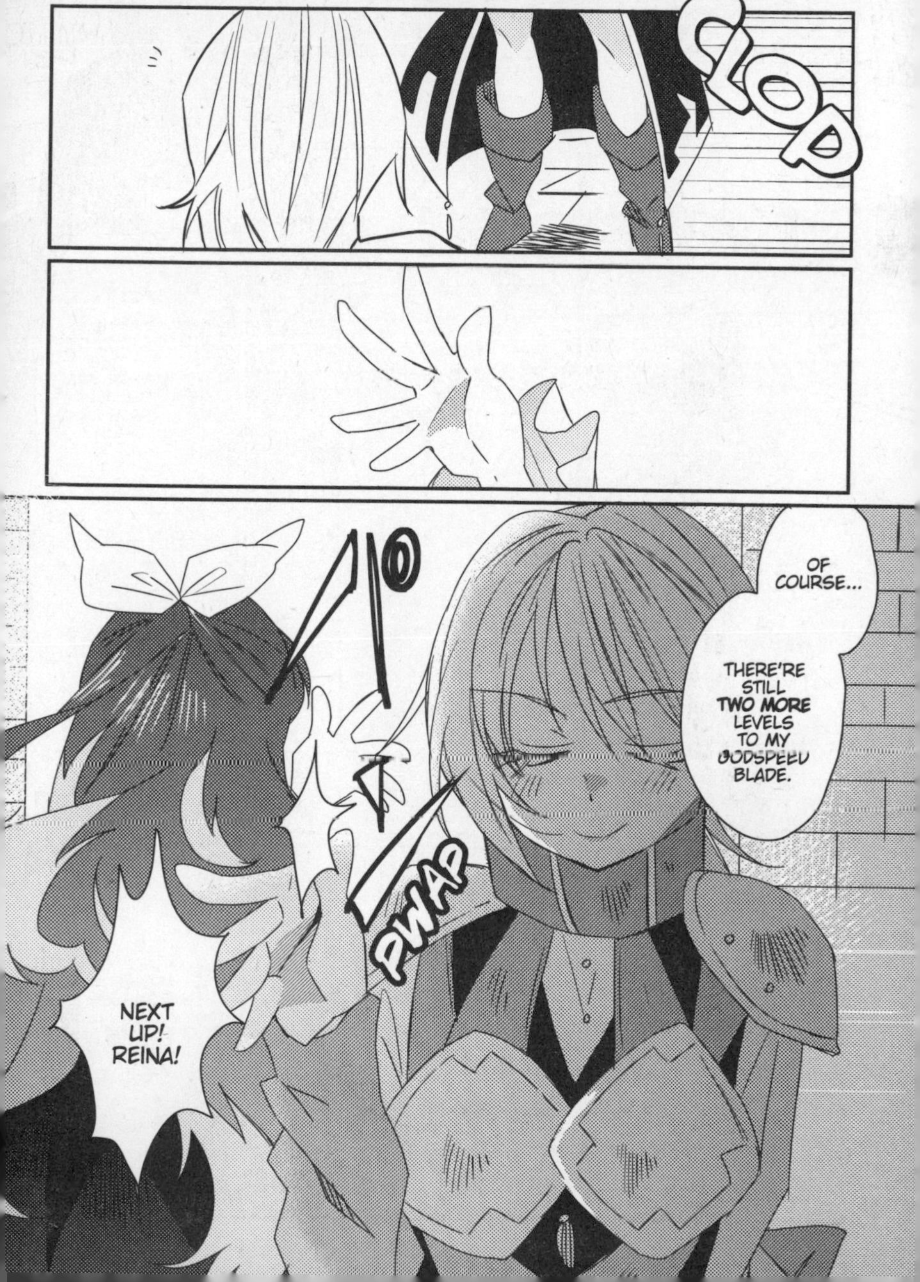
CLOP
OF COURSE...
THERE'RE STILL TWO MORE LEVELS TO MY GODSPEED BLADE.
PWAP
NEXT UP! REINA!

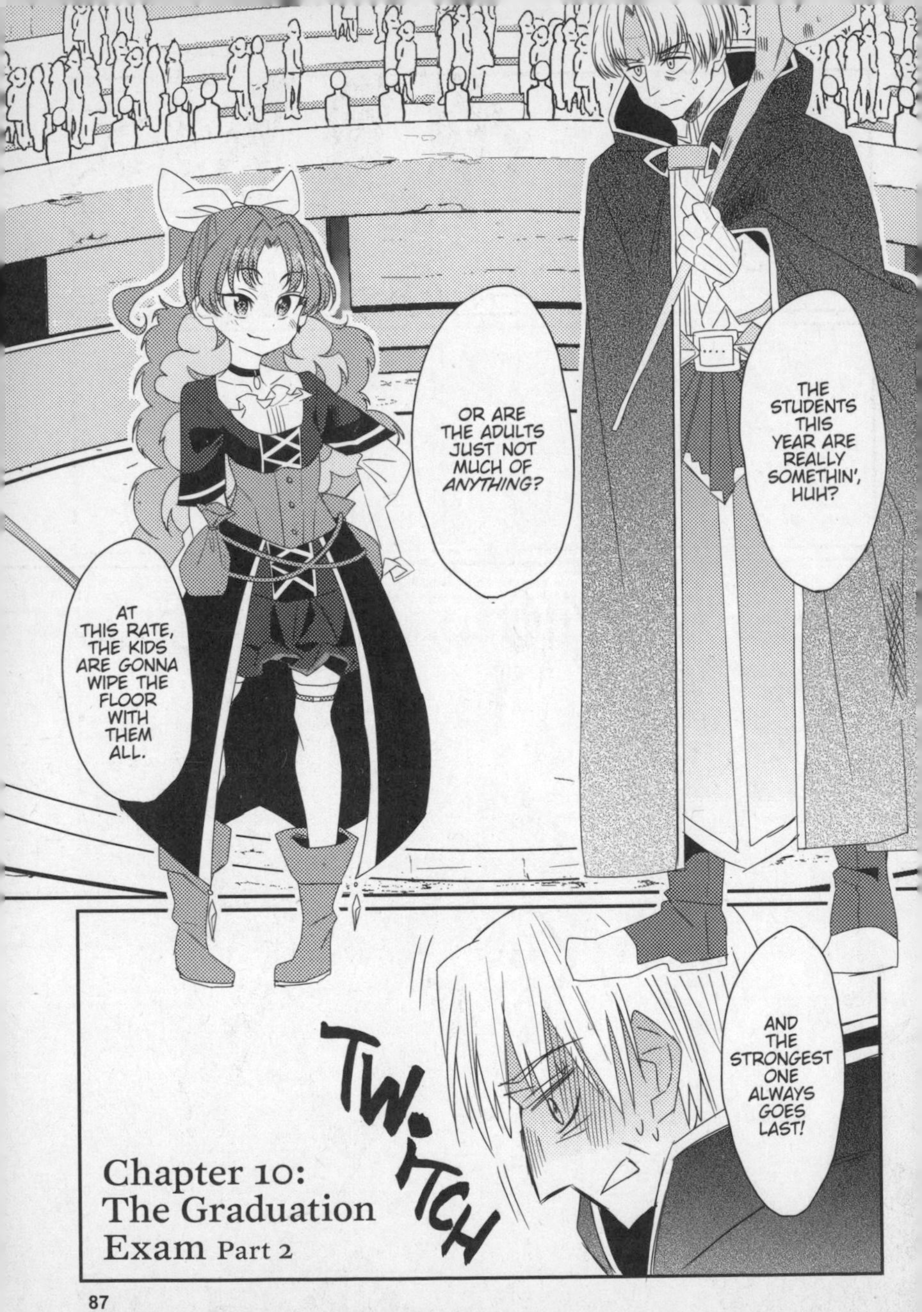
THE STUDENTS THIS YEAR ARE REALLY SOMETHIN', HUH?
....
OR ARE THE ADULTS JUST NOT MUCH OF *ANYTHING*?
AT THIS RATE, THE KIDS ARE GONNA WIPE THE FLOOR WITH THEM ALL.
AND THE STRONGEST ONE ALWAYS GOES LAST!
TWITCH

Chapter 10: The Graduation Exam Part 2

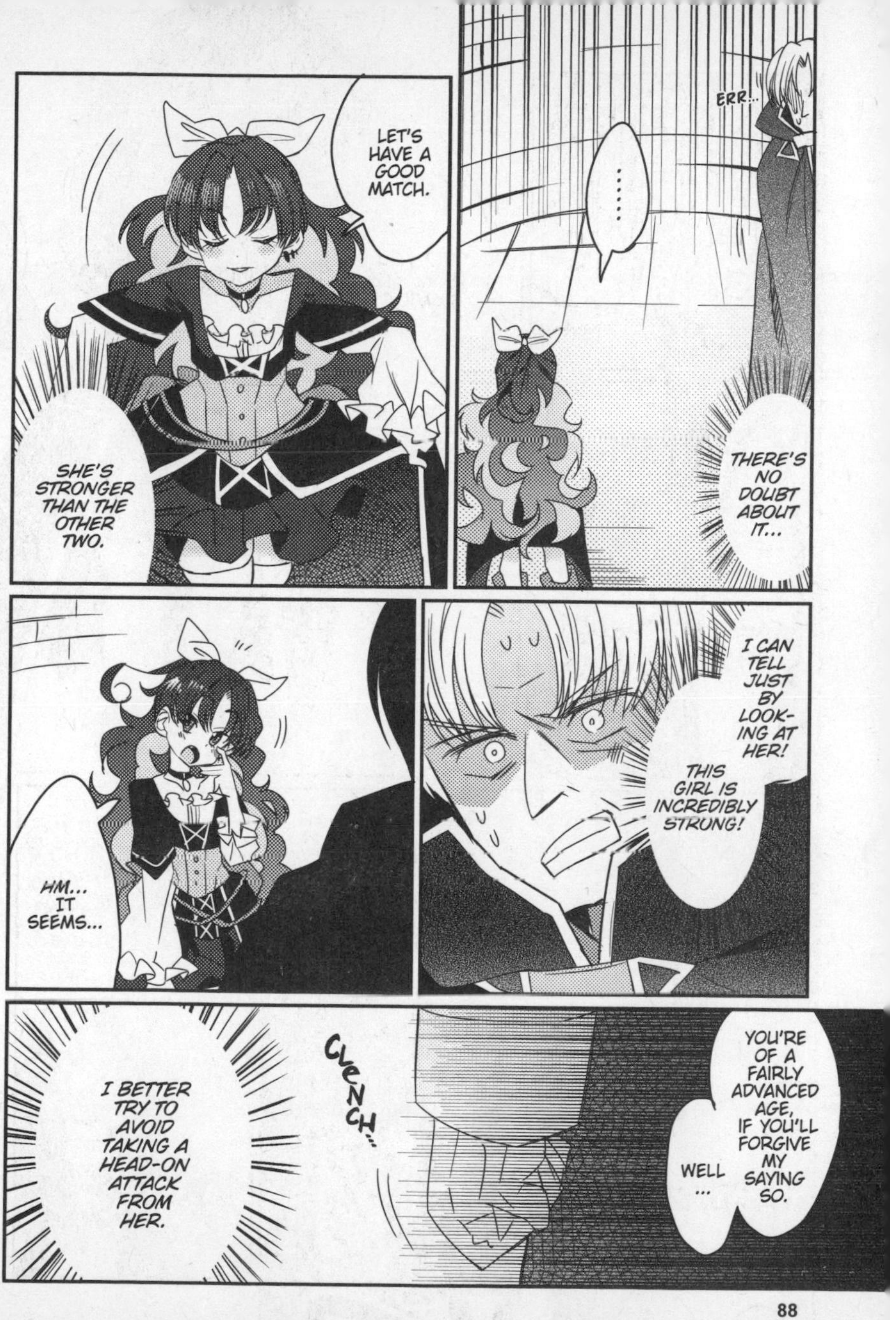
ERR...
......
THERE'S NO DOUBT ABOUT IT...
LET'S HAVE A GOOD MATCH.
SHE'S STRONGER THAN THE OTHER TWO.
I CAN TELL JUST BY LOOKING AT HER!
THIS GIRL IS INCREDIBLY STRONG!
HM... IT SEEMS...
YOU'RE OF A FAIRLY ADVANCED AGE, IF YOU'LL FORGIVE MY SAYING SO.
WELL ...
CLENCH...
I BETTER TRY TO AVOID TAKING A HEAD-ON ATTACK FROM HER.

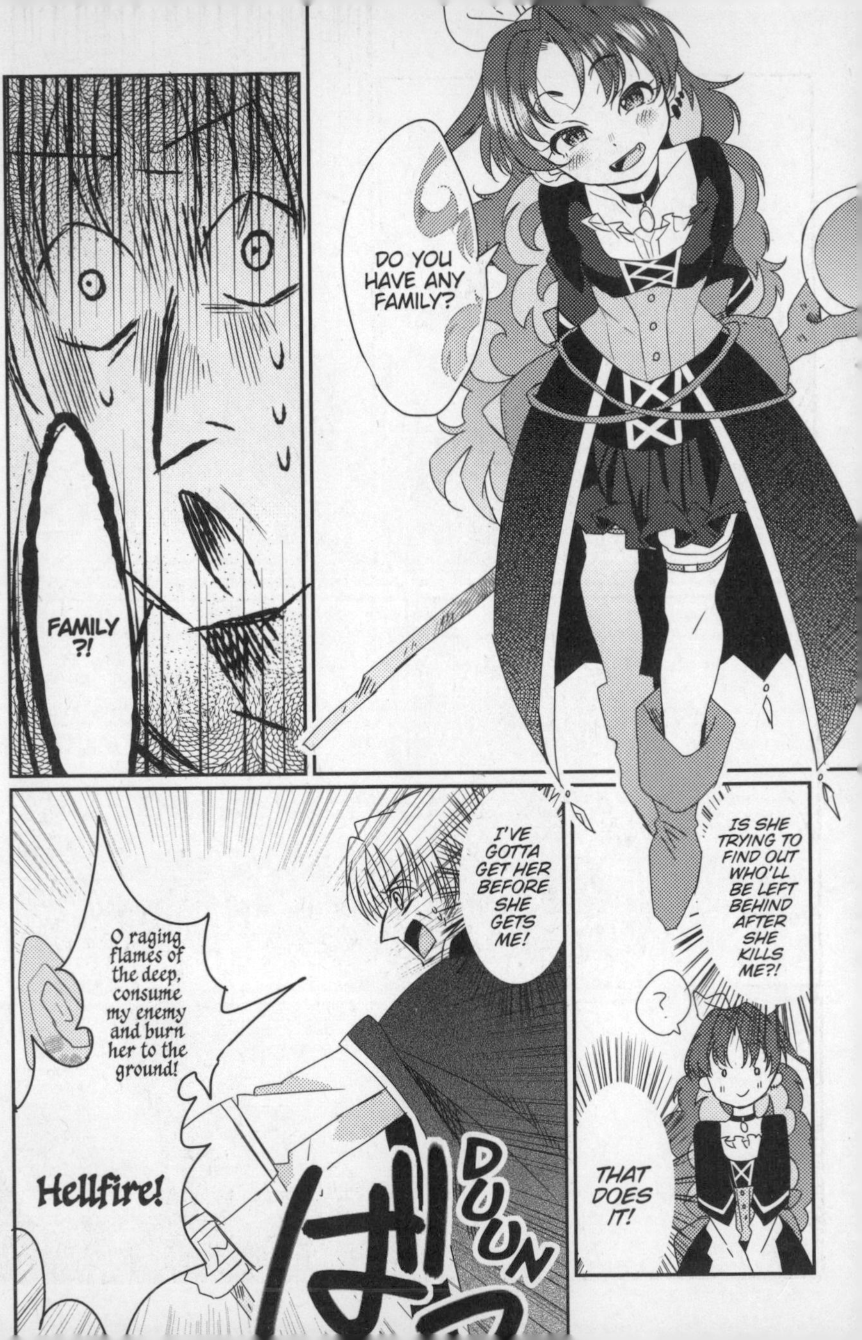
DO YOU HAVE ANY FAMILY?
FAMILY ?!
IS SHE TRYING TO FIND OUT WHO'LL BE LEFT BEHIND AFTER SHE KILLS ME?!
?
THAT DOES IT!
I'VE GOTTA GET HER BEFORE SHE GETS ME!
O raging flames of the deep, consume my enemy and burn her to the ground!
Hellfire!
DUUN

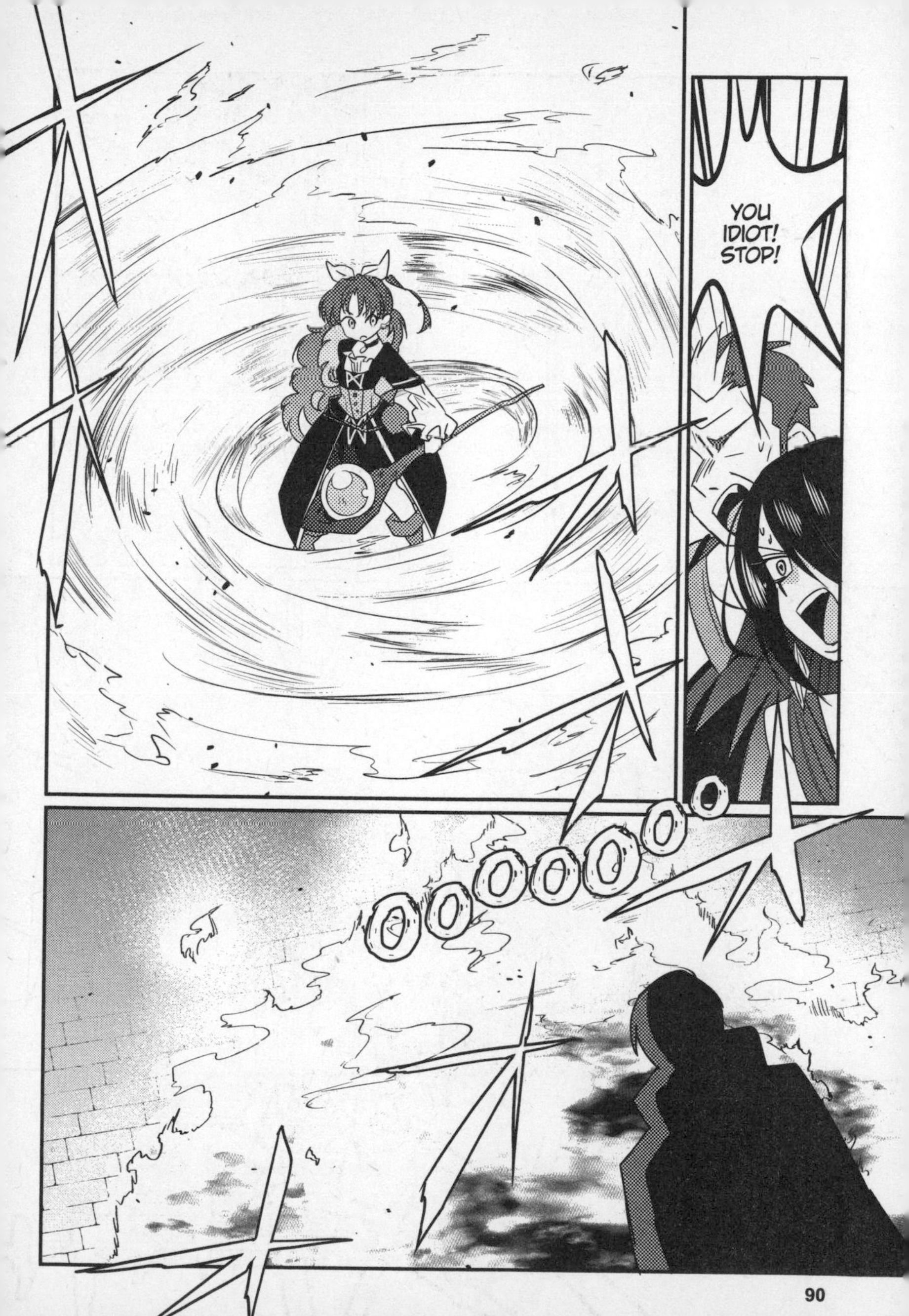
YOU IDIOT! STOP!
OOOOOOOOO

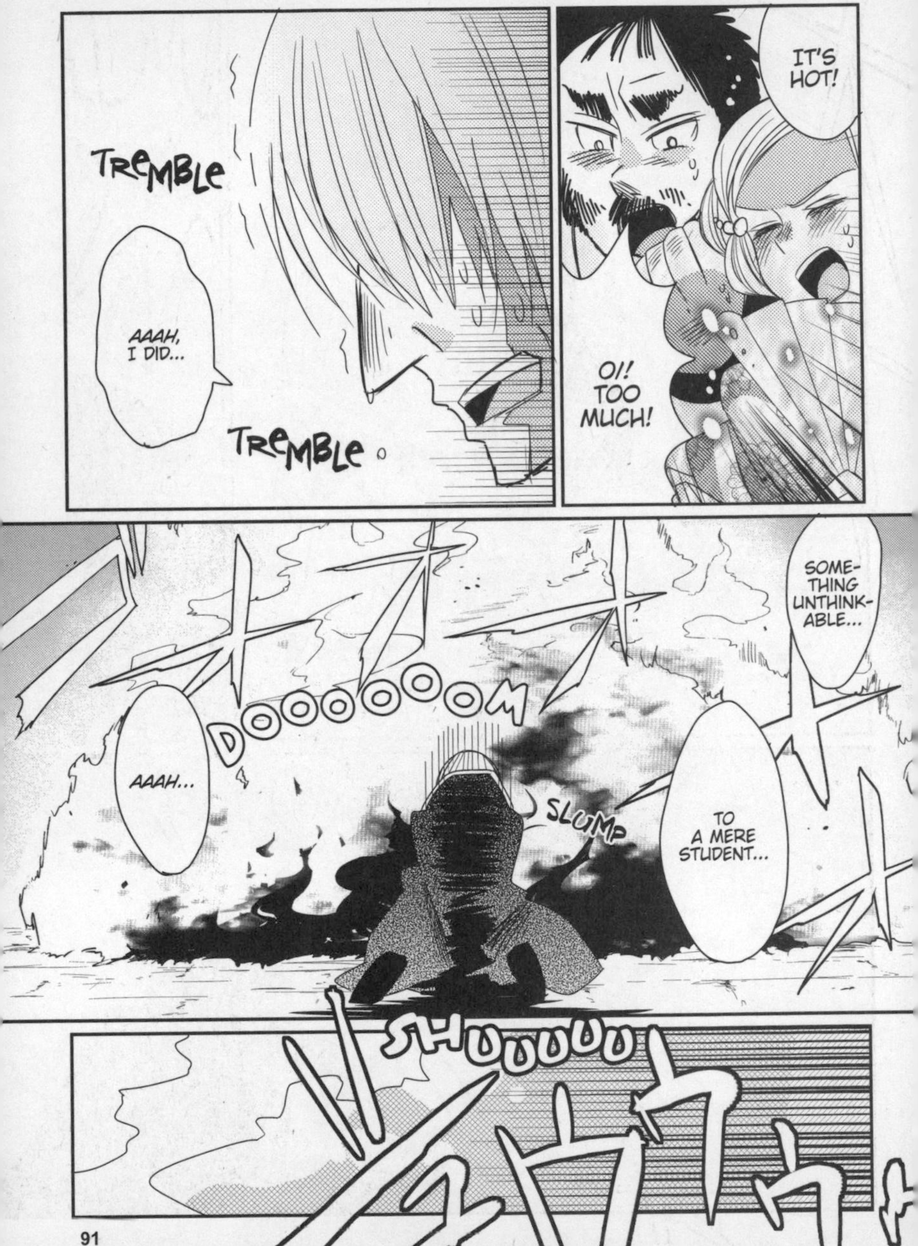
IT'S HOT!
OI! TOO MUCH!
TREMBLE
AAAH, I DID...
TREMBLE
SOME-THING UNTHINK-ABLE...
TO A MERE STUDENT...
DOOOOOOOM
SLUMP
AAAH...
SHUUUUU

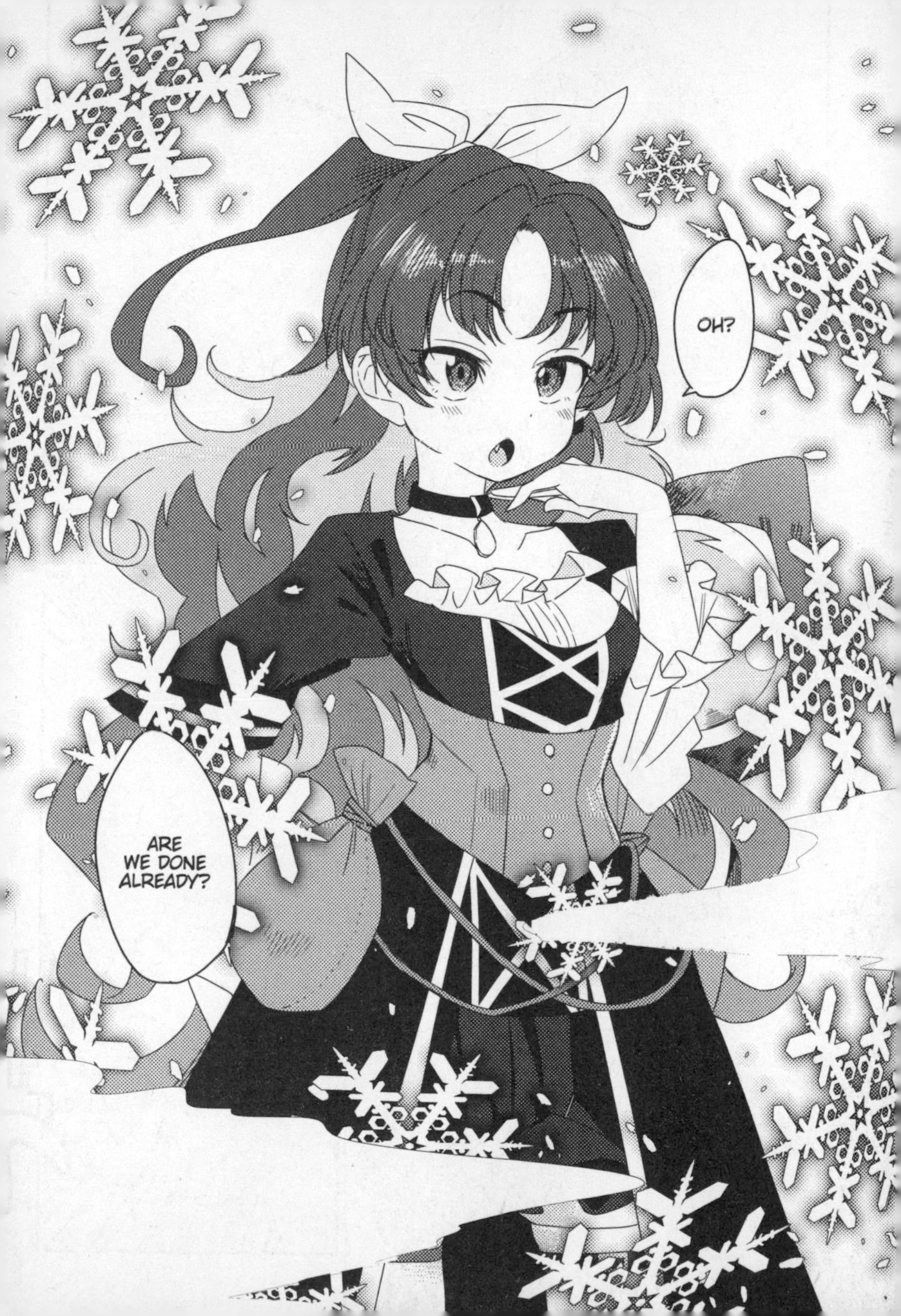
OH?
ARE WE DONE ALREADY?

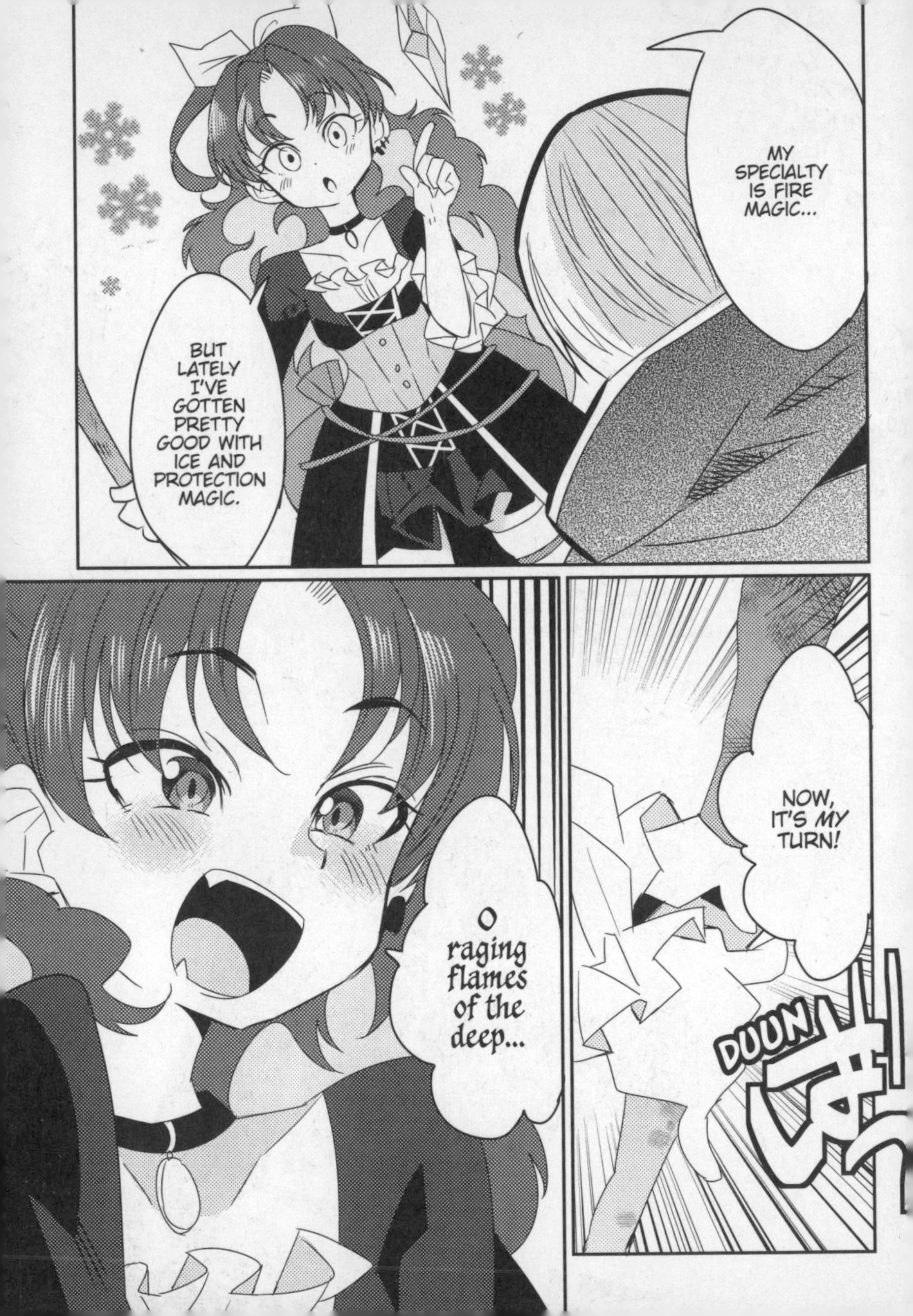
MY SPECIALTY IS FIRE MAGIC...
BUT LATELY I'VE GOTTEN PRETTY GOOD WITH ICE AND PROTECTION MAGIC.
NOW, IT'S MY TURN!
DUUN
O raging flames of the deep...

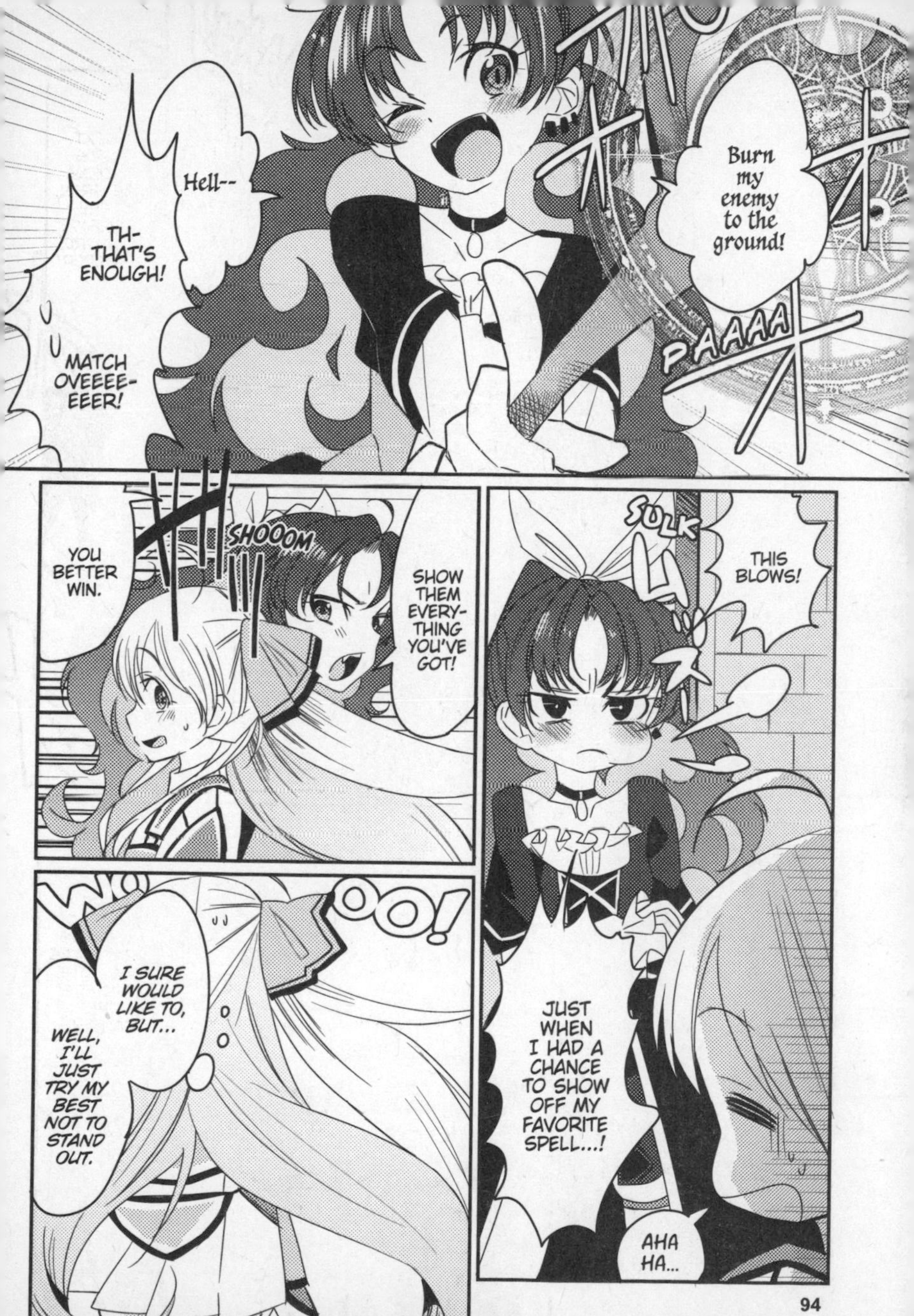
Burn my enemy to the ground!
PAAAA
Hell--
TH-THAT'S ENOUGH!
MATCH OVEEEEEEER!
SULK
THIS BLOWS!
JUST WHEN I HAD A CHANCE TO SHOW OFF MY FAVORITE SPELL...!
AHA HA...
SHOOOM
SHOW THEM EVERYTHING YOU'VE GOT!
YOU BETTER WIN.
WOOO!
I SURE WOULD LIKE TO, BUT...
WELL, I'LL JUST TRY MY BEST NOT TO STAND OUT.

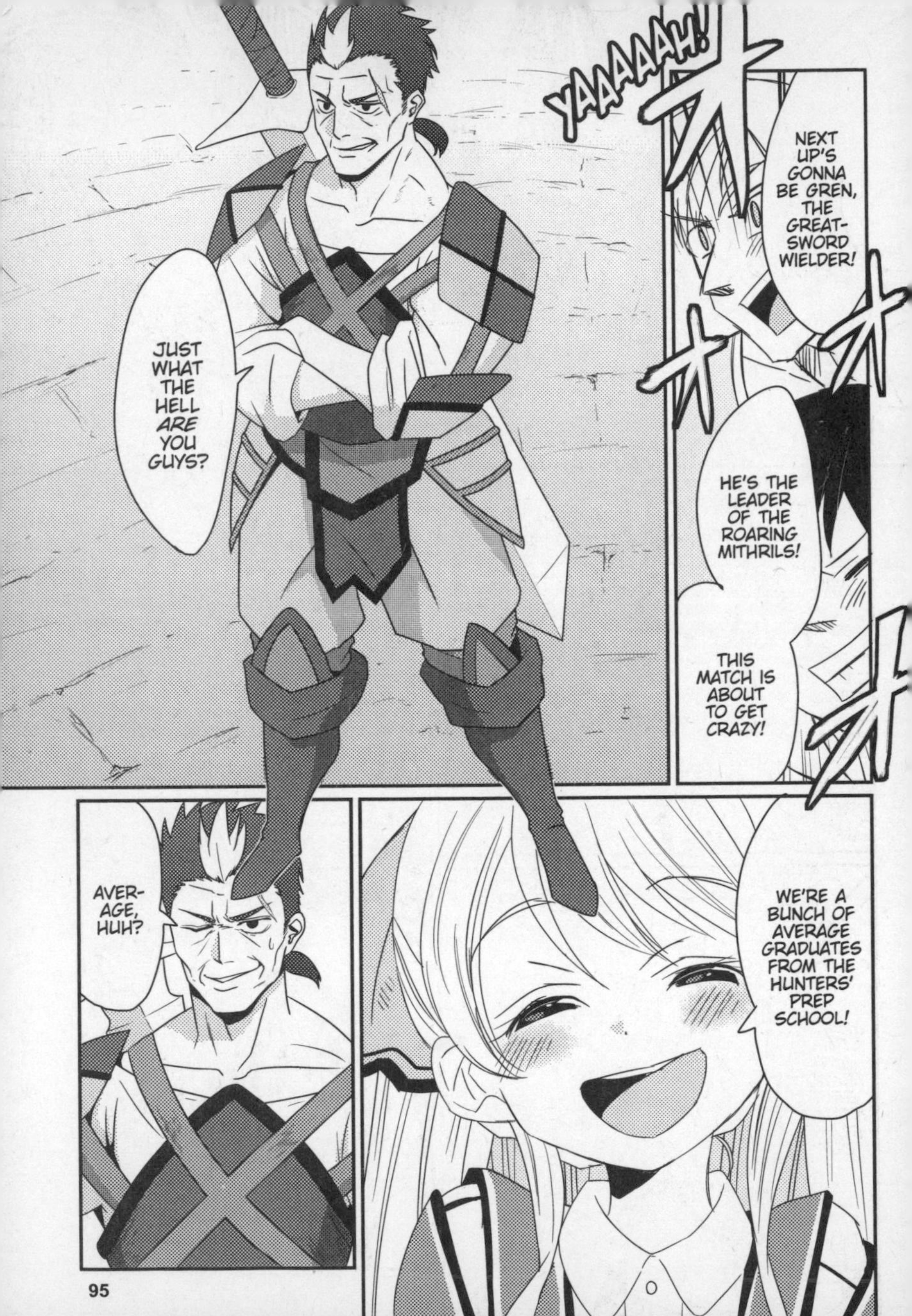
YAAAAAH!
NEXT UP'S GONNA BE GREN, THE GREAT-SWORD WIELDER!
HE'S THE LEADER OF THE ROARING MITHRILS!
THIS MATCH IS ABOUT TO GET CRAZY!
JUST WHAT THE HELL *ARE* YOU GUYS?
WE'RE A BUNCH OF AVERAGE GRADUATES FROM THE HUNTERS' PREP SCHOOL!
AVER-AGE, HUH?

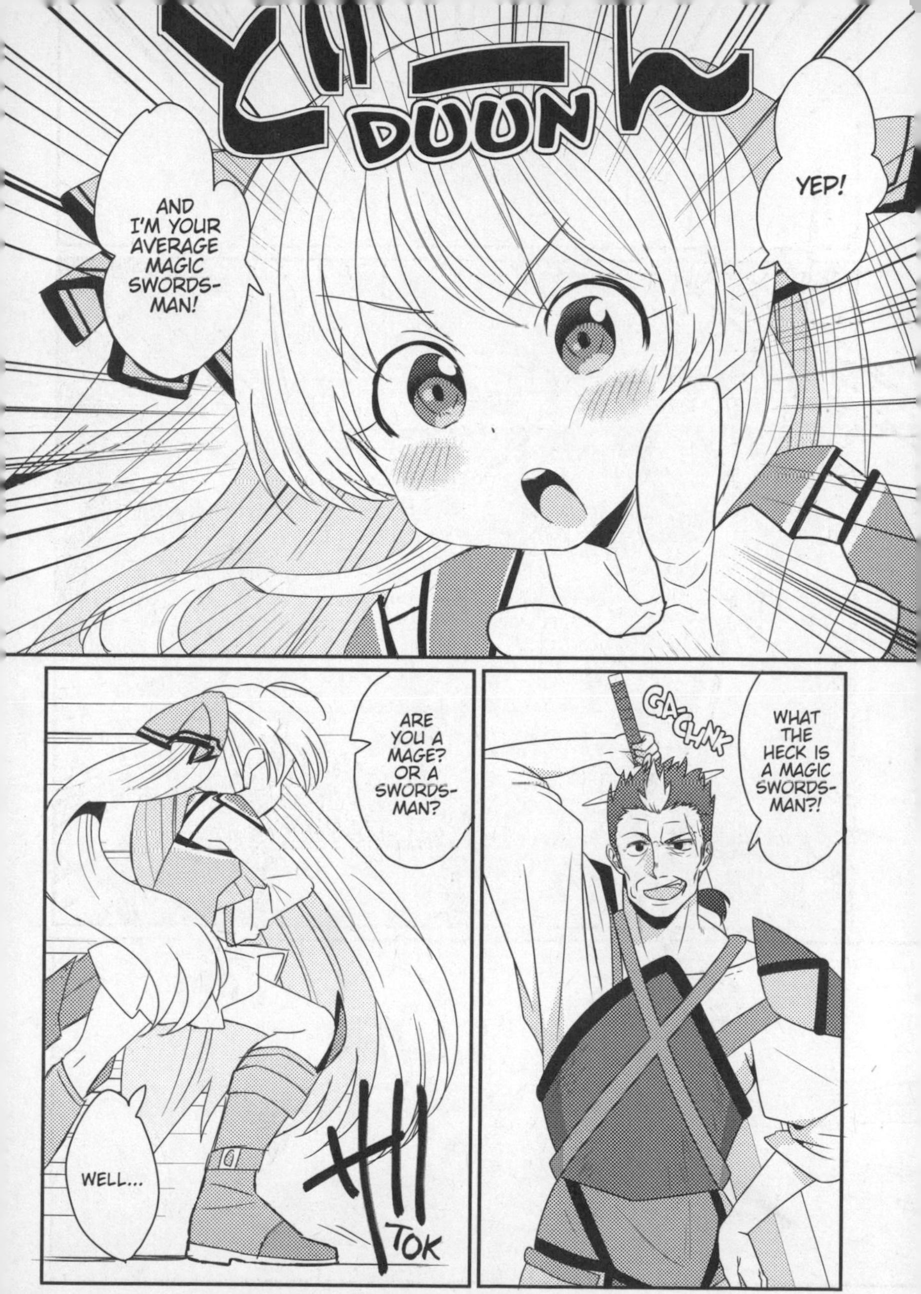
YEP!
どーん
DUUN
AND I'M YOUR AVERAGE MAGIC SWORDSMAN!
GA-CHNK
WHAT THE HECK IS A MAGIC SWORDSMAN?!
ARE YOU A MAGE? OR A SWORDSMAN?
TOK
WELL...

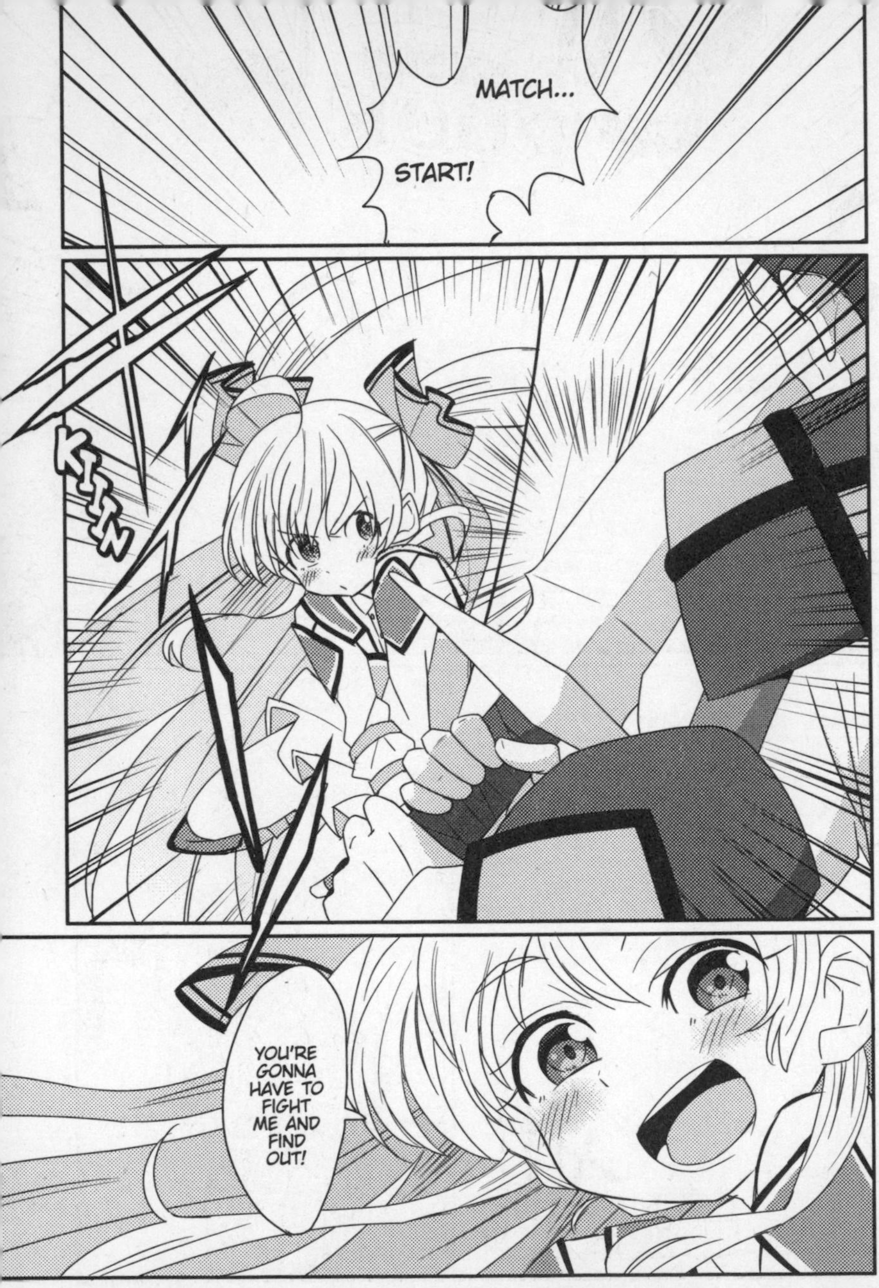
MATCH...
START!
KIIIN
YOU'RE GONNA HAVE TO FIGHT ME AND FIND OUT!

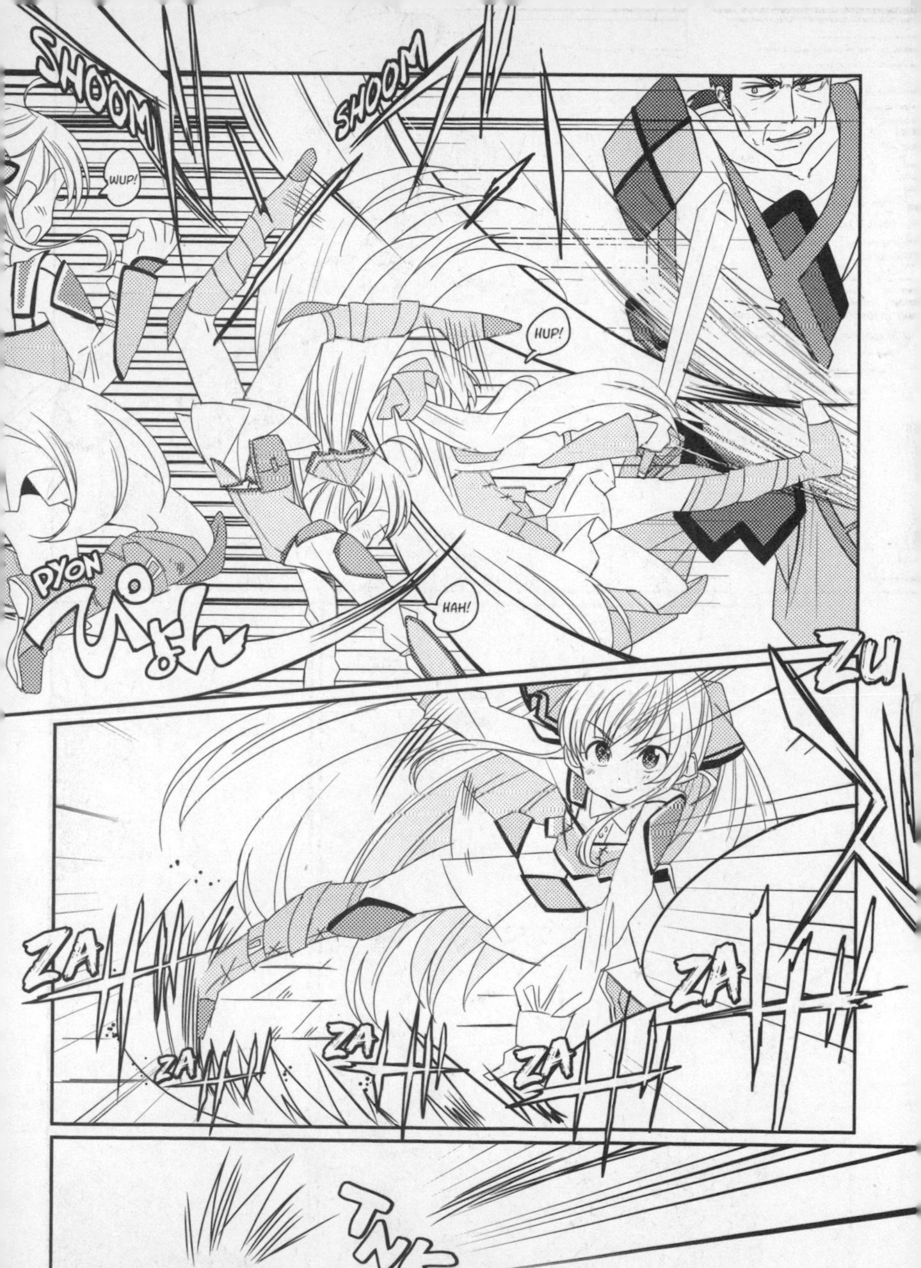
SHOOM
SHOOM
HUP!
WUP!
HAH!
PYON
ぴょん
ZU
ZA
ZA
ZA
ZA
ZA
TNK

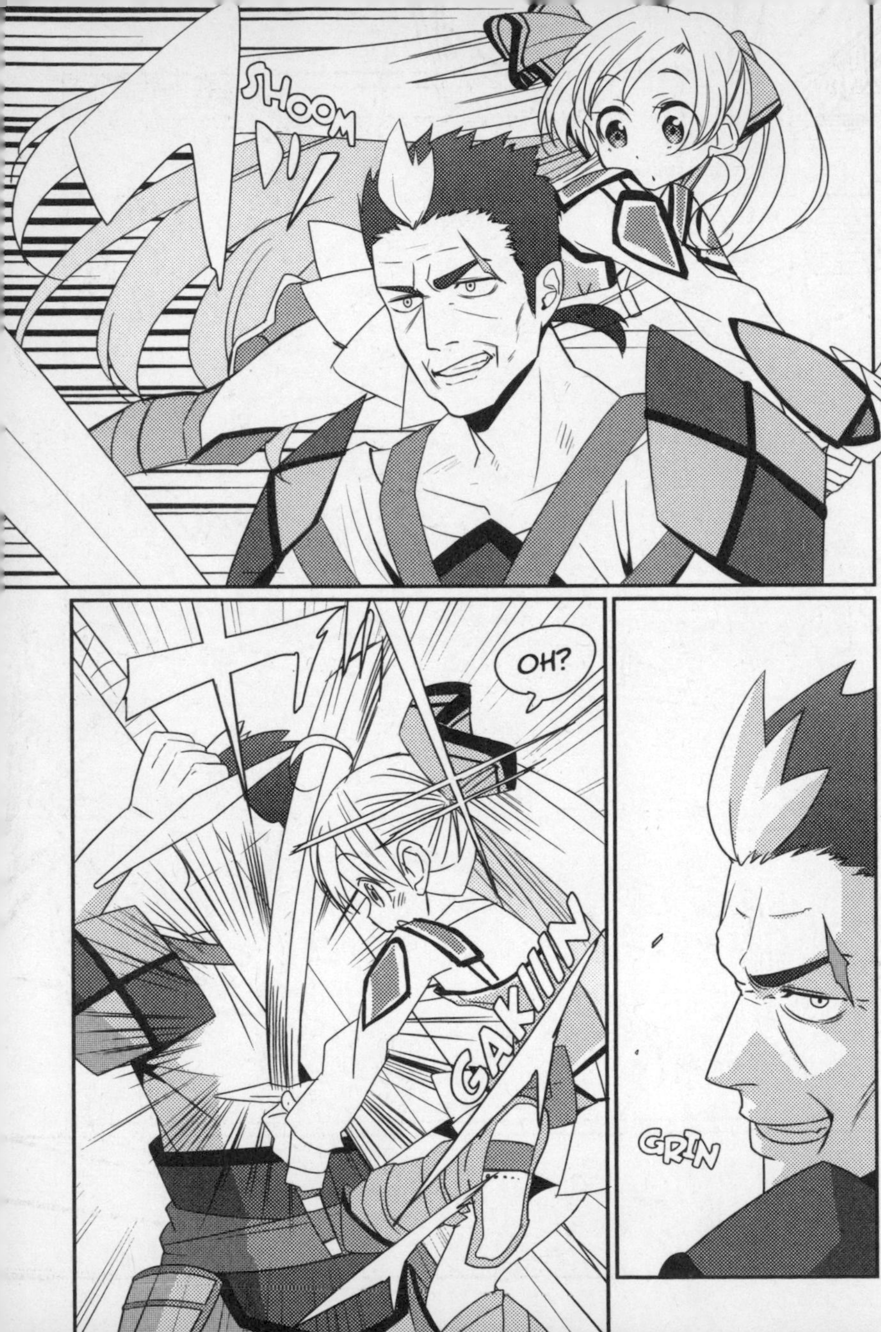
SHOOM
GRIN
OH?
GAKIIN

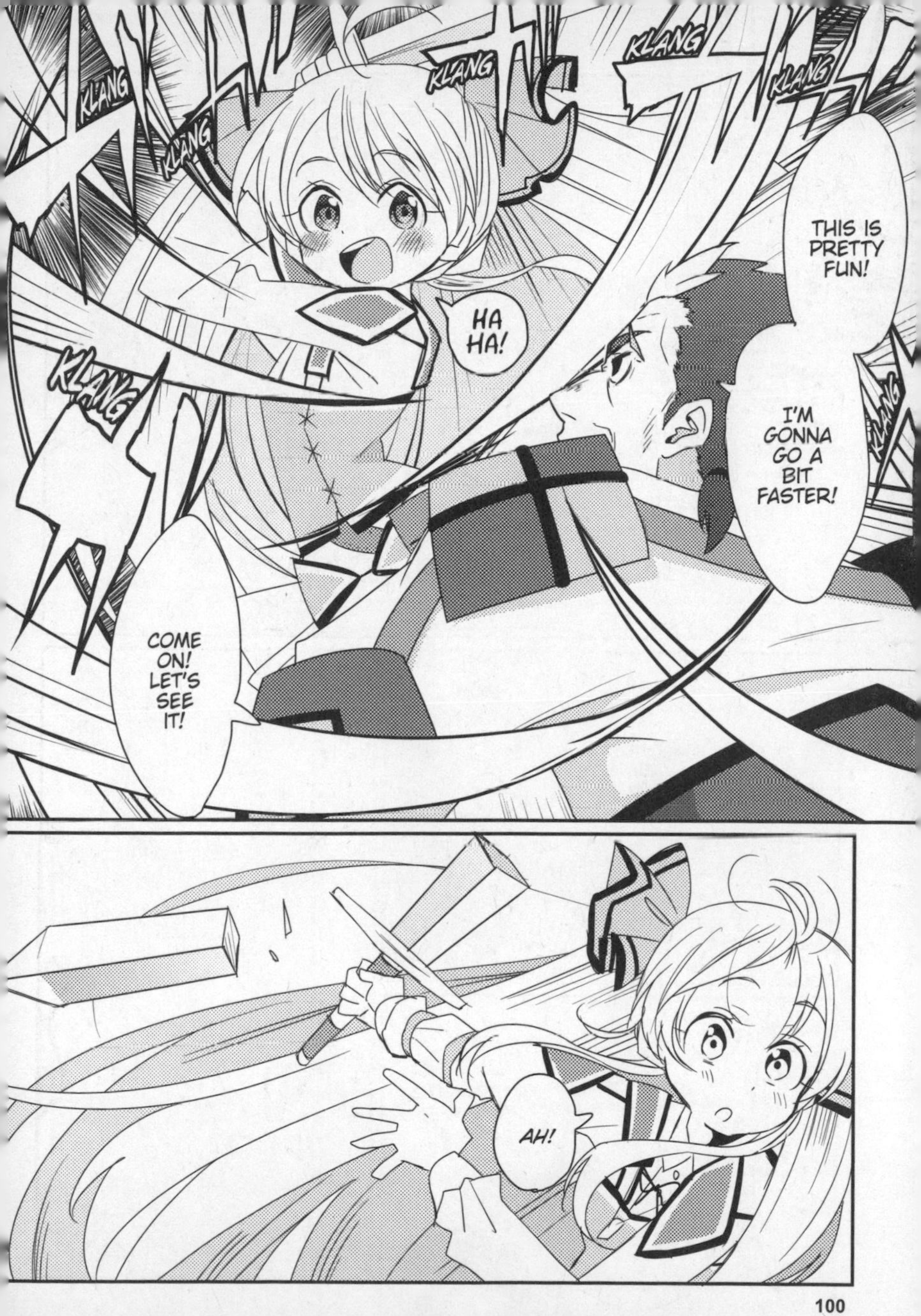
KLANG
KLANG
KLANG
KLANG
KLANG
KLANG
THIS IS PRETTY FUN!
I'M GONNA GO A BIT FASTER!
HA HA!
KLANG
COME ON! LET'S SEE IT!
AH!

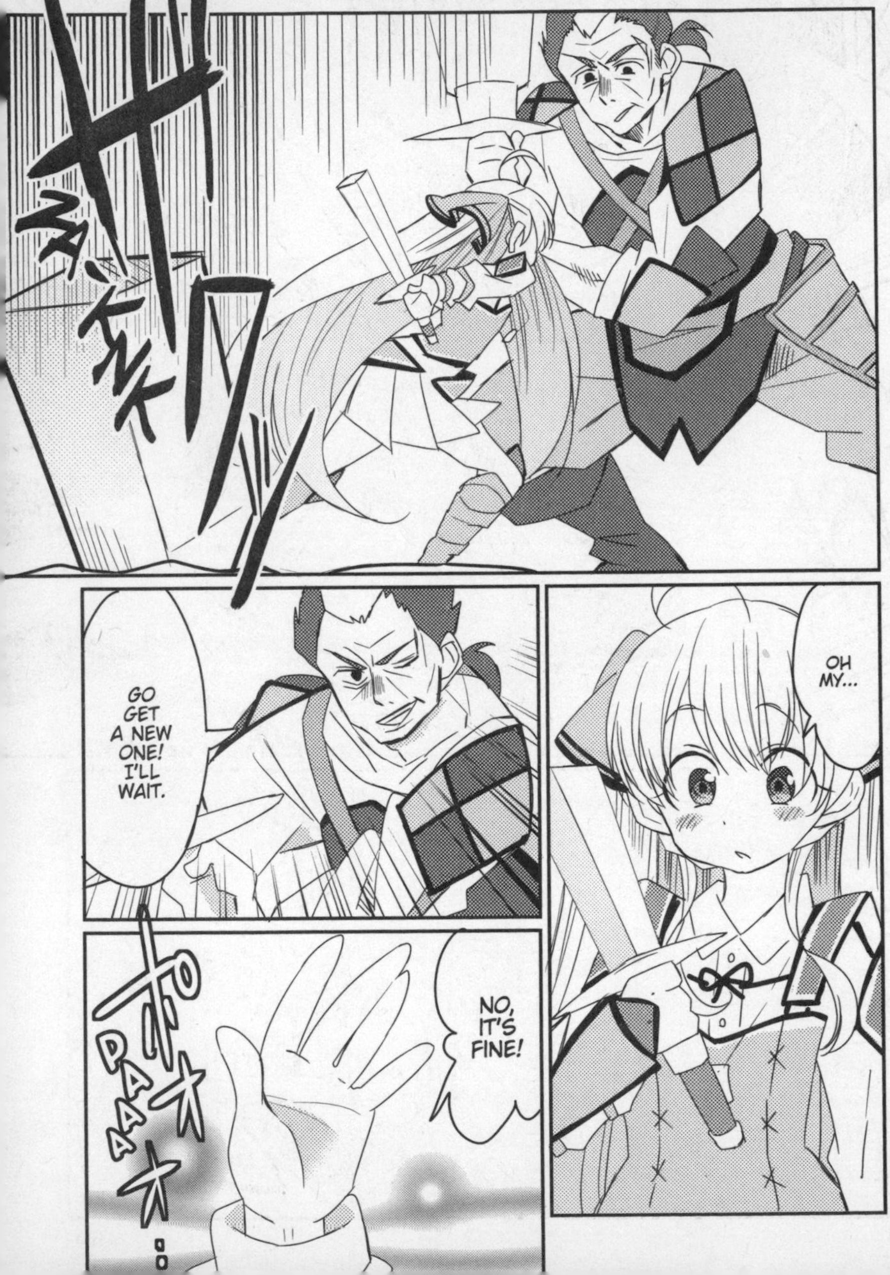
ZAKNK
OH MY...
GO GET A NEW ONE! I'LL WAIT.
NO, IT'S FINE!
PAAA

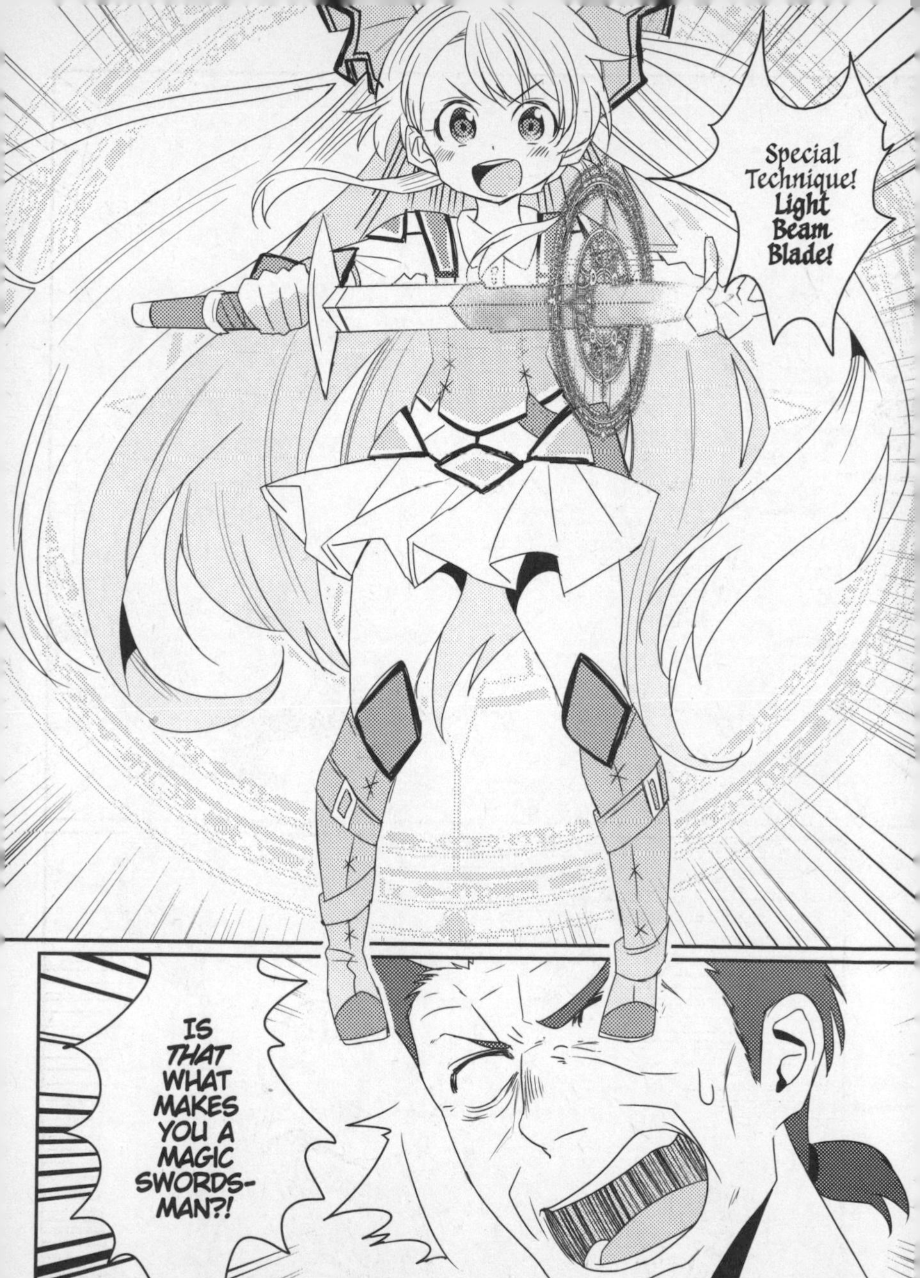
Special Technique! Light Beam Blade!
IS THAT WHAT MAKES YOU A MAGIC SWORDS-MAN?!

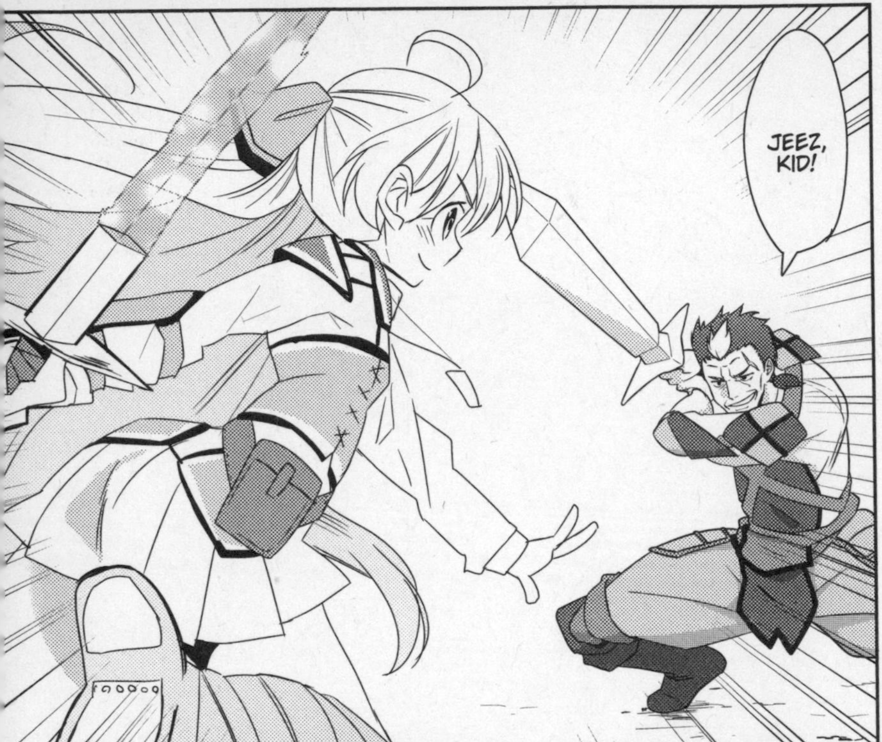
JEEZ, KID!

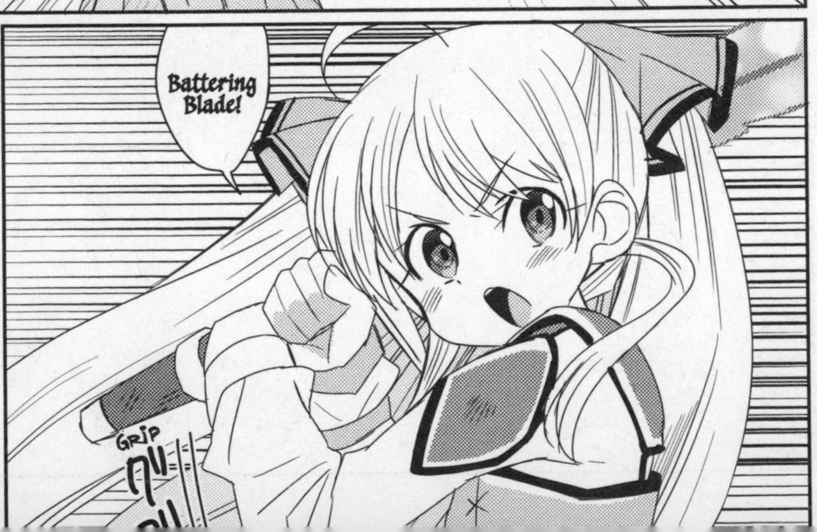
Battering Blade!
GRIP

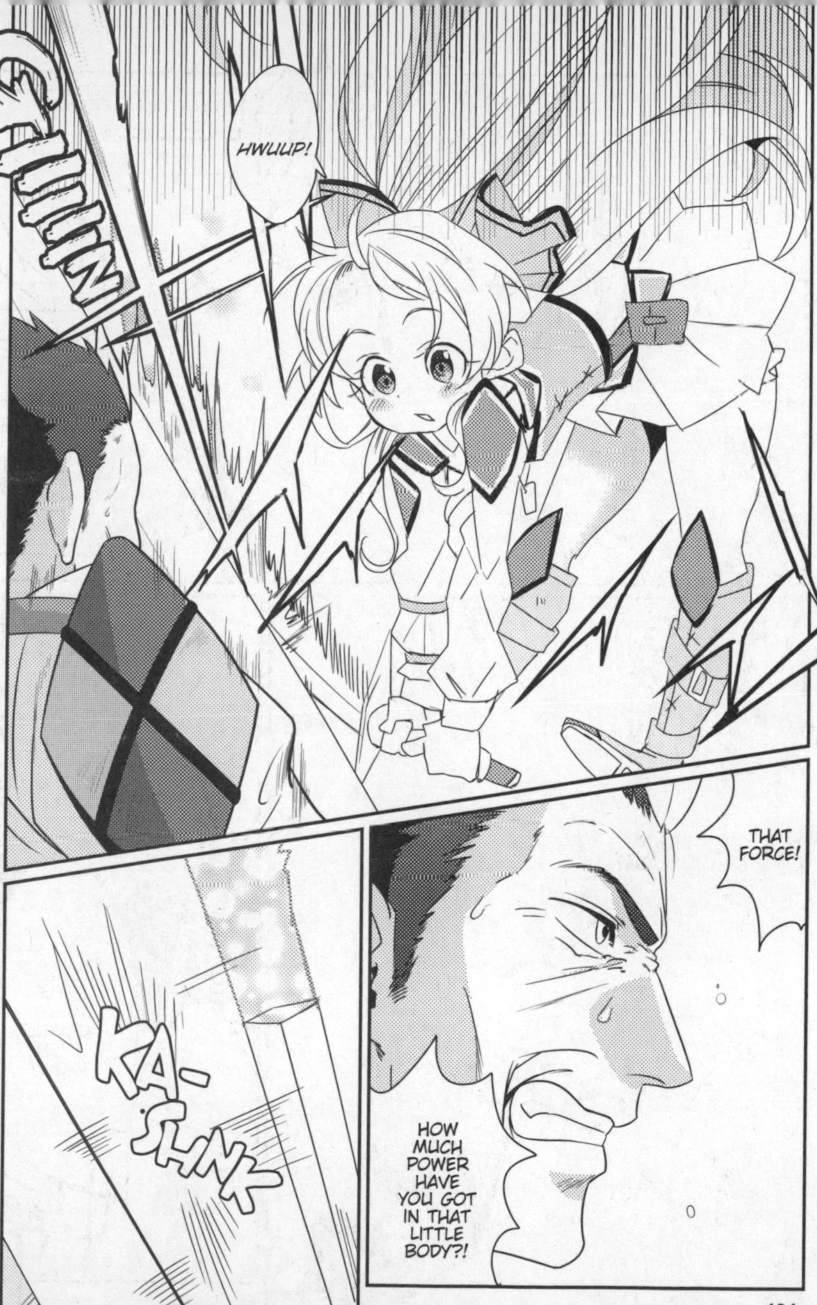
GUUIN
HWUUP!
THAT FORCE!
HOW MUCH POWER HAVE YOU GOT IN THAT LITTLE BODY?!
KA-SHNK

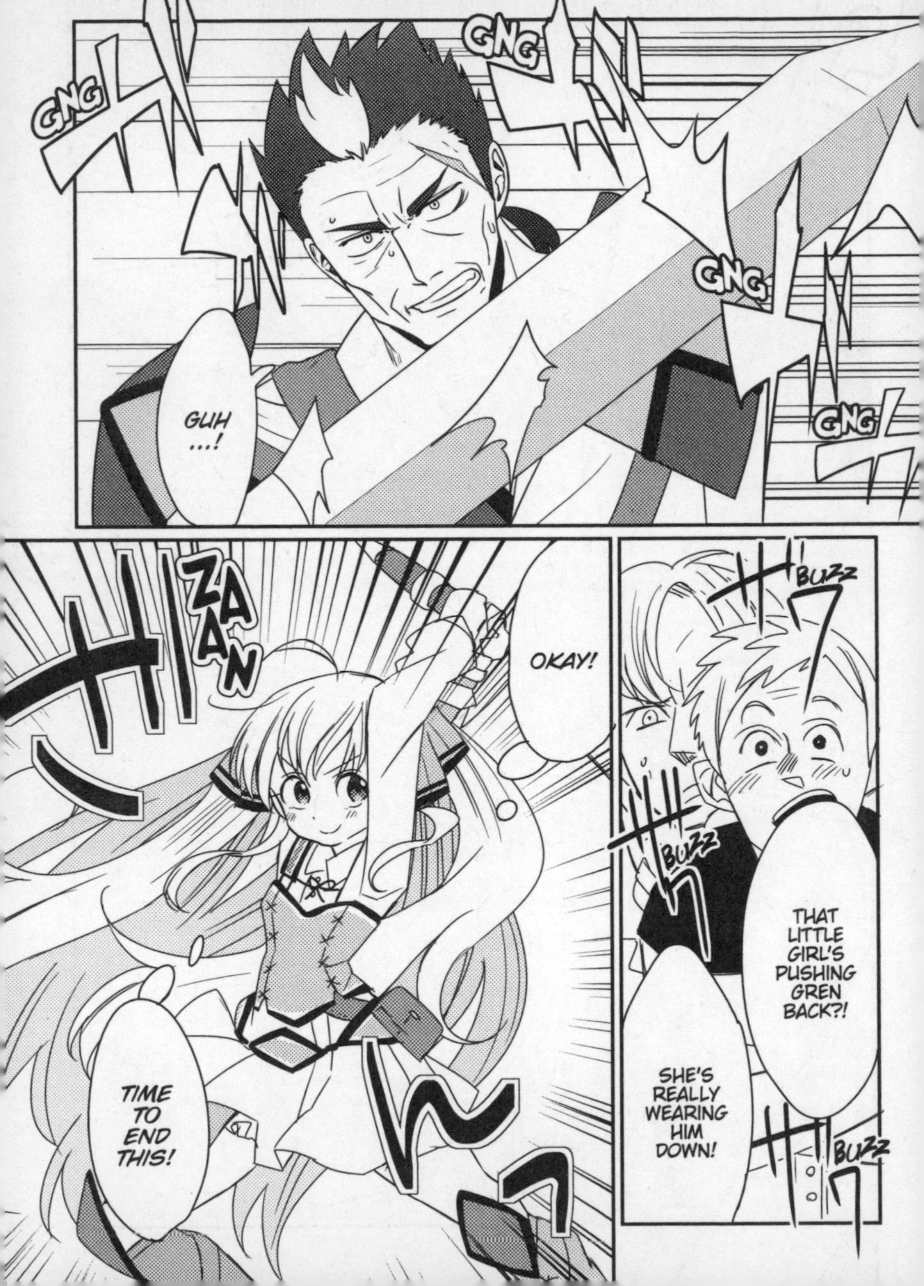
GNG
GNG
GNG
GNG
GUH ...!
BUZZ
BUZZ
THAT LITTLE GIRL'S PUSHING GREN BACK?!
SHE'S REALLY WEARING HIM DOWN!
BUZZ
OKAY!
ZAAAN
TIME TO END THIS!

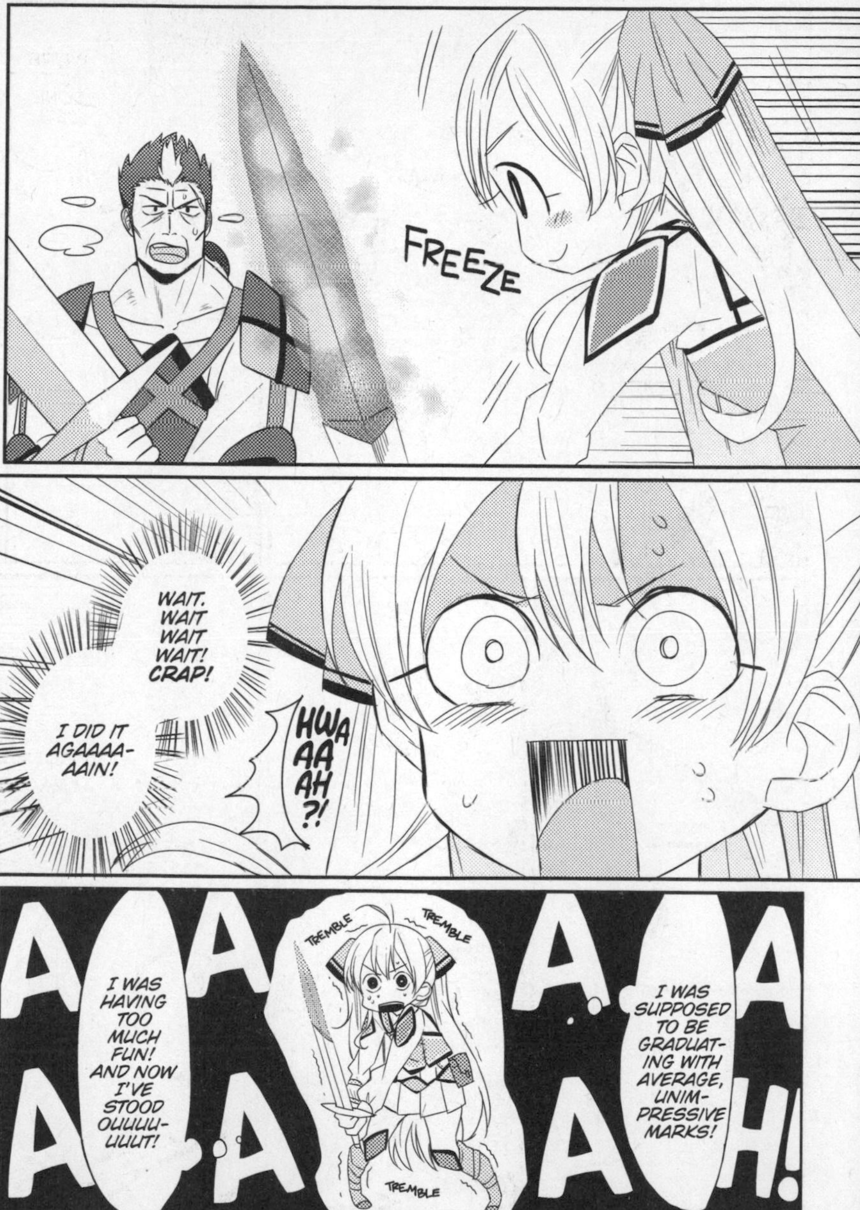
FREEZE
HWAAAAAH?!
WAIT. WAIT WAIT WAIT! CRAP!
I DID IT AGAAAAAAIN!
AAAAAAAAH!
TREMBLE TREMBLE
I WAS SUPPOSED TO BE GRADUATING WITH AVERAGE, UNIMPRESSIVE MARKS!
I WAS HAVING TOO MUCH FUN! AND NOW I'VE STOOD OUUUUUUUT!
TREMBLE

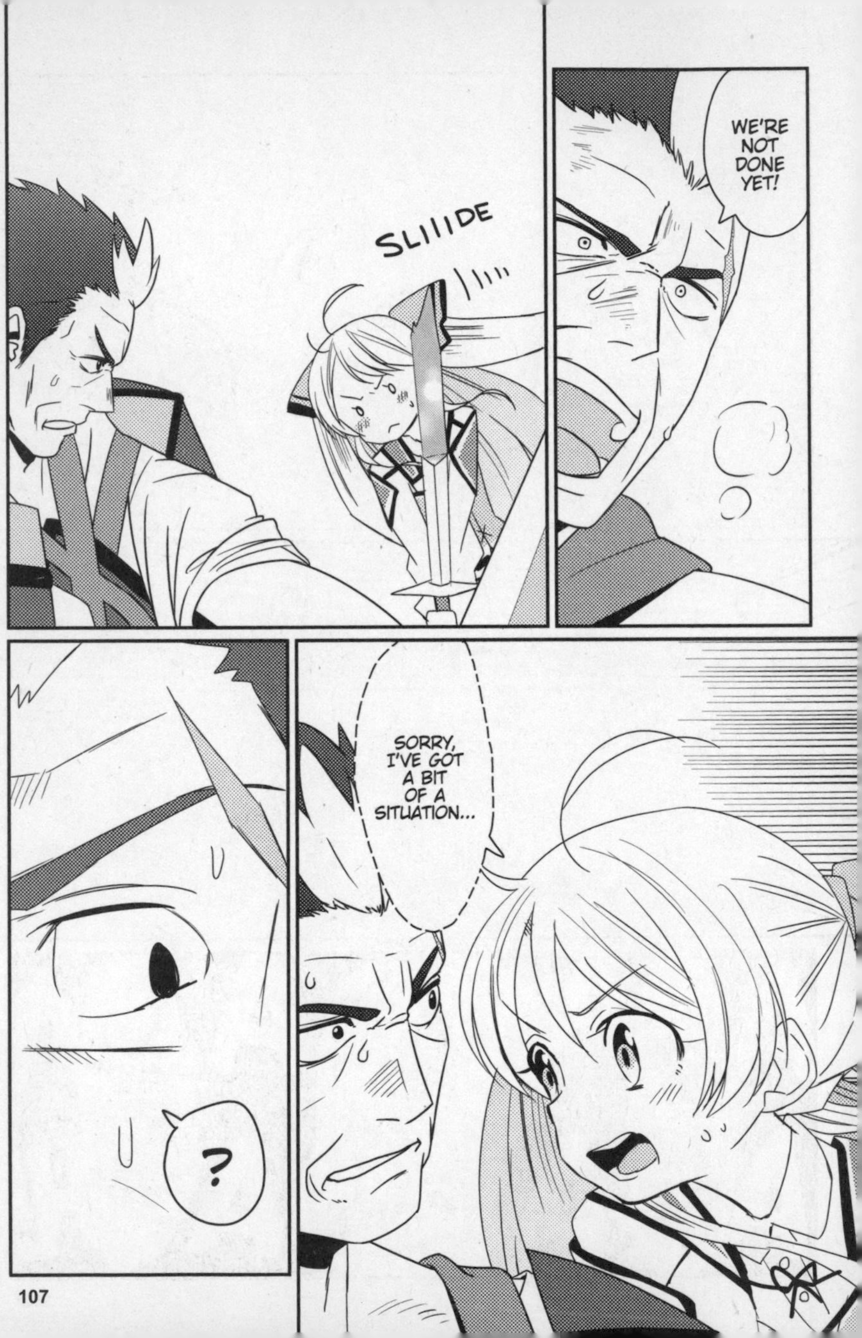
WE'RE NOT DONE YET!
SLIIIDE
SORRY, I'VE GOT A BIT OF A SITUATION...
?

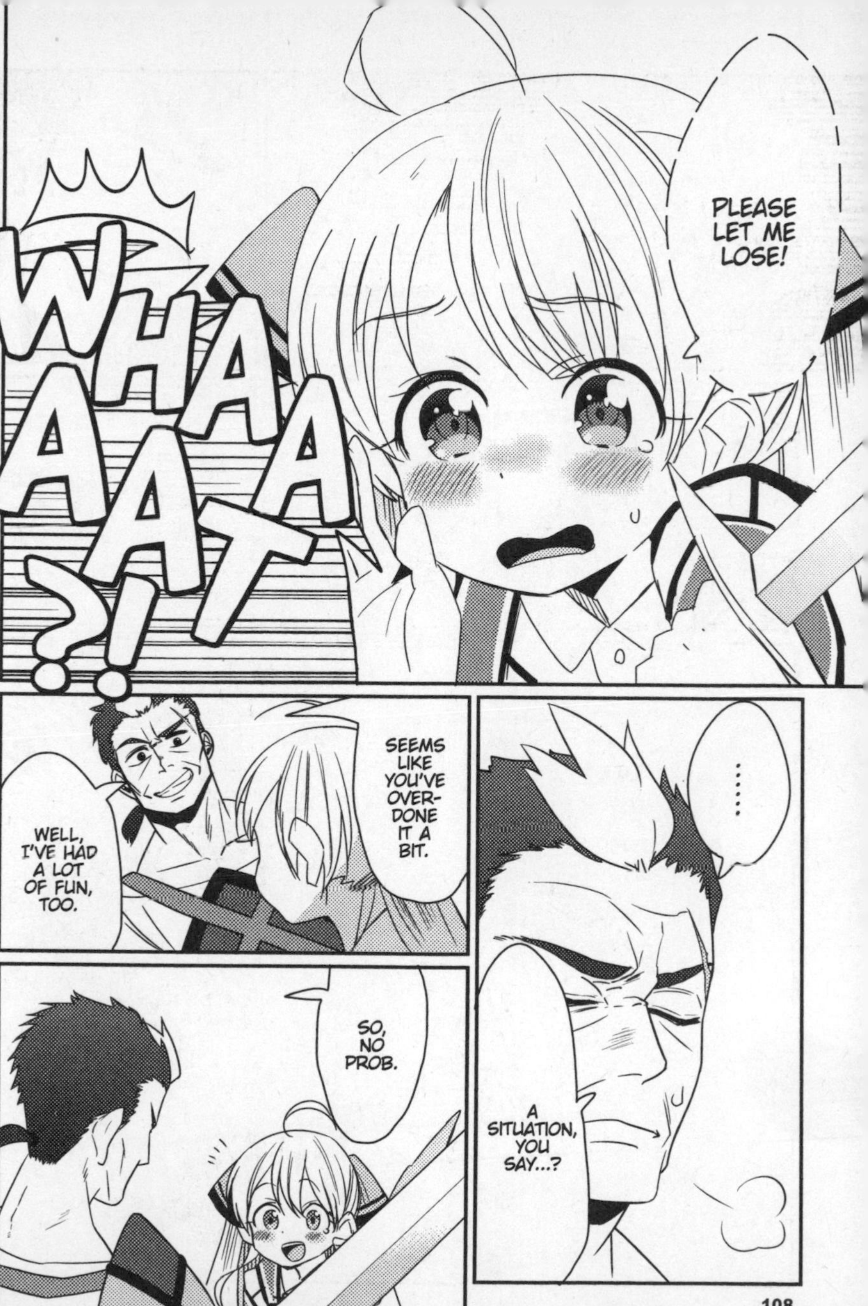
PLEASE LET ME LOSE!
WHAAAAAT?!
......
A SITUATION, YOU SAY...?
SEEMS LIKE YOU'VE OVER-DONE IT A BIT.
WELL, I'VE HAD A LOT OF FUN, TOO.
SO, NO PROB.

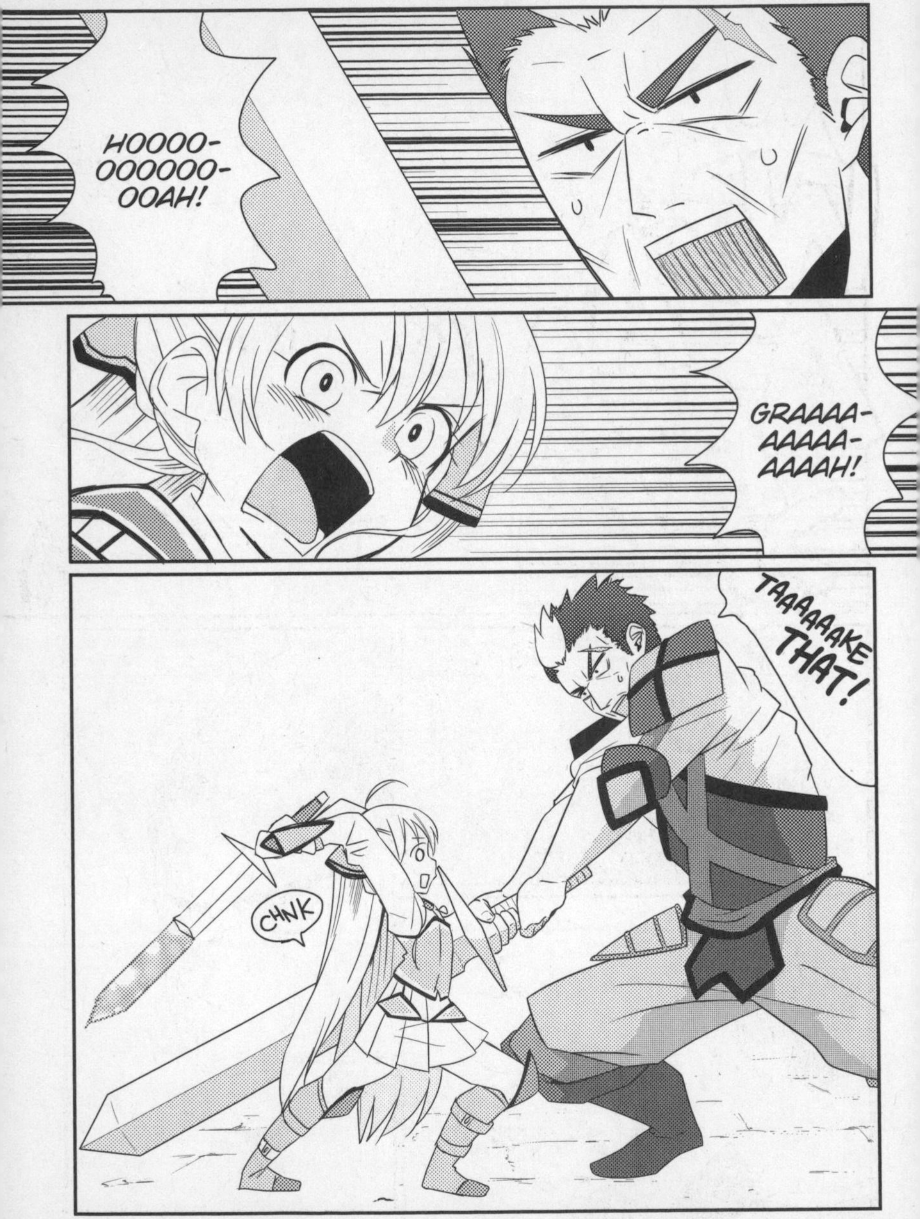
HOOOO-OOOOOO-OOAH!
GRAAAA-AAAAA-AAAAH!
TAAAAAAKE THAT!
CHNK

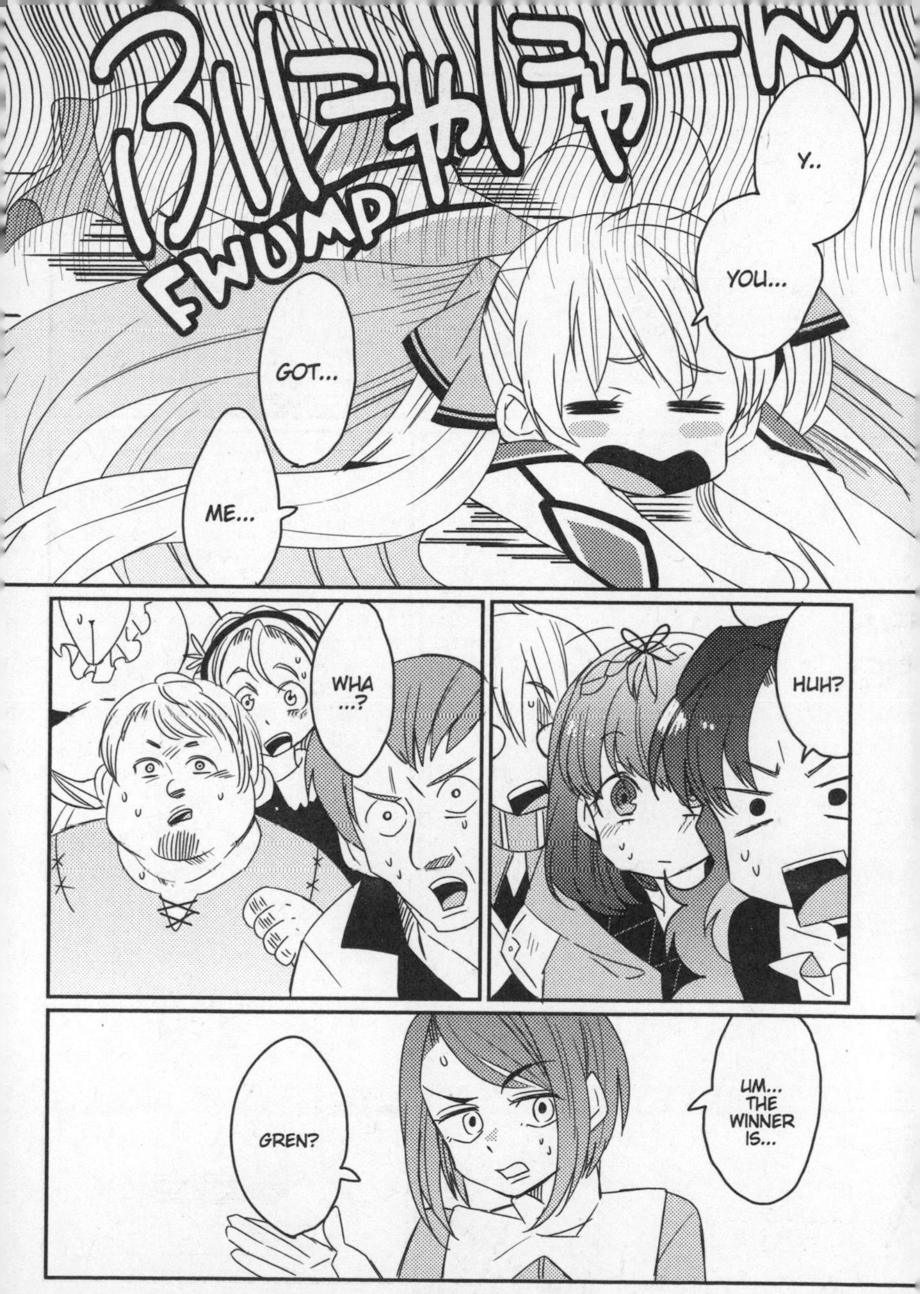
Y..
YOU...
FWUMP
GOT...
ME...
HUH?
WHA ...?
UM... THE WINNER IS...
GREN?

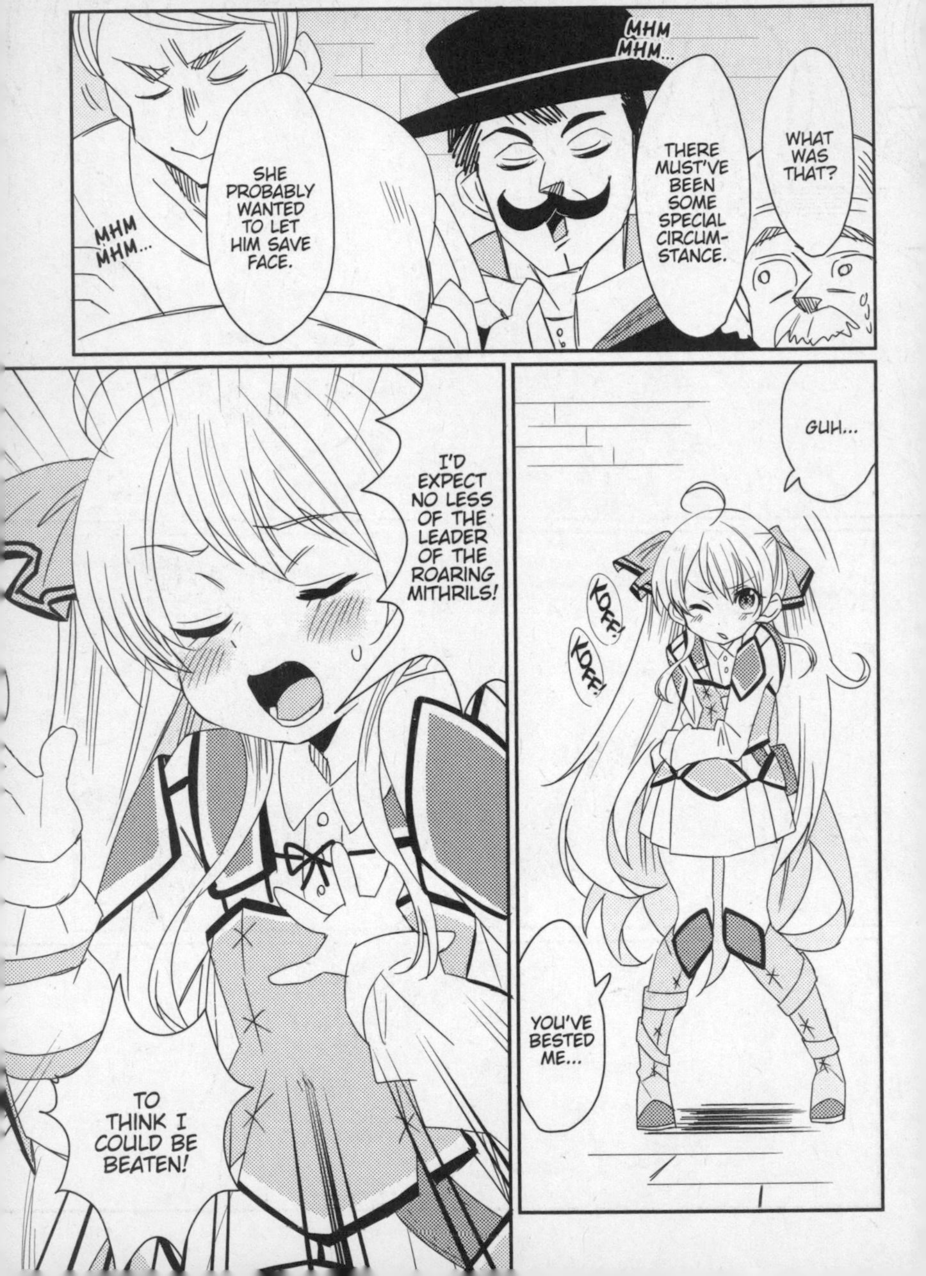
MHM MHM...
WHAT WAS THAT?
THERE MUST'VE BEEN SOME SPECIAL CIRCUM-STANCE.
SHE PROBABLY WANTED TO LET HIM SAVE FACE.
MHM MHM...
GUH...
KOFF!
KOFF!
YOU'VE BESTED ME...
I'D EXPECT NO LESS OF THE LEADER OF THE ROARING MITHRILS!
TO THINK I COULD BE BEATEN!

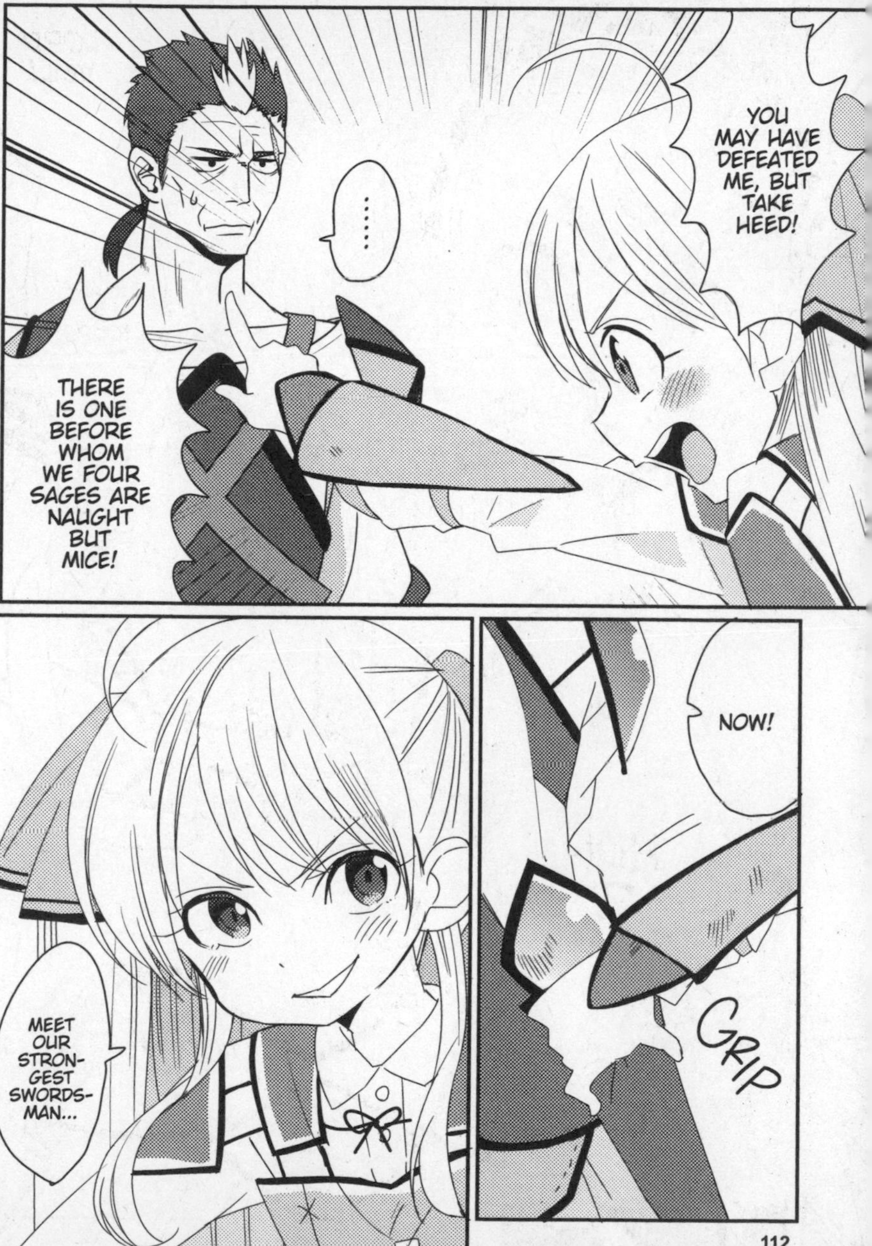
YOU MAY HAVE DEFEATED ME, BUT TAKE HEED!
......
THERE IS ONE BEFORE WHOM WE FOUR SAGES ARE NAUGHT BUT MICE!
NOW!
GRIP
MEET OUR STRONGEST SWORDSMAN...

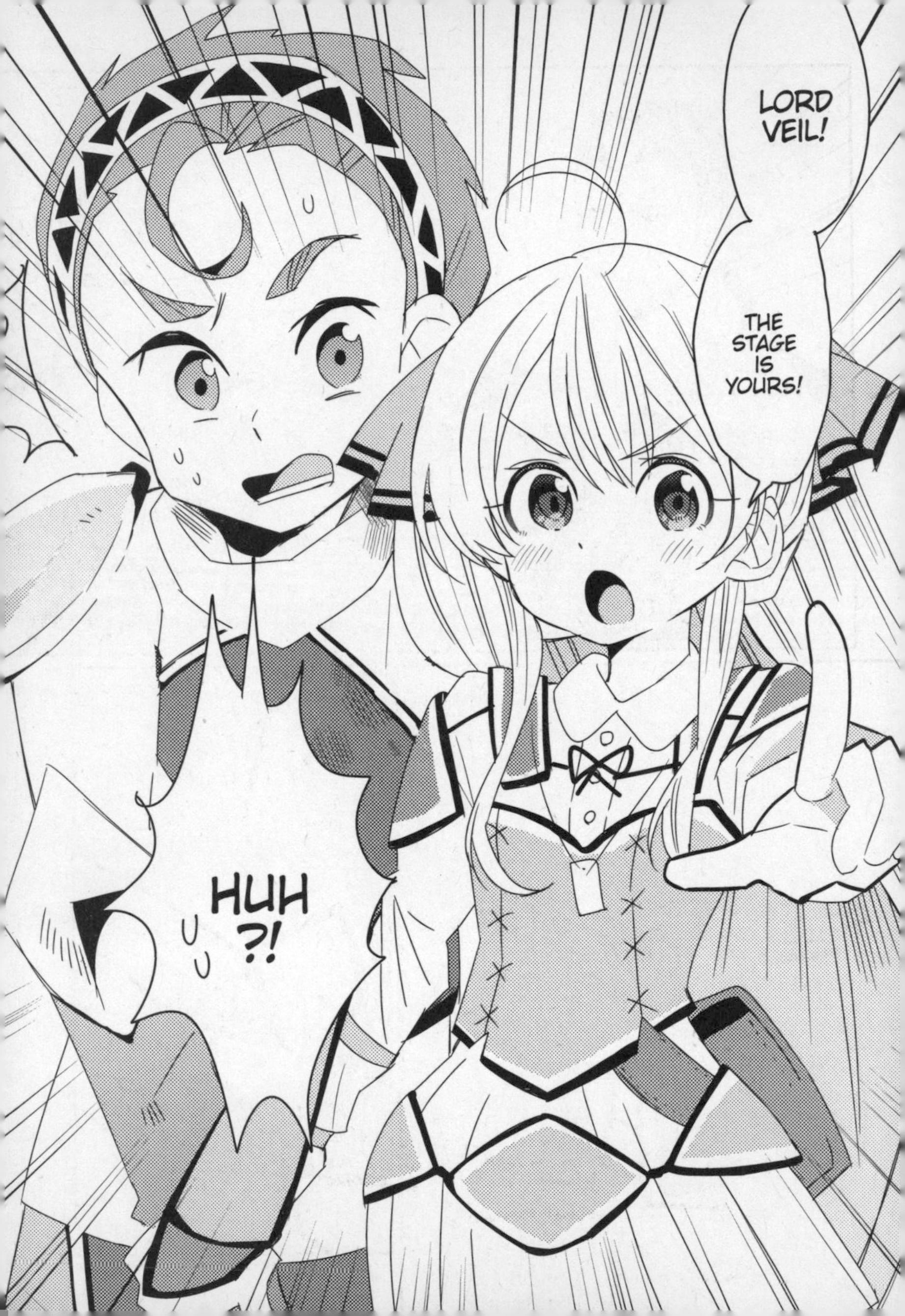
LORD VEIL!
THE STAGE IS YOURS!
HUH ?!

Didn't I Say to Make My Abilities Average in the Next Life?!

Chapter 11: The Graduation Exam Part 3

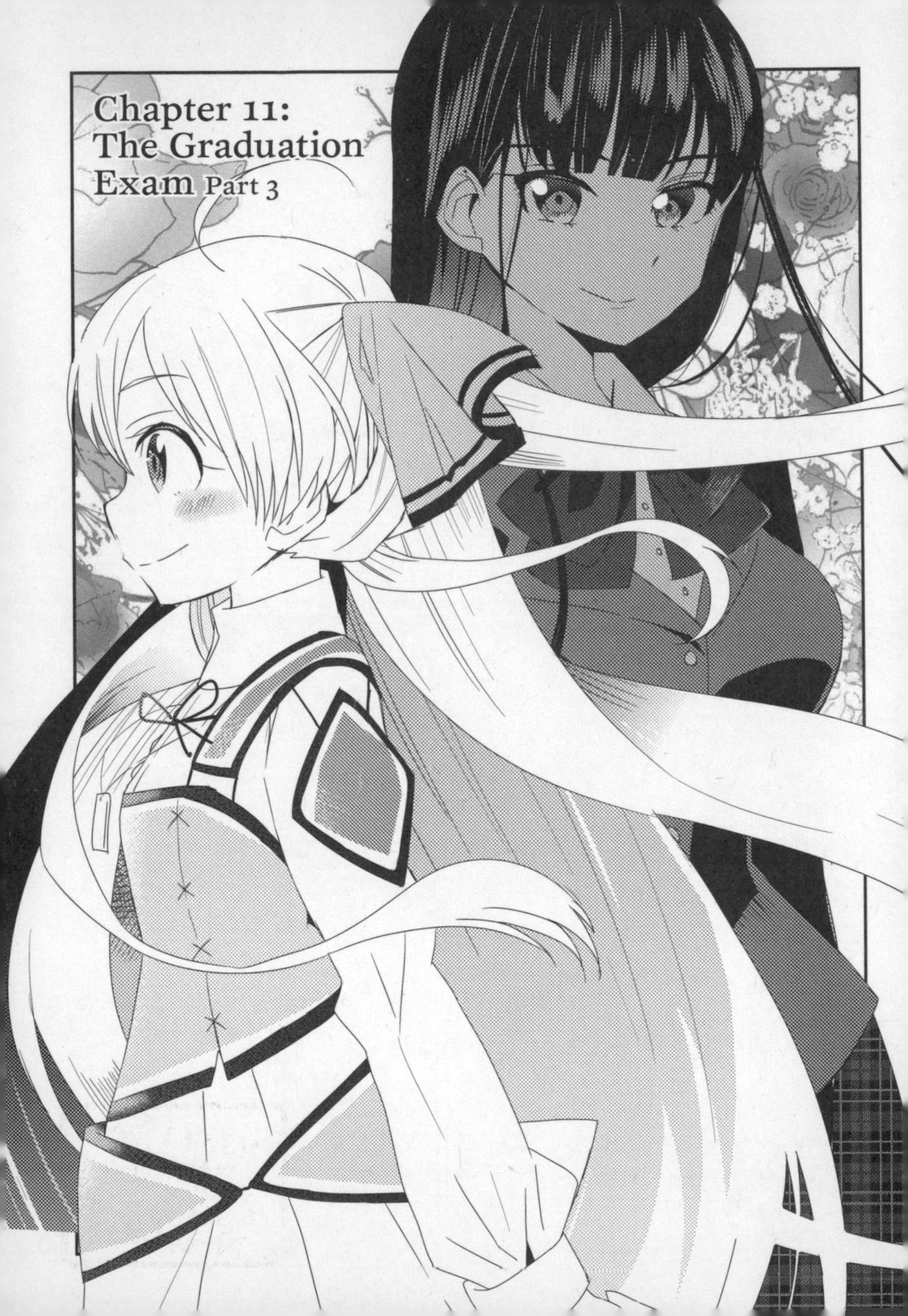

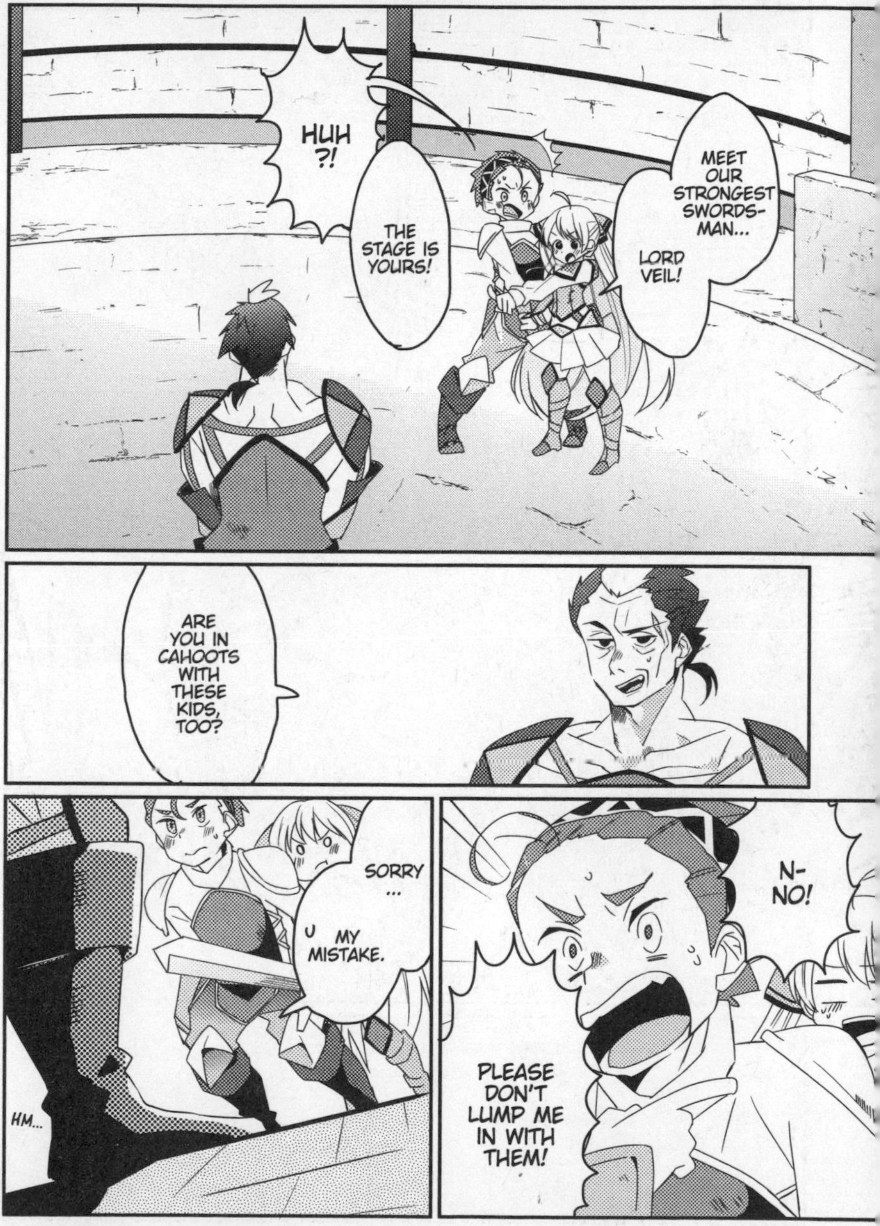
MEET OUR STRONGEST SWORDS-MAN...
LORD VEIL!
THE STAGE IS YOURS!
HUH?!
ARE YOU IN CAHOOTS WITH THESE KIDS, TOO?
N-NO!
PLEASE DON'T LUMP ME IN WITH THEM!
SORRY... MY MISTAKE.
HM...

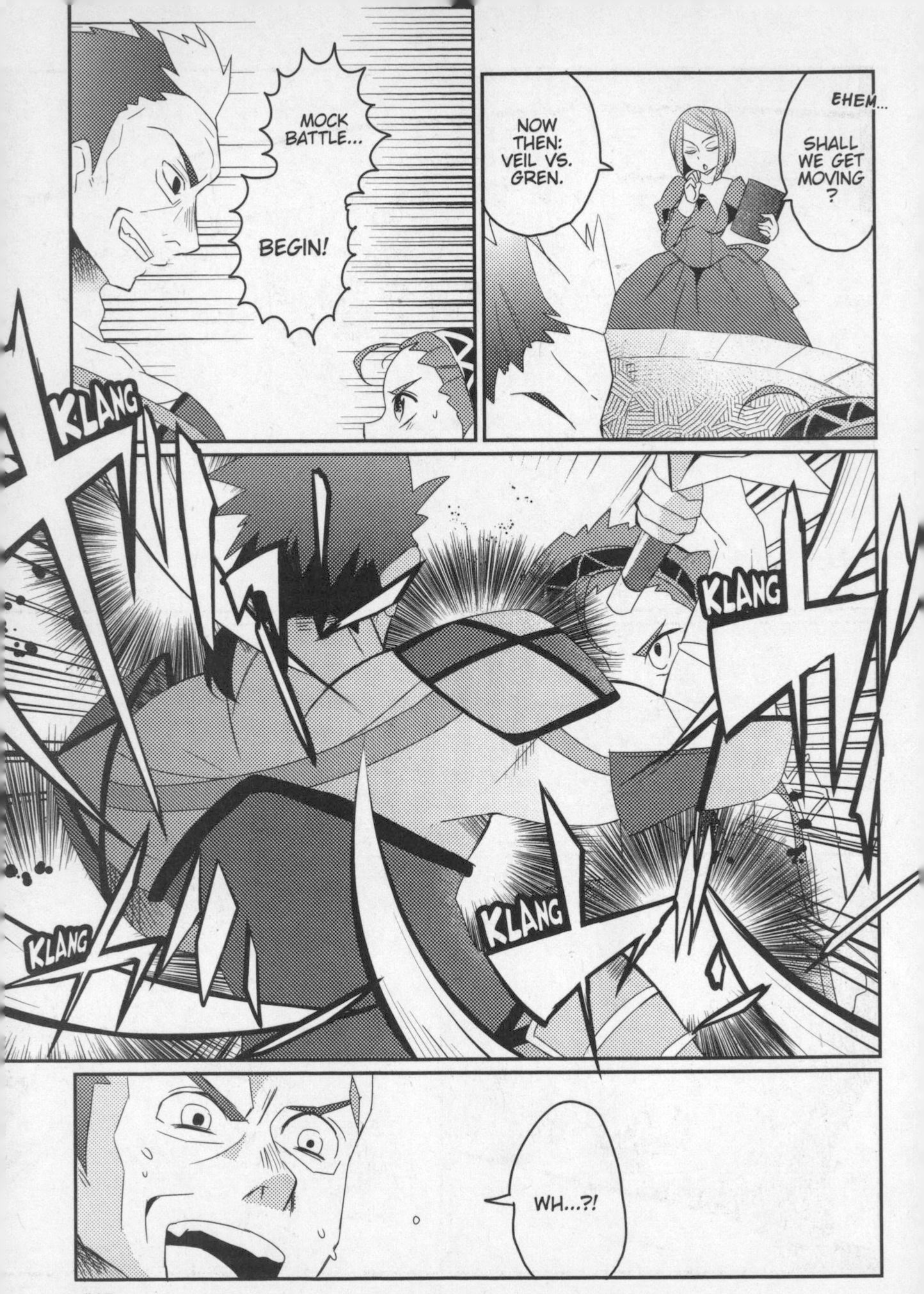
EHEM...
SHALL WE GET MOVING?
NOW THEN: VEIL VS. GREN.
MOCK BATTLE...
BEGIN!
KLANG
KLANG
KLANG
KLANG
WH...?!

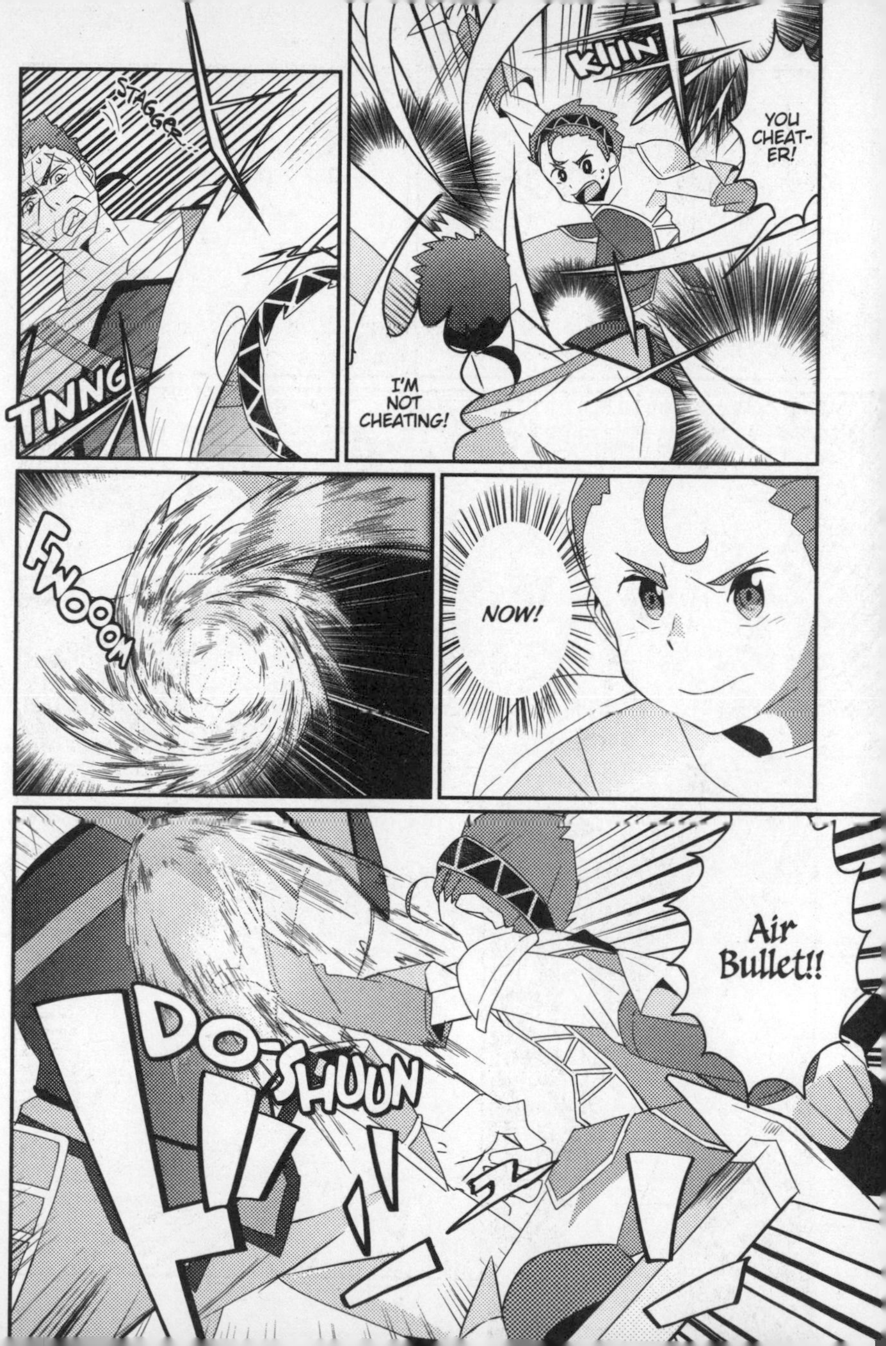
KIIIN
YOU CHEAT-ER!
I'M NOT CHEATING!
STAGGER
TNNG
NOW!
FWOOOM
Air Bullet!!
DO-SHUUN

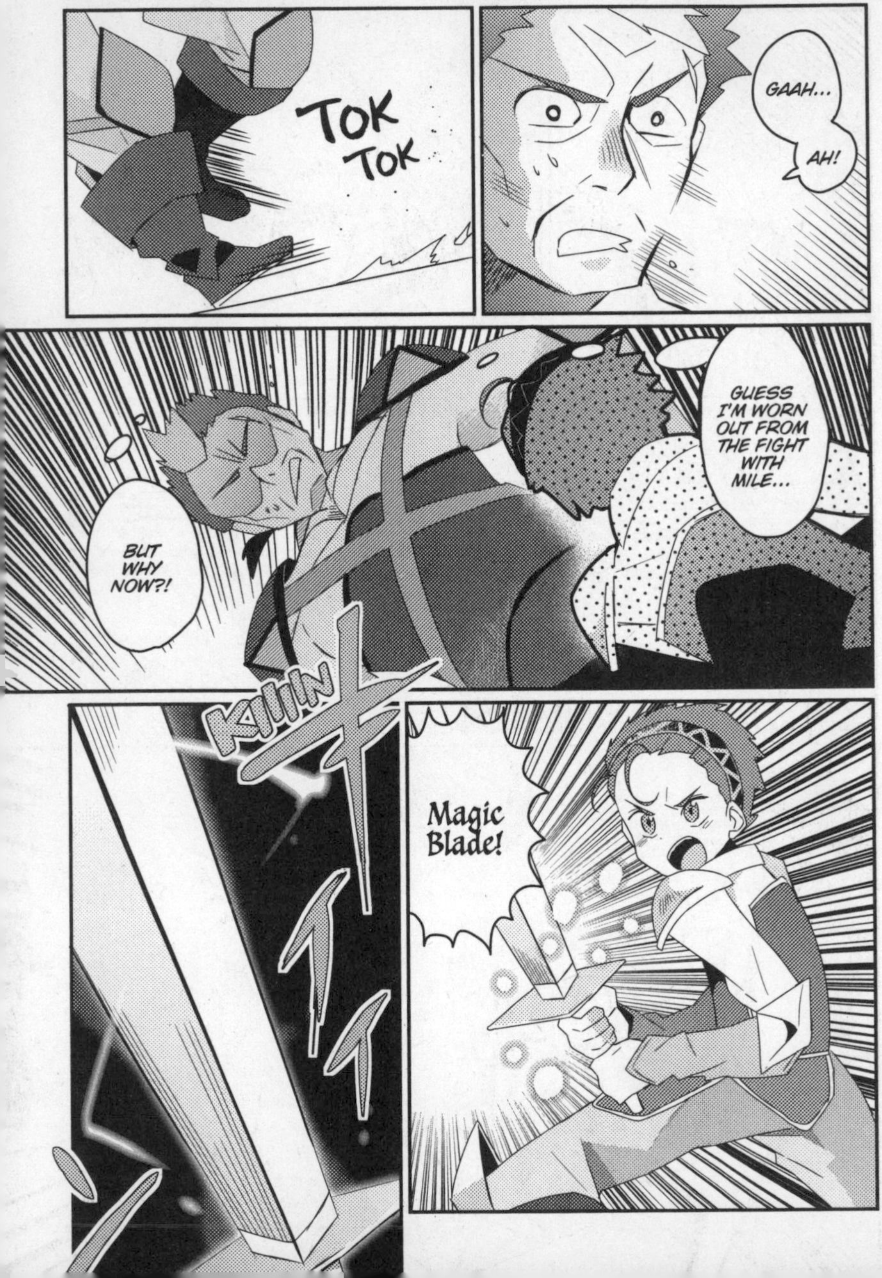
GAAH...
AH!
TOK TOK
GUESS I'M WORN OUT FROM THE FIGHT WITH MILE...
BUT WHY NOW?!
Magic Blade!
KIIIN

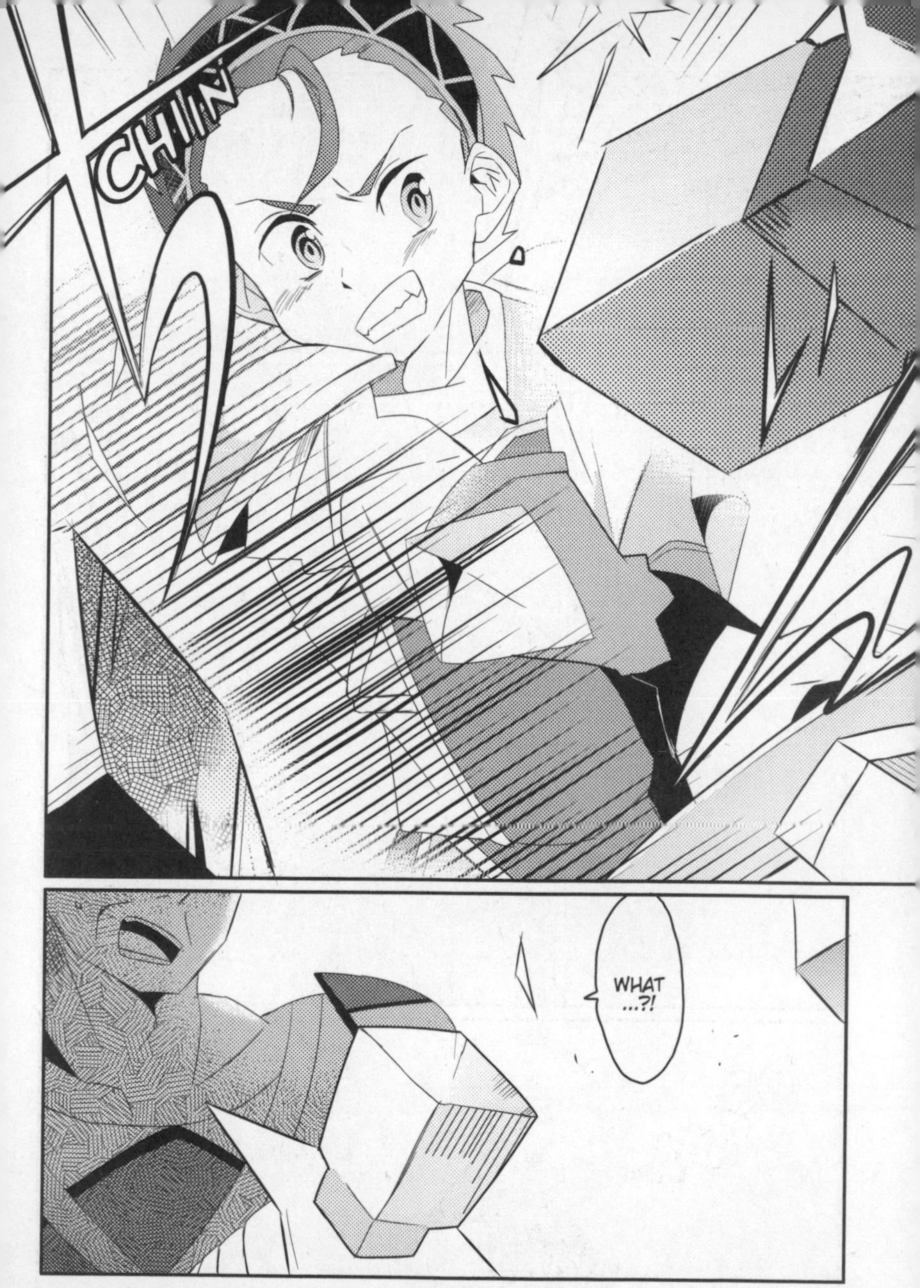
CHIN
WHAT
...?!

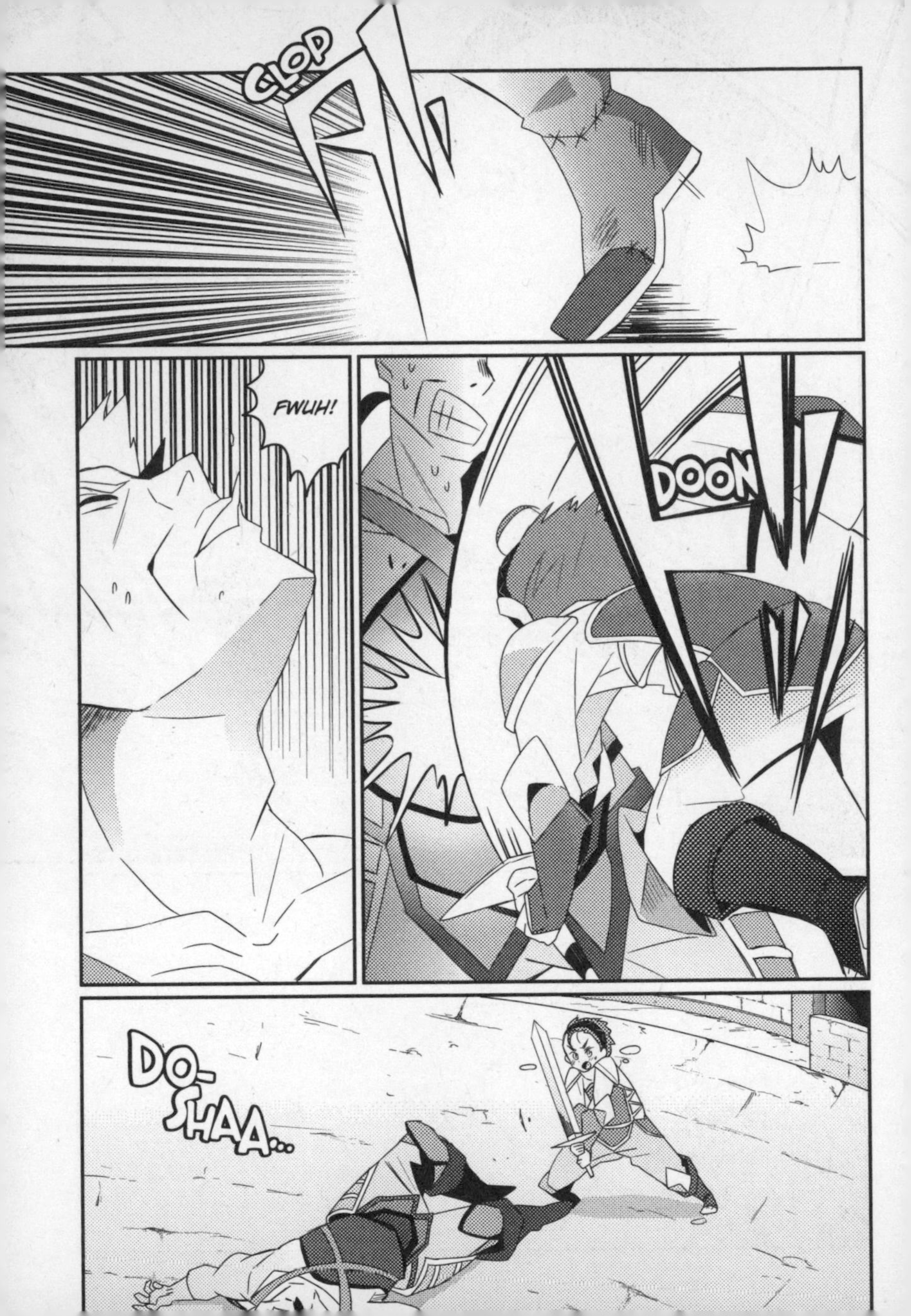
CLOP
DOON
FWUH!
DO-SHAA...

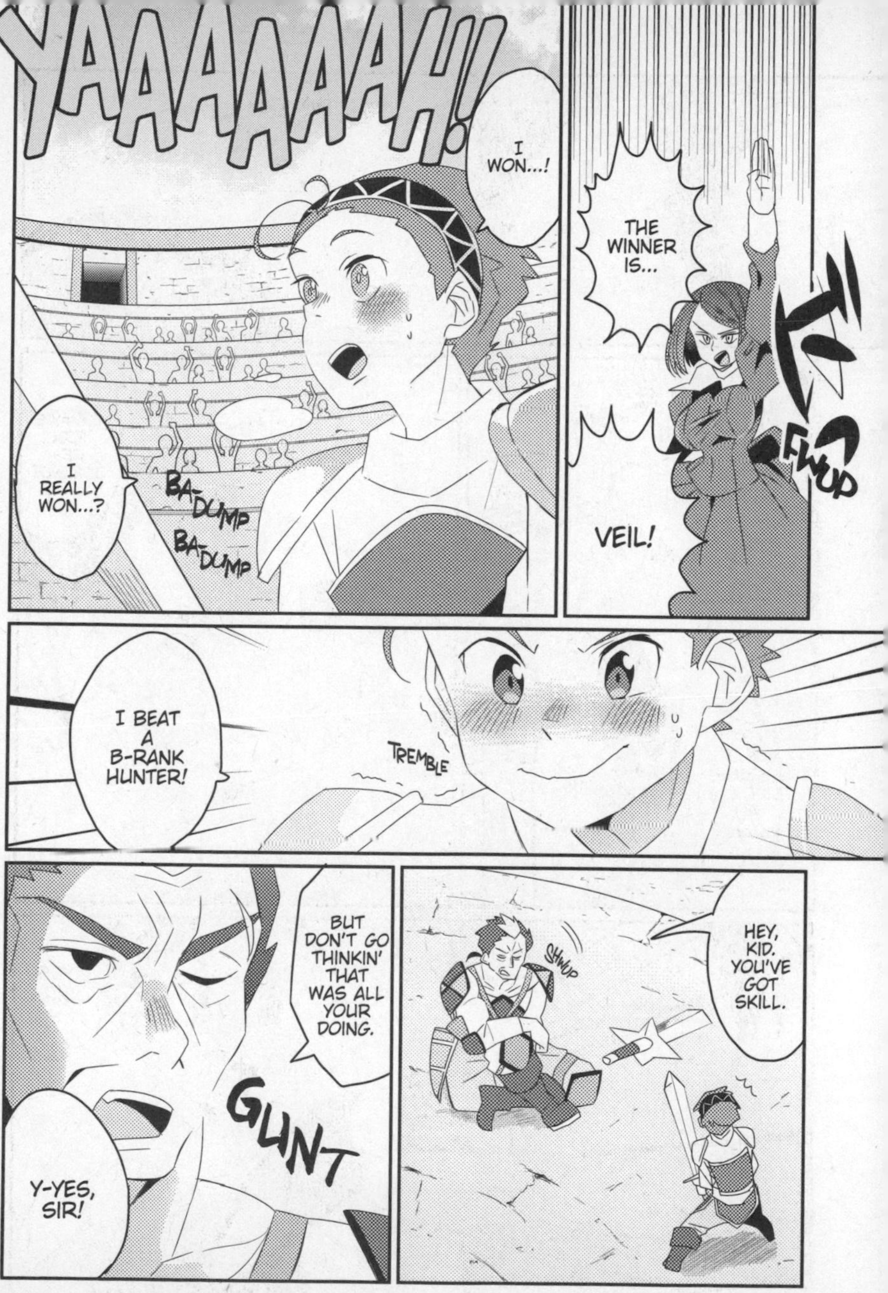

THE WINNER IS...
VEIL!
FWUP
YAAAAAAH!!
I WON...!
I REALLY WON...?
BA-DUMP
BA-DUMP
I BEAT A B-RANK HUNTER!
TREMBLE
HEY, KID. YOU'VE GOT SKILL.
SHWUP
BUT DON'T GO THINKIN' THAT WAS ALL YOUR DOING.
GLINT
Y-YES, SIR!

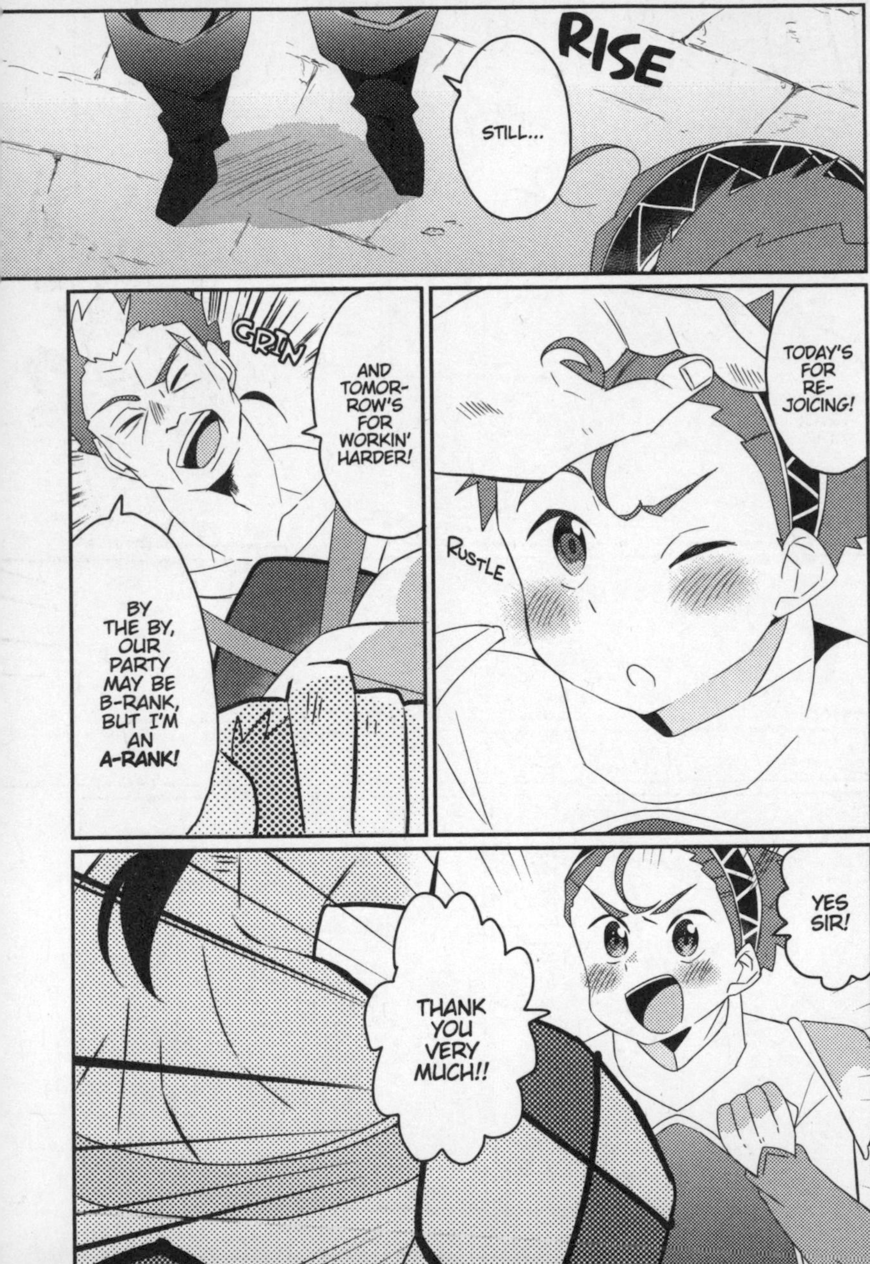
RISE
STILL...
TODAY'S FOR RE-JOICING!
RUSTLE
GRIN
AND TOMOR-ROW'S FOR WORKIN' HARDER!
BY THE BY, OUR PARTY MAY BE B-RANK, BUT I'M AN A-RANK!
YES SIR!
THANK YOU VERY MUCH!!

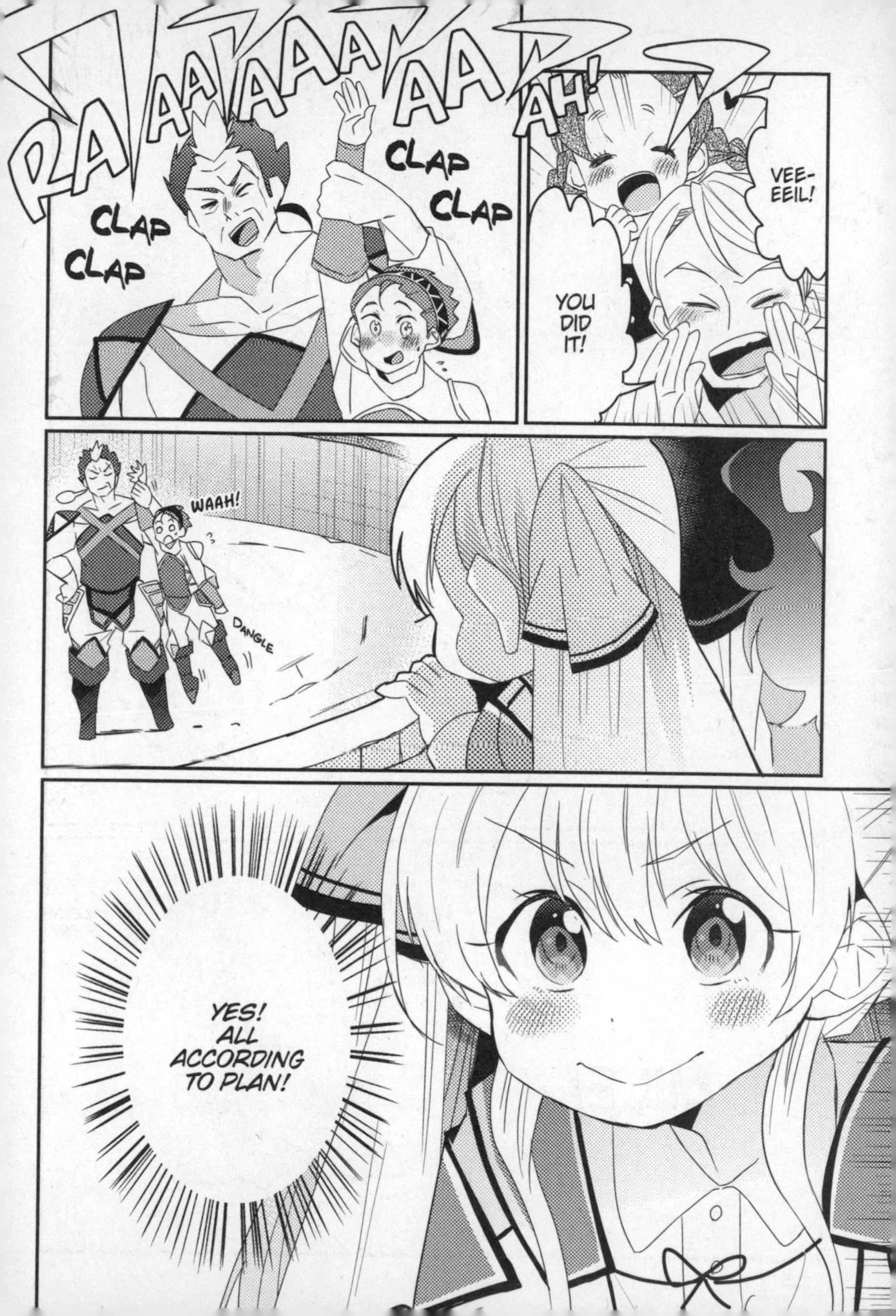
VEEE-
EEIL!
YOU DID IT!
RAAAAAAAAAH!
CLAP CLAP
CLAP CLAP
WAAH!
DANGLE
YES! ALL ACCORDING TO PLAN!

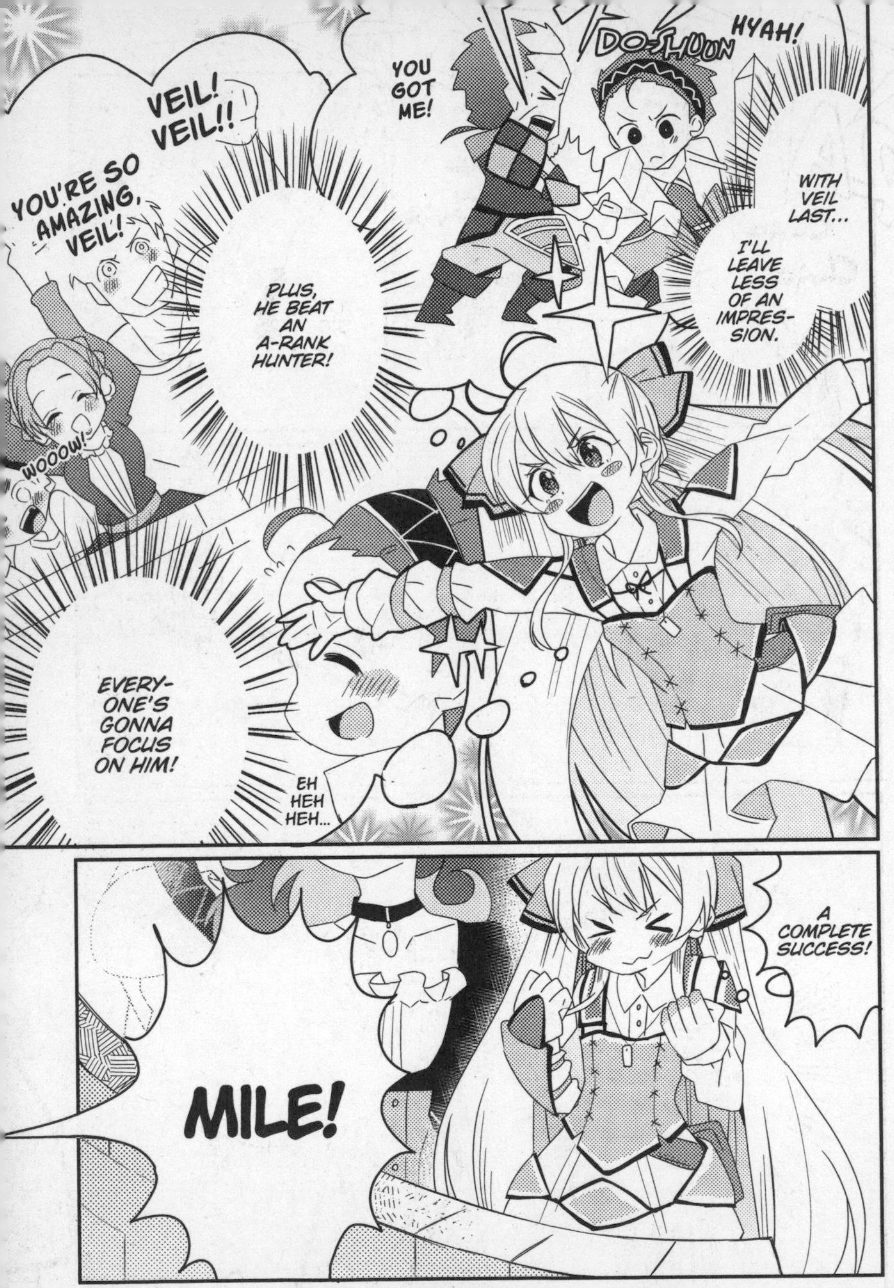
HYAH!
DO-SHUUN
YOU GOT ME!
WITH VEIL LAST...
I'LL LEAVE LESS OF AN IMPRES-SION.
VEIL! VEIL!!
YOU'RE SO AMAZING, VEIL!
PLUS, HE BEAT AN A-RANK HUNTER!
WOOOW!
EVERY-ONE'S GONNA FOCUS ON HIM!
EH HEH HEH...
A COMPLETE SUCCESS!
MILE!

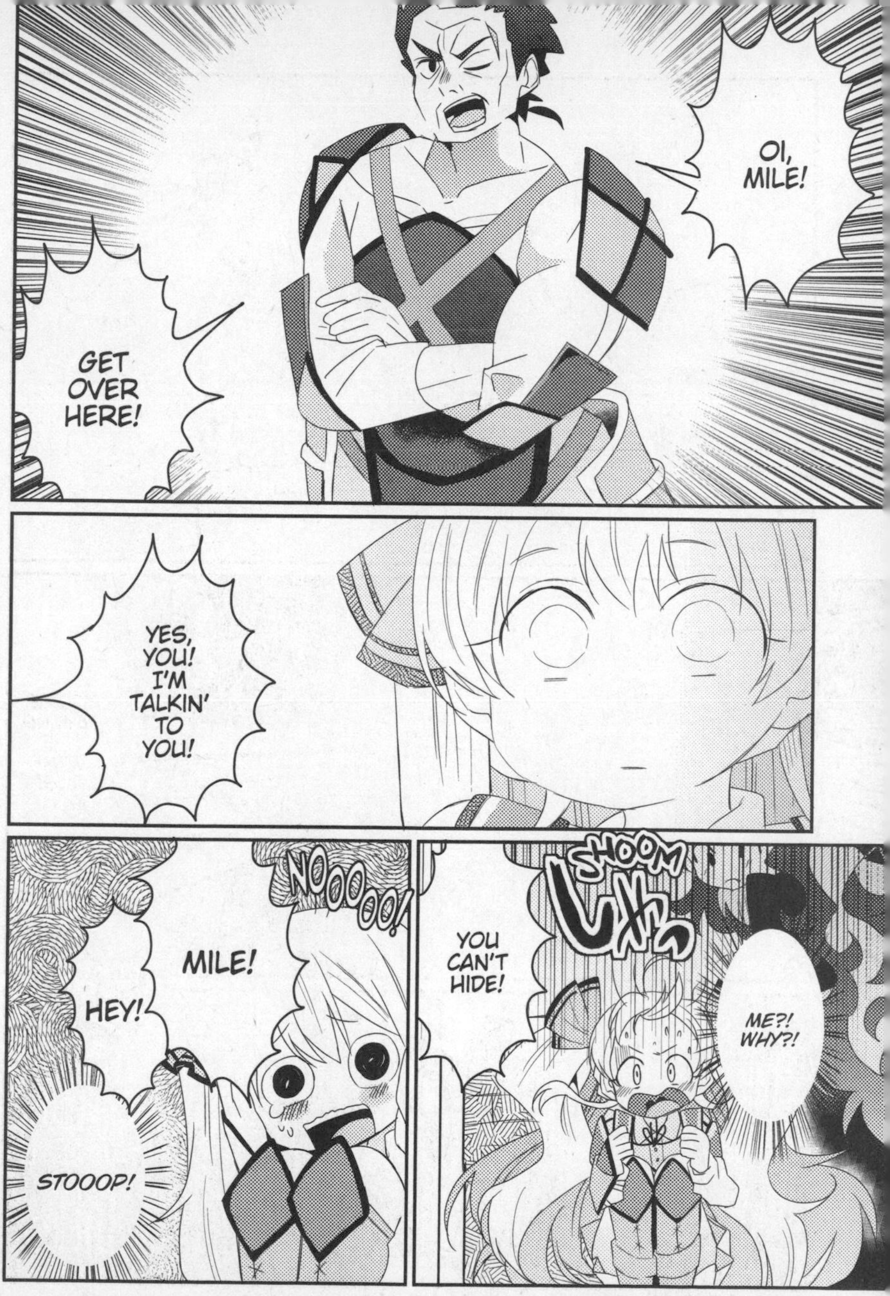
OI, MILE!
GET OVER HERE!
YES, YOU! I'M TALKIN' TO YOU!
SHOOM
ME?! WHY?!
YOU CAN'T HIDE!
NOOOOO!
MILE!
HEY!
STOOOP!

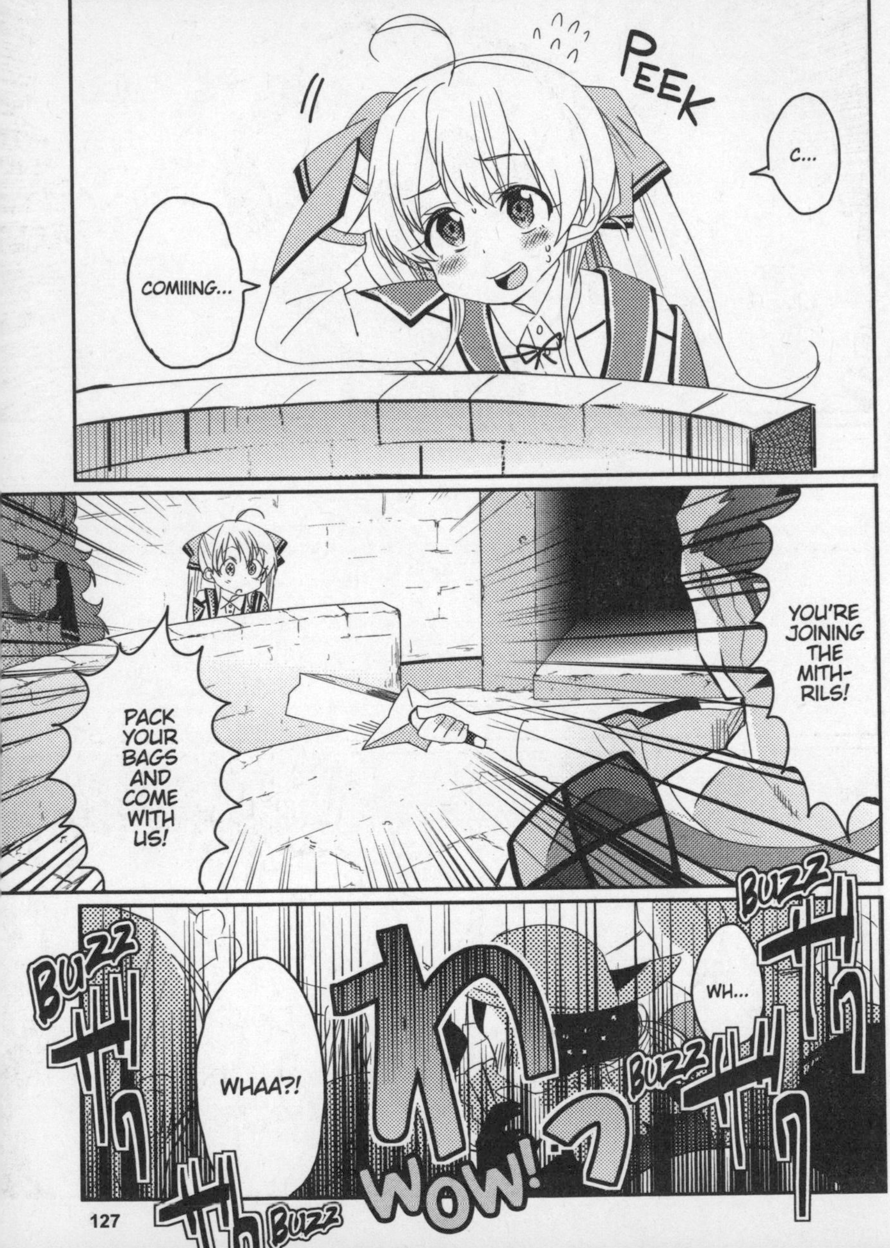
PEEK
C...
COMIIING...
YOU'RE JOINING THE MITH-RILS!
PACK YOUR BAGS AND COME WITH US!
BUZZ
WH...
BUZZ
WOW!
WHAA?!
BUZZ
BUZZ

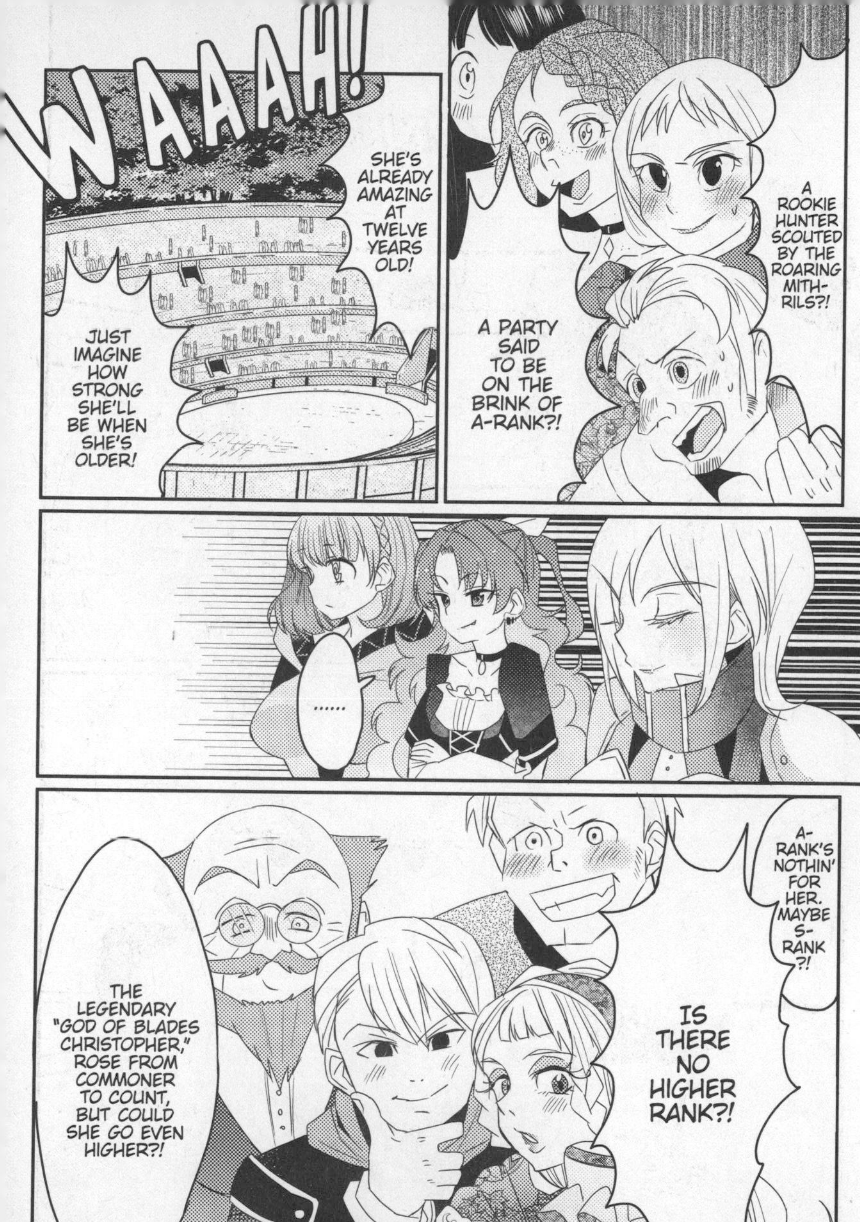
A ROOKIE HUNTER SCOUTED BY THE ROARING MITH-RILS?!
A PARTY SAID TO BE ON THE BRINK OF A-RANK?!
WAAAH!
SHE'S ALREADY AMAZING AT TWELVE YEARS OLD!
JUST IMAGINE HOW STRONG SHE'LL BE WHEN SHE'S OLDER!
......
A-RANK'S NOTHIN' FOR HER. MAYBE S-RANK?!
IS THERE NO HIGHER RANK?!
THE LEGENDARY "GOD OF BLADES CHRISTOPHER," ROSE FROM COMMONER TO COUNT, BUT COULD SHE GO EVEN HIGHER?!

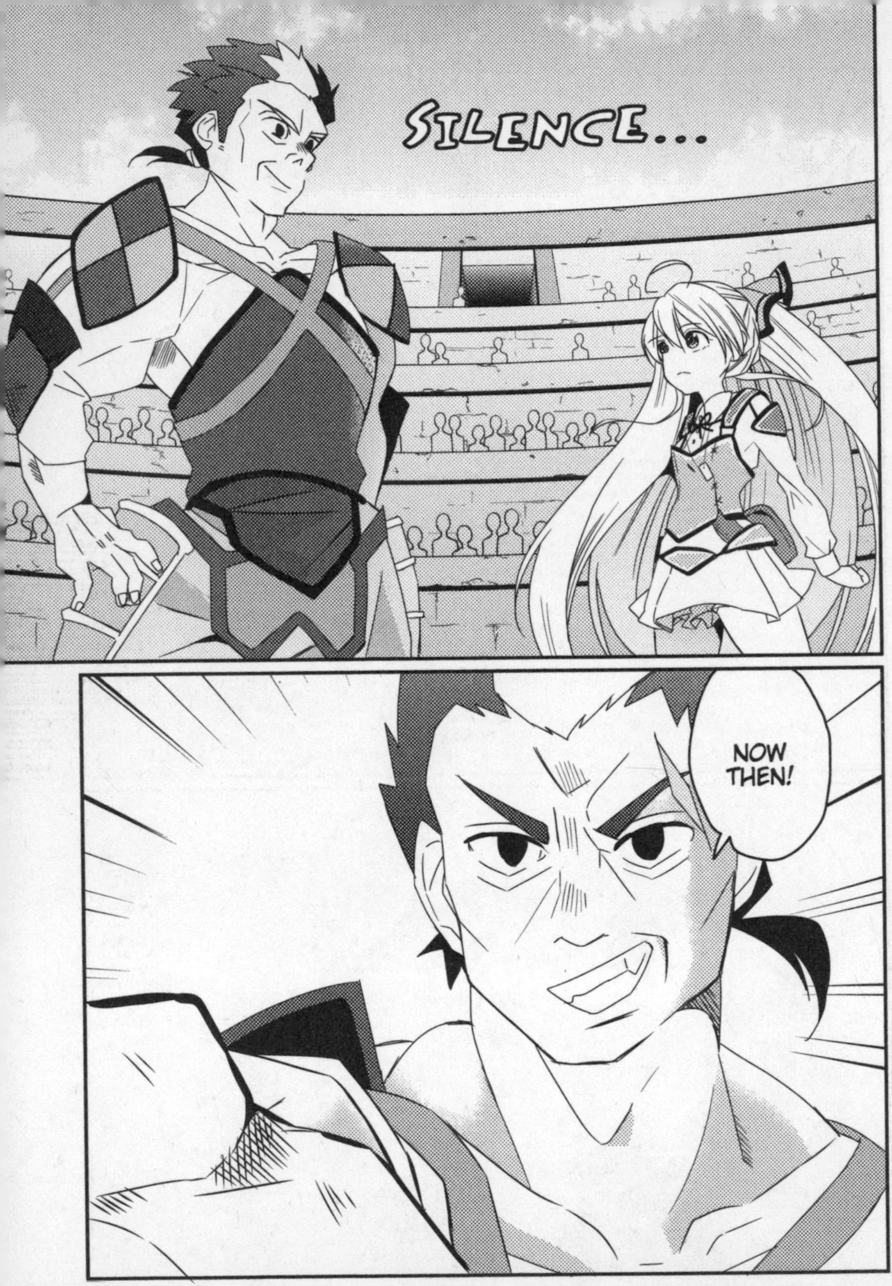
SILENCE...
NOW THEN!

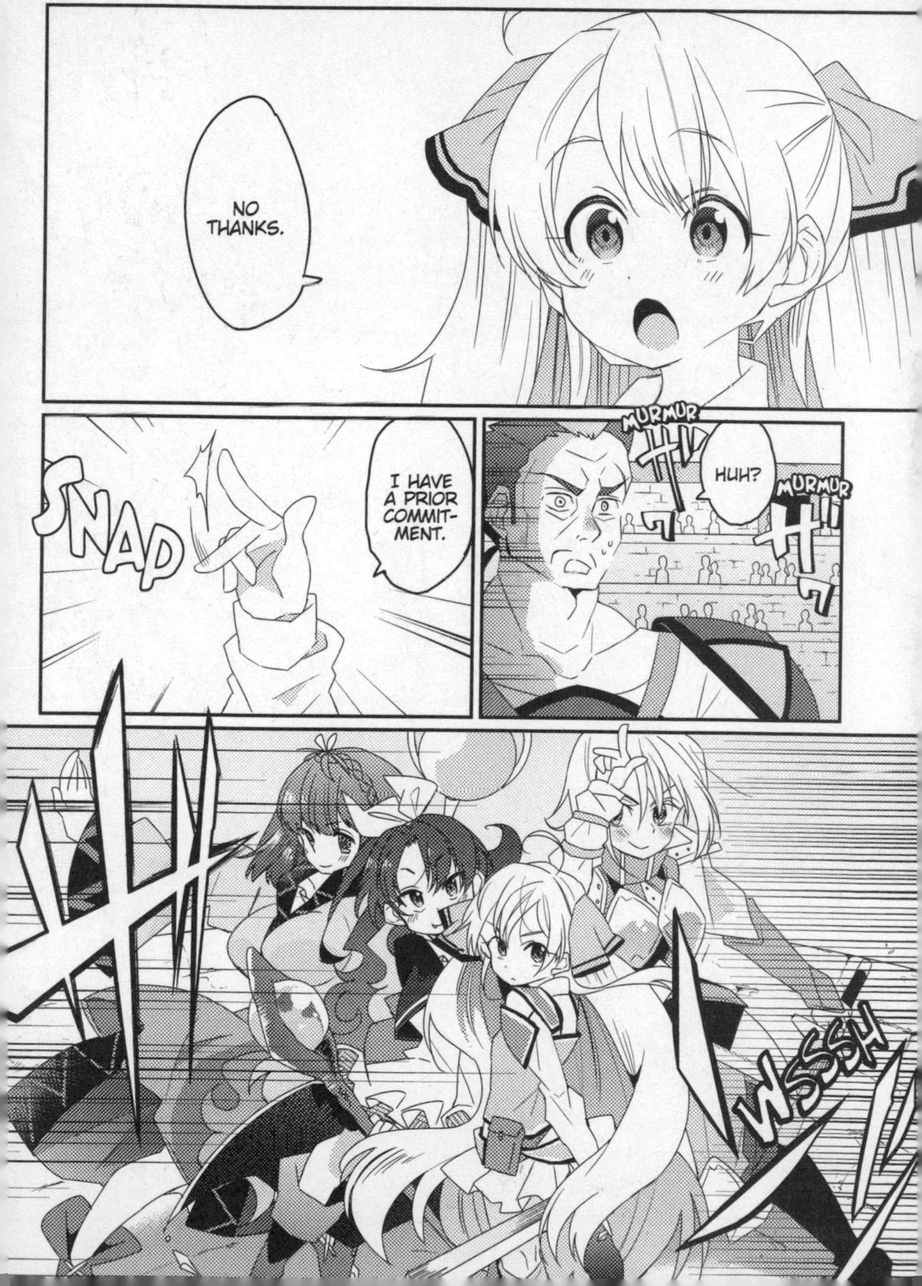
NO THANKS.
MURMUR
HUH?
MURMUR
I HAVE A PRIOR COMMIT-MENT.
SNAP
WSSSH

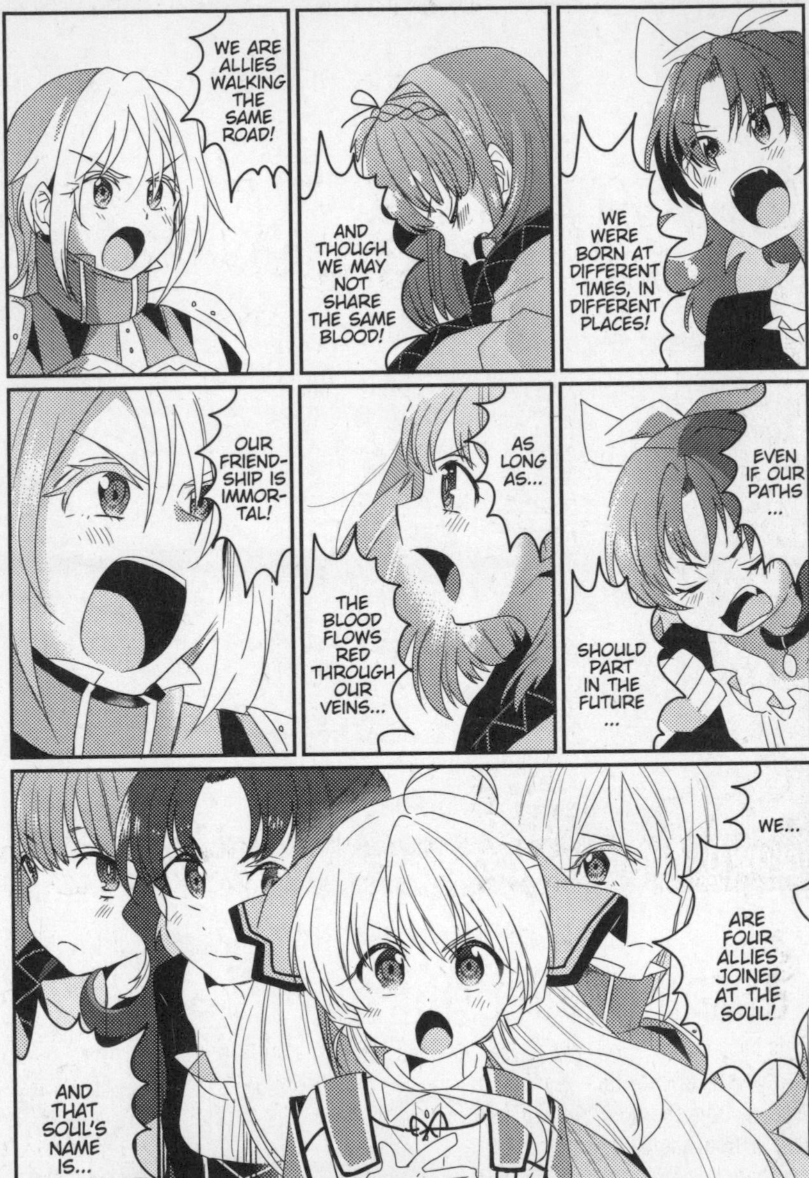
WE WERE BORN AT DIFFERENT TIMES, IN DIFFERENT PLACES!
AND THOUGH WE MAY NOT SHARE THE SAME BLOOD!
WE ARE ALLIES WALKING THE SAME ROAD!
EVEN IF OUR PATHS ...
SHOULD PART IN THE FUTURE ...
AS LONG AS...
THE BLOOD FLOWS RED THROUGH OUR VEINS...
OUR FRIEND-SHIP IS IMMOR-TAL!
WE...
ARE FOUR ALLIES JOINED AT THE SOUL!
AND THAT SOUL'S NAME IS...

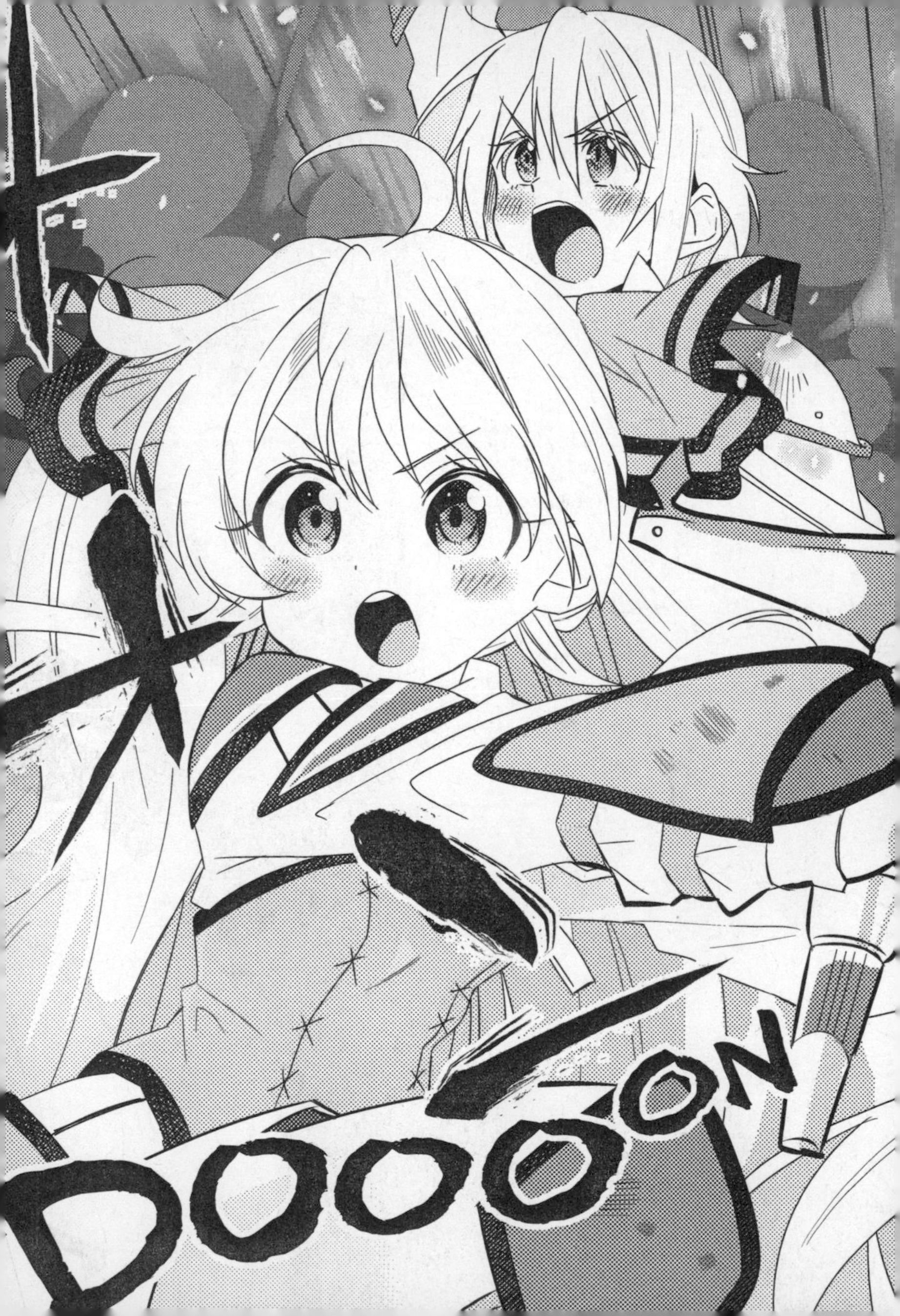
DOOOOON

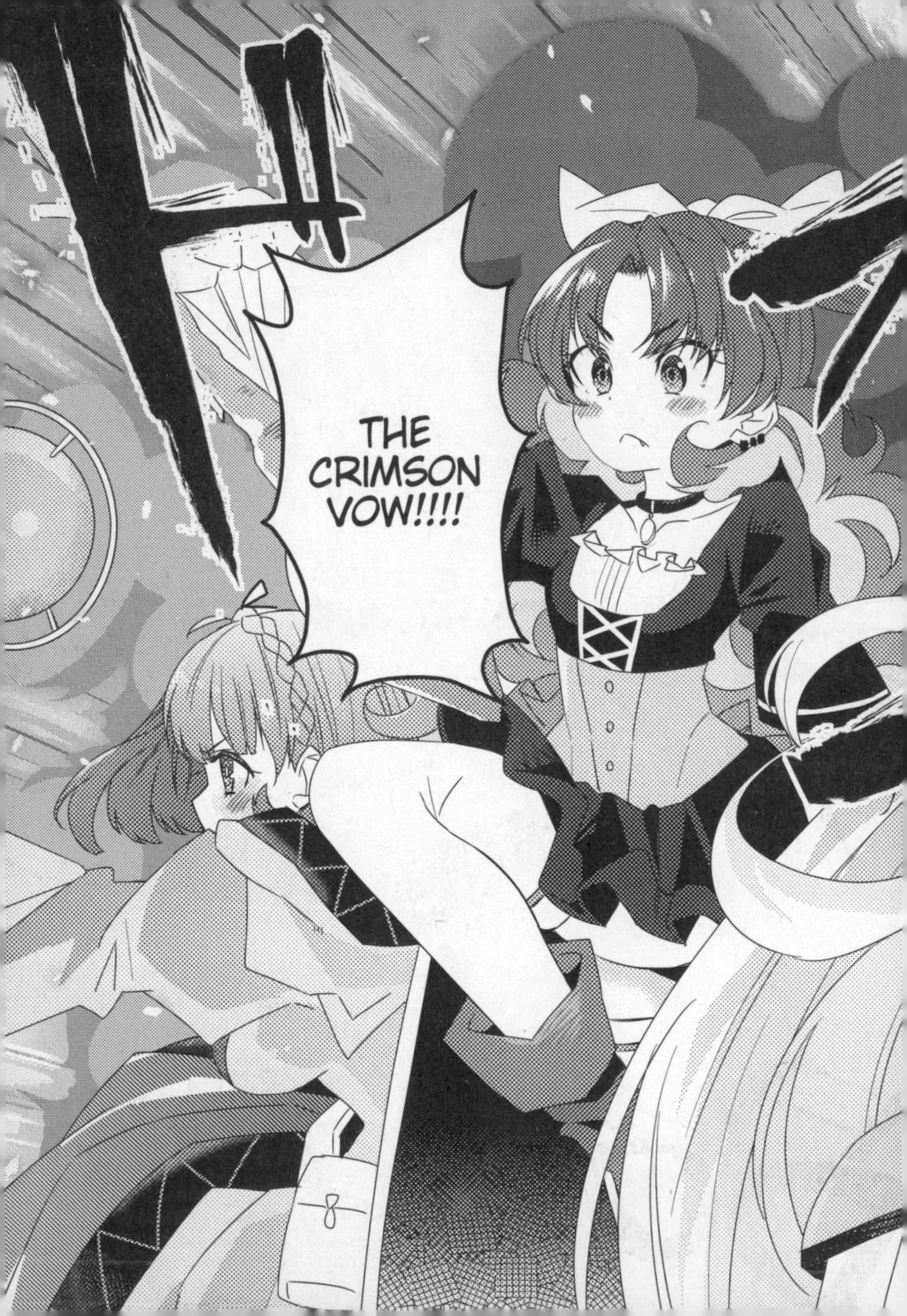
THE CRIMSON VOW!!!!

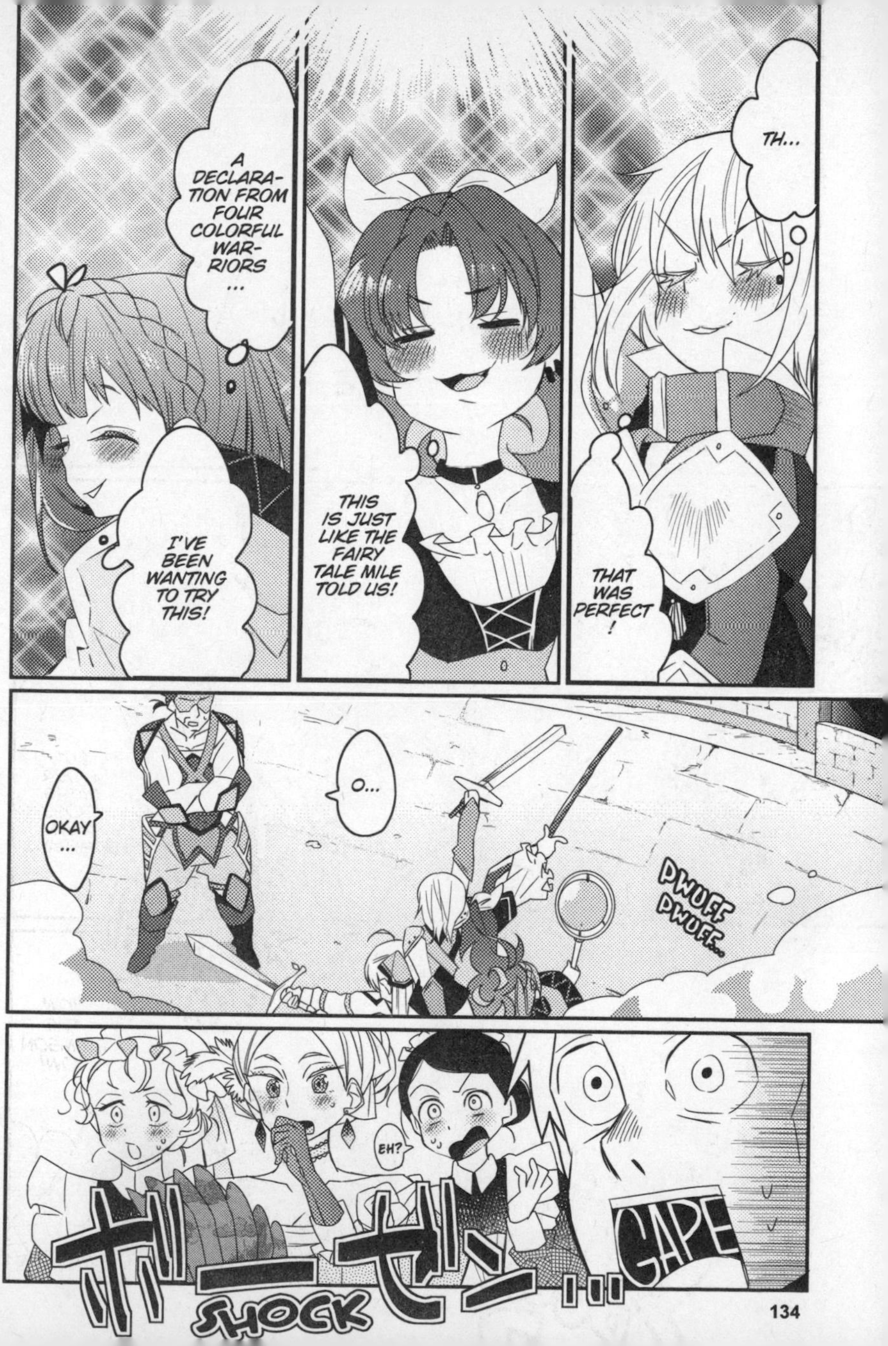
TH...
THAT WAS PERFECT!
THIS IS JUST LIKE THE FAIRY TALE MILE TOLD US!
A DECLARATION FROM FOUR COLORFUL WARRIORS...
I'VE BEEN WANTING TO TRY THIS!
PWUFF PWUFF...
O...
OKAY...
GAPE
EH?
SHOCK

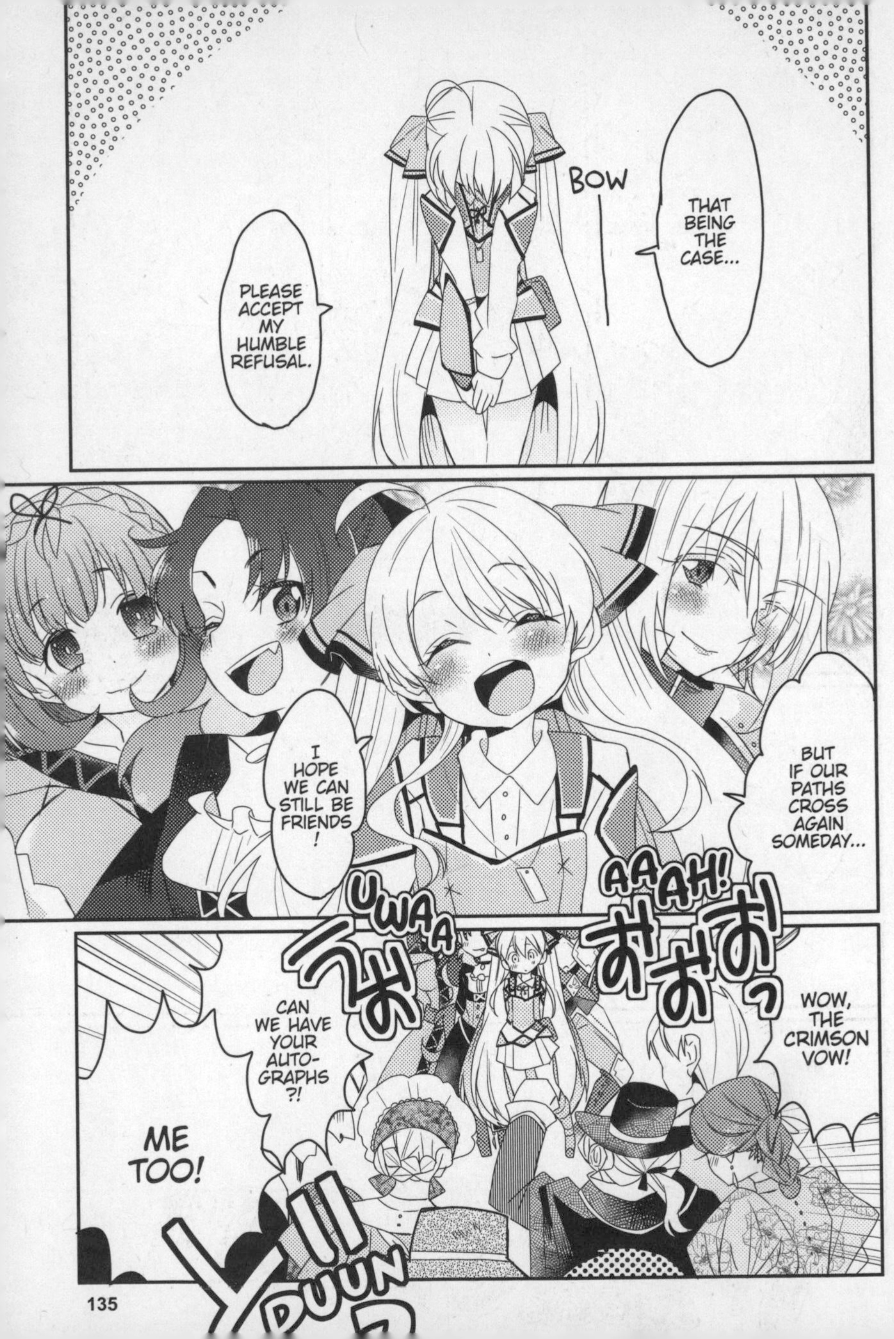
THAT BEING THE CASE...
BOW
PLEASE ACCEPT MY HUMBLE REFUSAL.
BUT IF OUR PATHS CROSS AGAIN SOMEDAY...
I HOPE WE CAN STILL BE FRIENDS!
AAAH!
おおおっ
WOW, THE CRIMSON VOW!
UWAA
CAN WE HAVE YOUR AUTO-GRAPHS?!
ME TOO!
DUUN

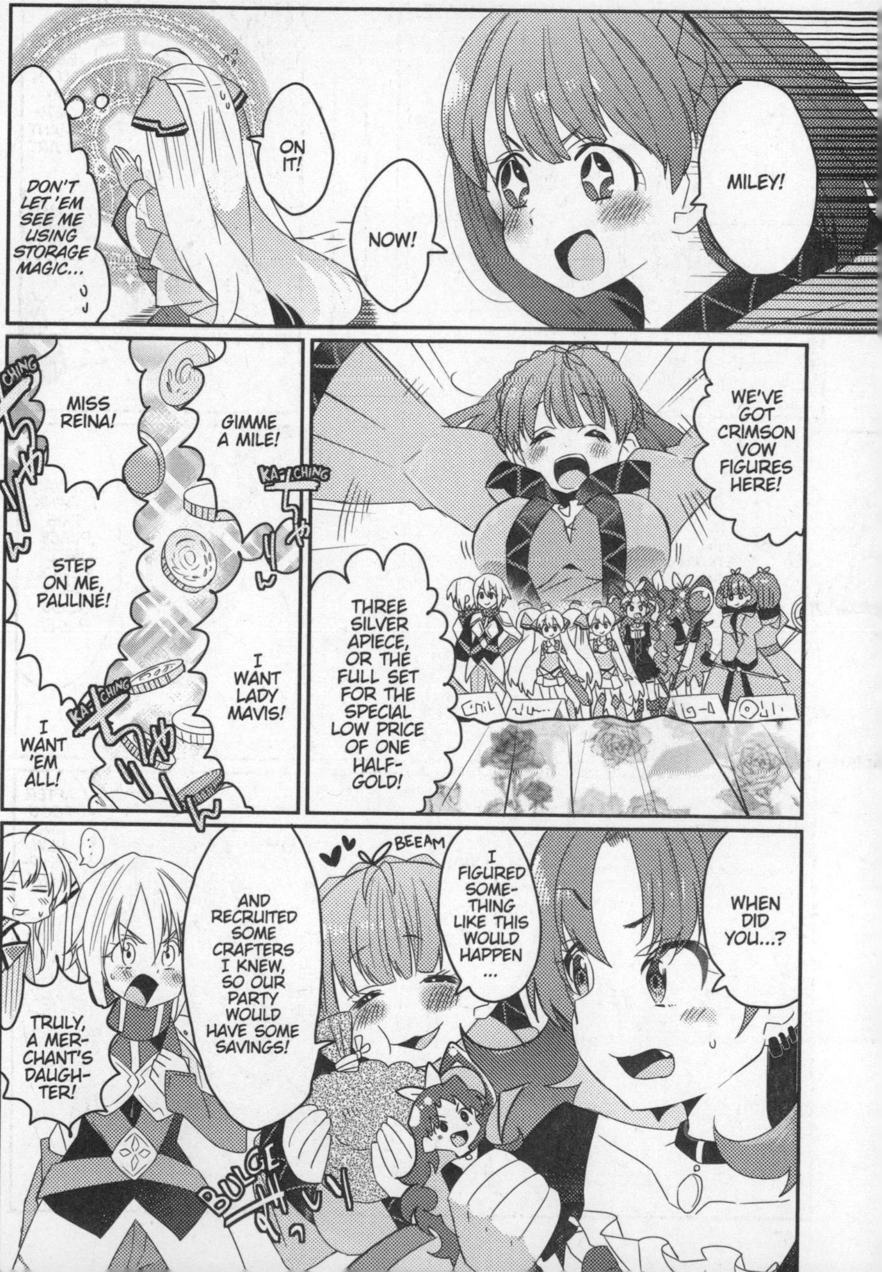
MILEY!
NOW!
ON IT!
DON'T LET 'EM SEE ME USING STORAGE MAGIC...
WE'VE GOT CRIMSON VOW FIGURES HERE!
THREE SILVER APIECE, OR THE FULL SET FOR THE SPECIAL LOW PRICE OF ONE HALF-GOLD!
KA-CHING
GIMME A MILE!
KA-CHING
MISS REINA!
I WANT LADY MAVIS!
STEP ON ME, PAULINE!
KA-CHING
I WANT 'EM ALL!
WHEN DID YOU...?
I FIGURED SOMETHING LIKE THIS WOULD HAPPEN...
BEEAM
AND RECRUITED SOME CRAFTERS I KNEW, SO OUR PARTY WOULD HAVE SOME SAVINGS!
TRULY, A MERCHANT'S DAUGHTER!
BULGE

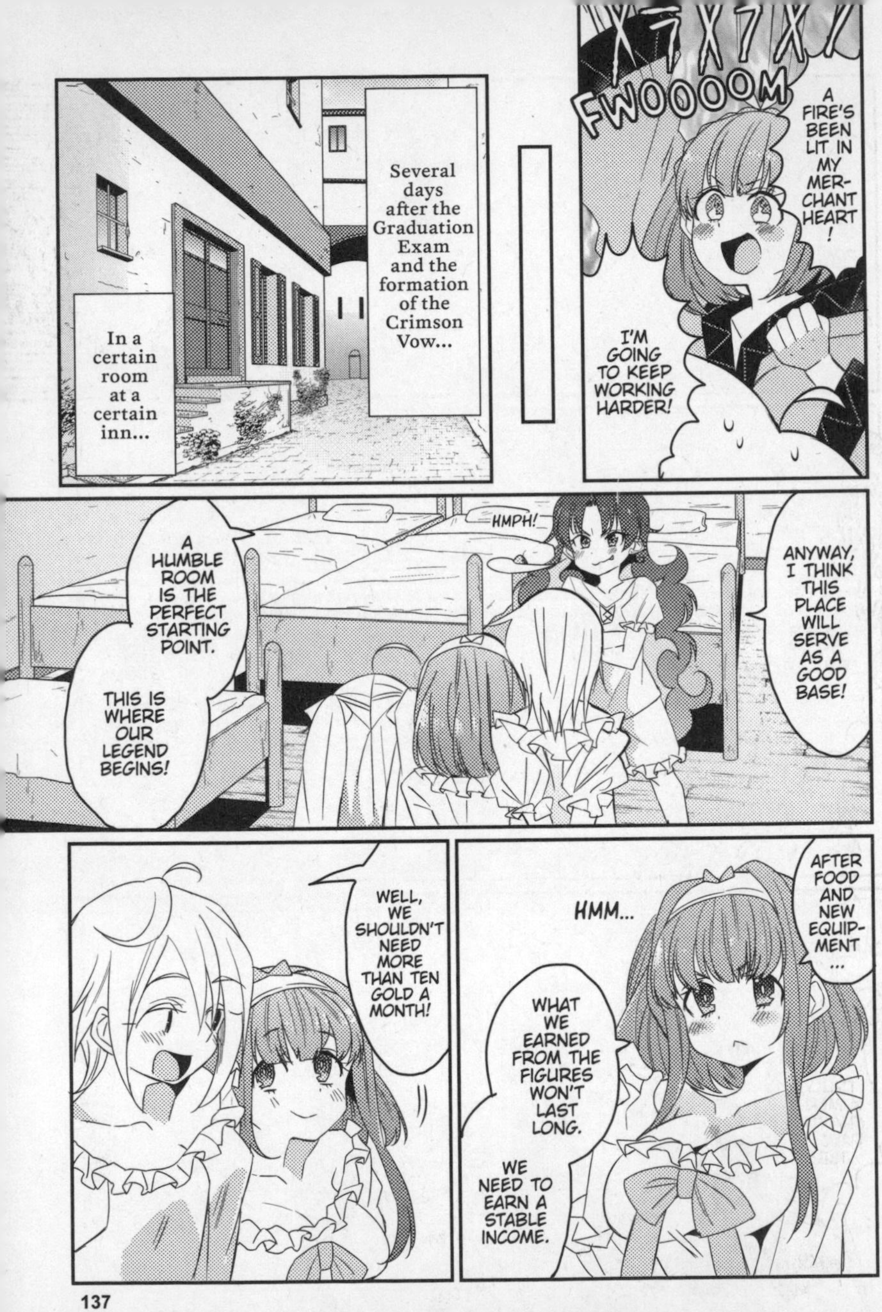
FWOOOOM
A FIRE'S BEEN LIT IN MY MERCHANT HEART!
I'M GOING TO KEEP WORKING HARDER!
Several days after the Graduation Exam and the formation of the Crimson Vow...
In a certain room at a certain inn...
ANYWAY, I THINK THIS PLACE WILL SERVE AS A GOOD BASE!
HMPH!
A HUMBLE ROOM IS THE PERFECT STARTING POINT.
THIS IS WHERE OUR LEGEND BEGINS!
AFTER FOOD AND NEW EQUIPMENT...
HMM...
WHAT WE EARNED FROM THE FIGURES WON'T LAST LONG.
WE NEED TO EARN A STABLE INCOME.
WELL, WE SHOULDN'T NEED MORE THAN TEN GOLD A MONTH!

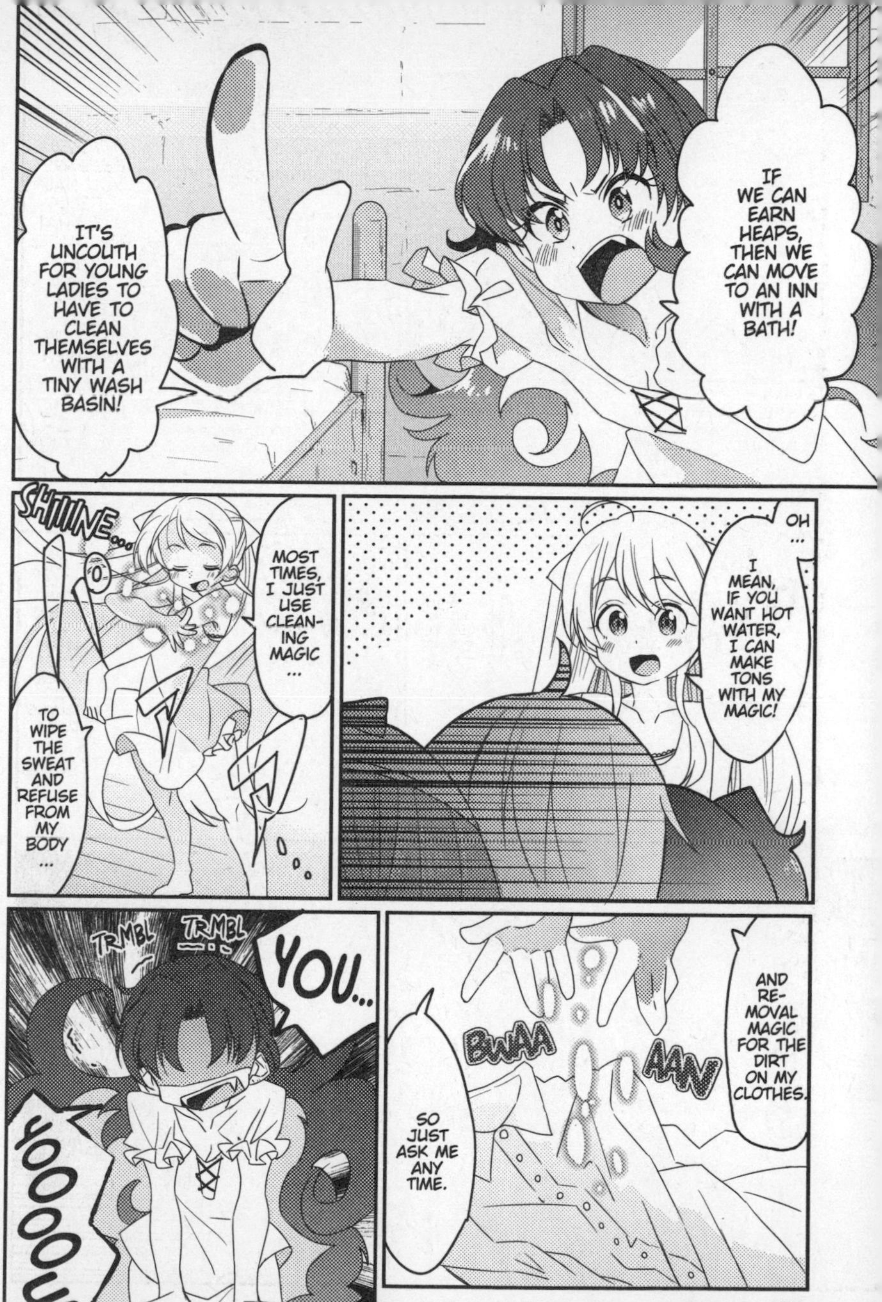
IF WE CAN EARN HEAPS, THEN WE CAN MOVE TO AN INN WITH A BATH!
IT'S UNCOUTH FOR YOUNG LADIES TO HAVE TO CLEAN THEMSELVES WITH A TINY WASH BASIN!
OH ...
I MEAN, IF YOU WANT HOT WATER, I CAN MAKE TONS WITH MY MAGIC!
SHIIIINE...
MOST TIMES, I JUST USE CLEANING MAGIC ...
TO WIPE THE SWEAT AND REFUSE FROM MY BODY ...
AND REMOVAL MAGIC FOR THE DIRT ON MY CLOTHES.
BWAA AAN
SO JUST ASK ME ANY TIME.
TRMBL TRMBL
YOU...
YOOOOUU...

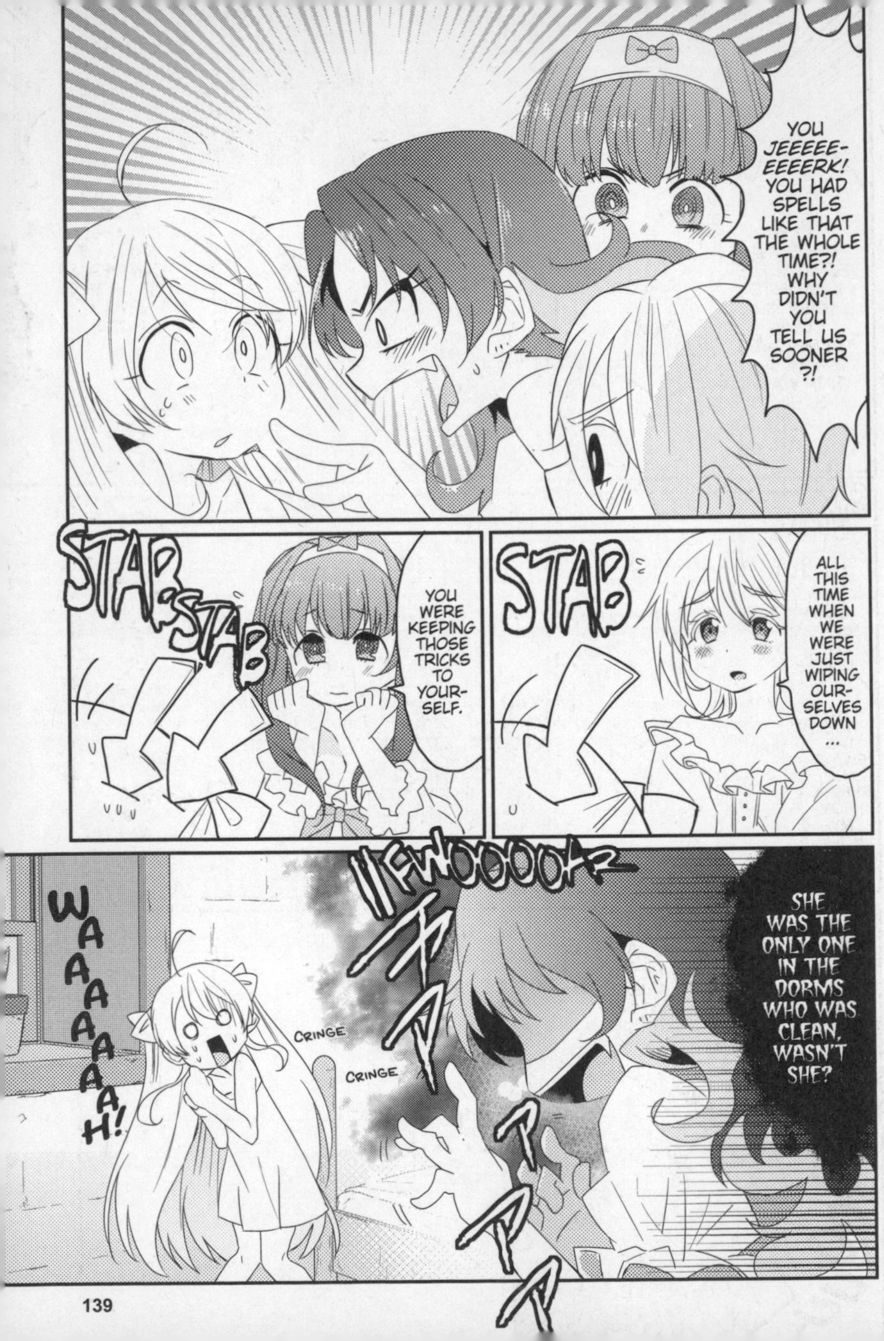
YOU JEEEEE-EEEERK! YOU HAD SPELLS LIKE THAT THE WHOLE TIME?! WHY DIDN'T YOU TELL US SOONER?!
STAB
ALL THIS TIME WHEN WE WERE JUST WIPING OUR-SELVES DOWN...
STAB STAB
YOU WERE KEEPING THOSE TRICKS TO YOUR-SELF.
SHE WAS THE ONLY ONE IN THE DORMS WHO WAS CLEAN, WASN'T SHE?
CRINGE
CRINGE
WAAAAAAAH!

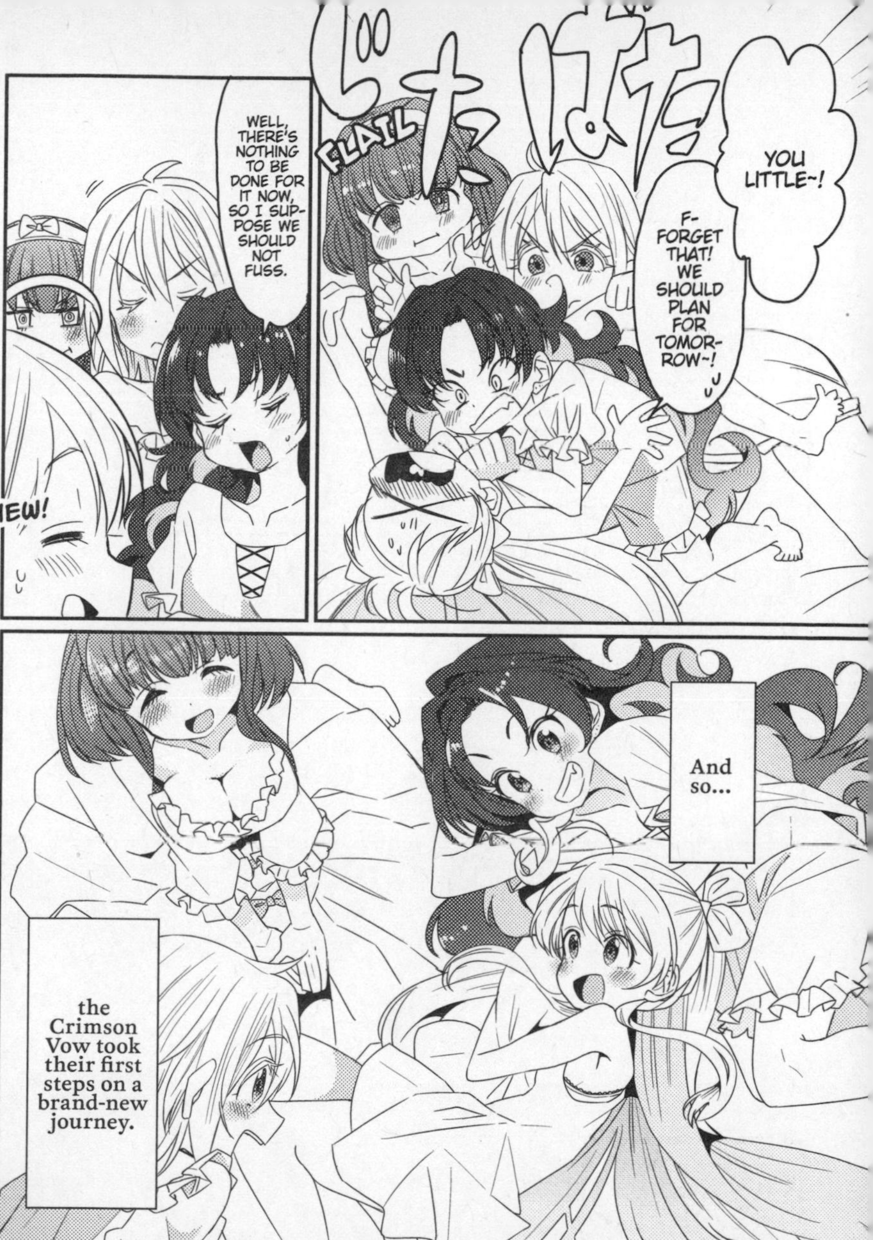
じたばた
FLAIL
YOU LITTLE~!
F-FORGET THAT! WE SHOULD PLAN FOR TOMORROW~!
WELL, THERE'S NOTHING TO BE DONE FOR IT NOW, SO I SUPPOSE WE SHOULD NOT FUSS.
PHEW!
And so...
the Crimson Vow took their first steps on a brand-new journey.

Didn't I Say to Make My Abilities Average in the Next Life?!

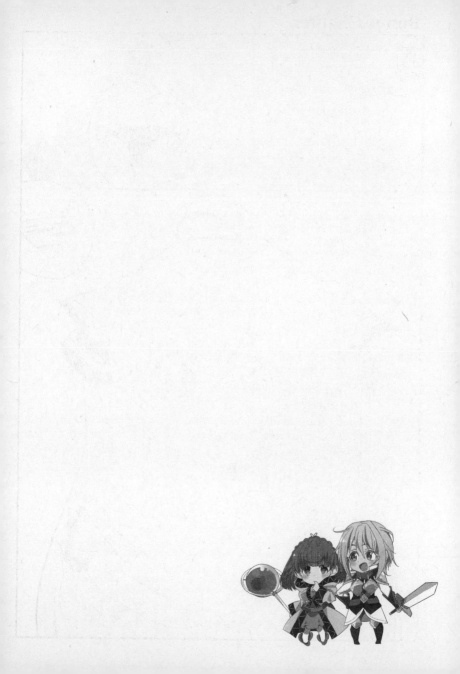

Bonus Chapter

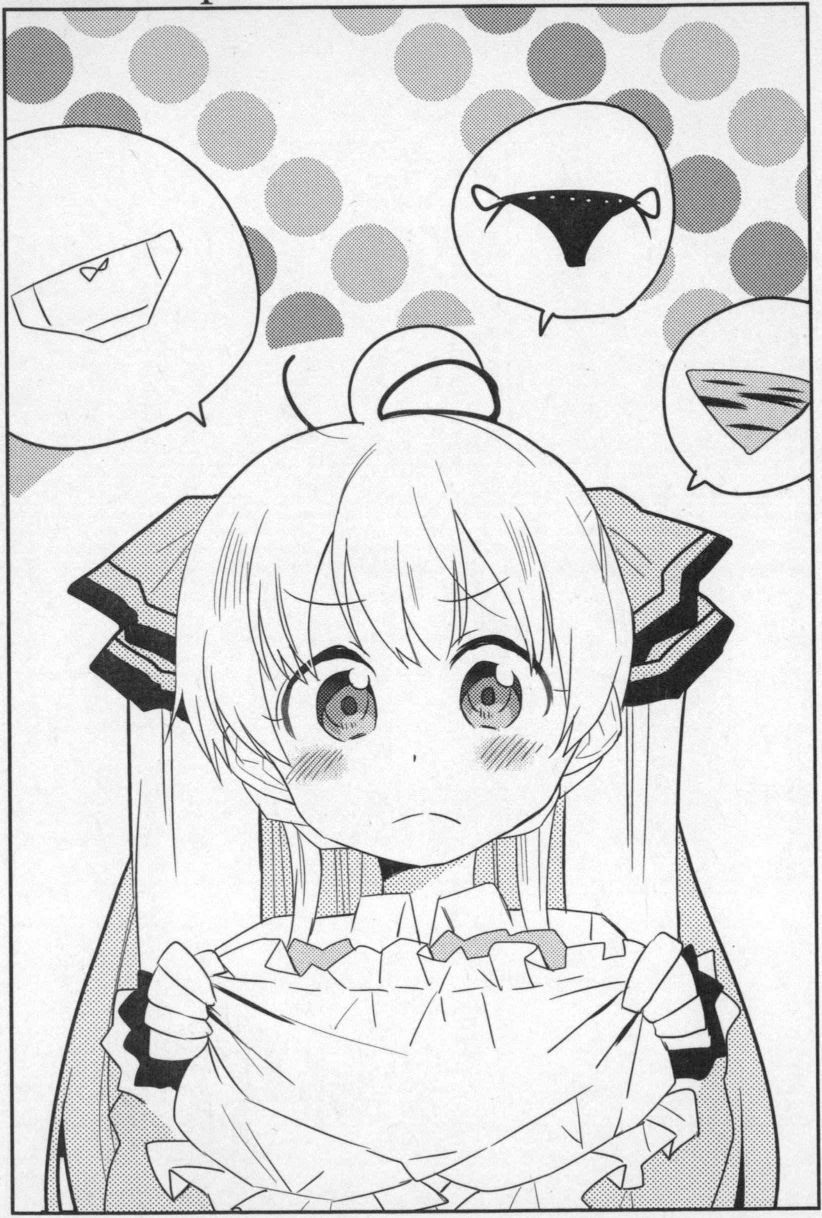

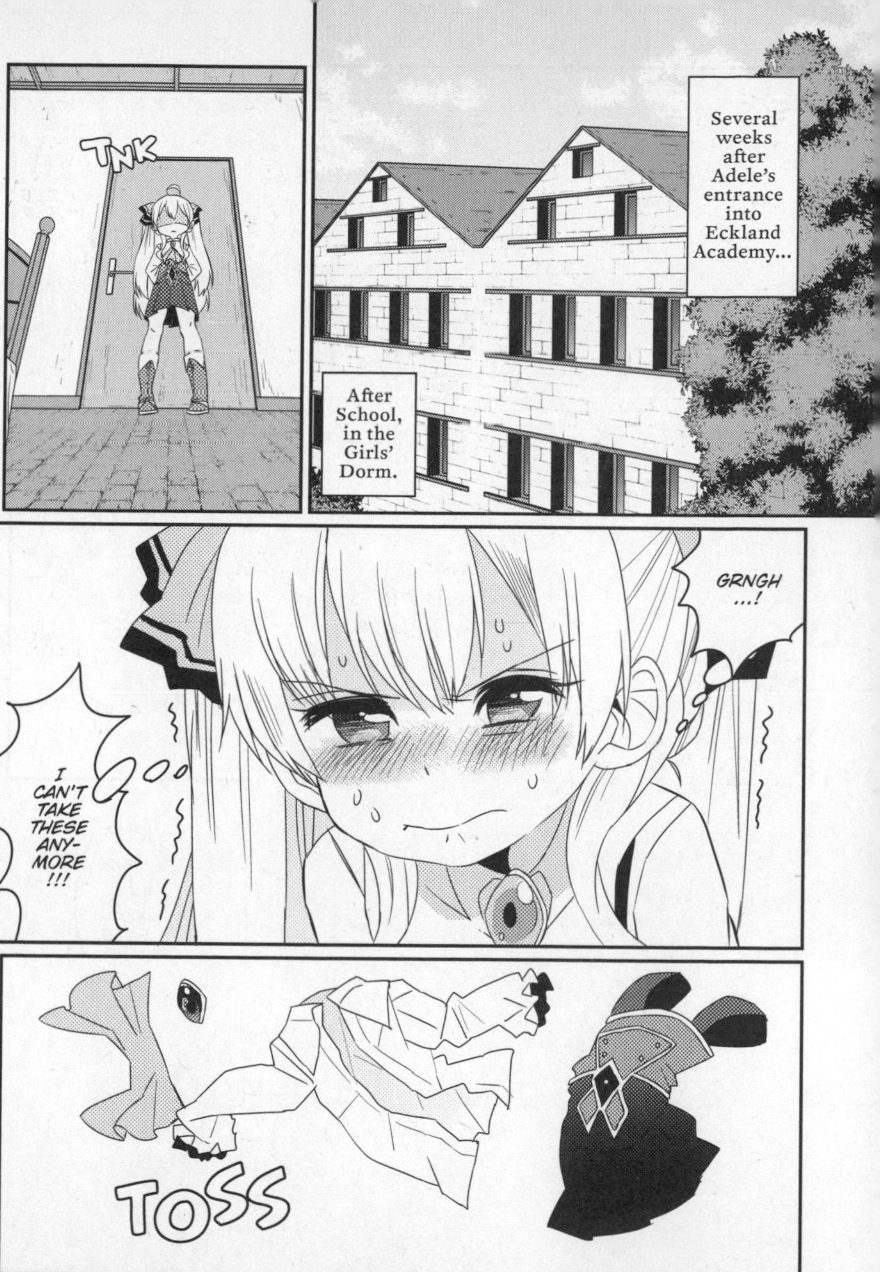
Several weeks after Adele's entrance into Eckland Academy...
After School, in the Girls' Dorm.
TNK
GRNGH ...!
I CAN'T TAKE THESE ANYMORE !!!
TOSS

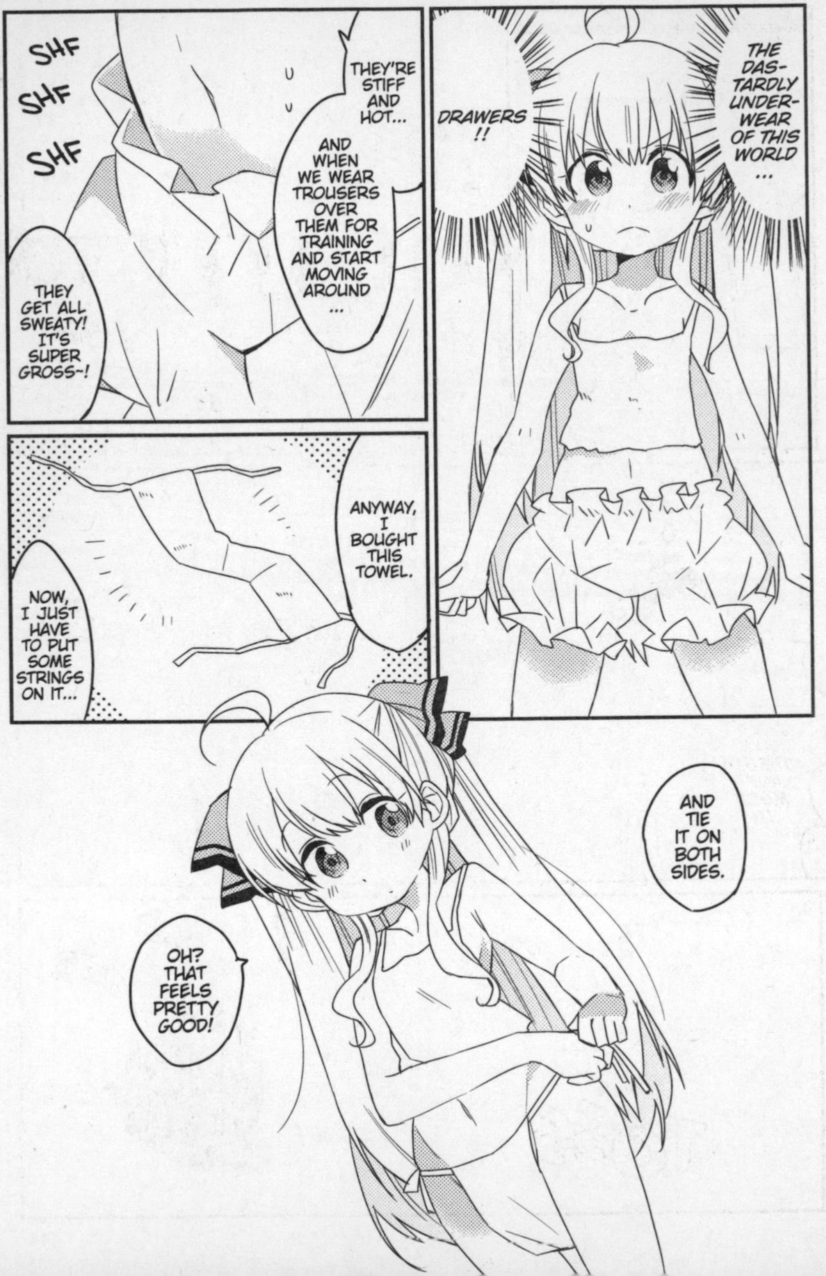
THE DAS-TARDLY UNDER-WEAR OF THIS WORLD ...
DRAWERS !!
THEY'RE STIFF AND HOT...
AND WHEN WE WEAR TROUSERS OVER THEM FOR TRAINING AND START MOVING AROUND ...
SHF
SHF
SHF
THEY GET ALL SWEATY! IT'S SUPER GROSS~!
ANYWAY, I BOUGHT THIS TOWEL.
NOW, I JUST HAVE TO PUT SOME STRINGS ON IT...
AND TIE IT ON BOTH SIDES.
OH? THAT FEELS PRETTY GOOD!

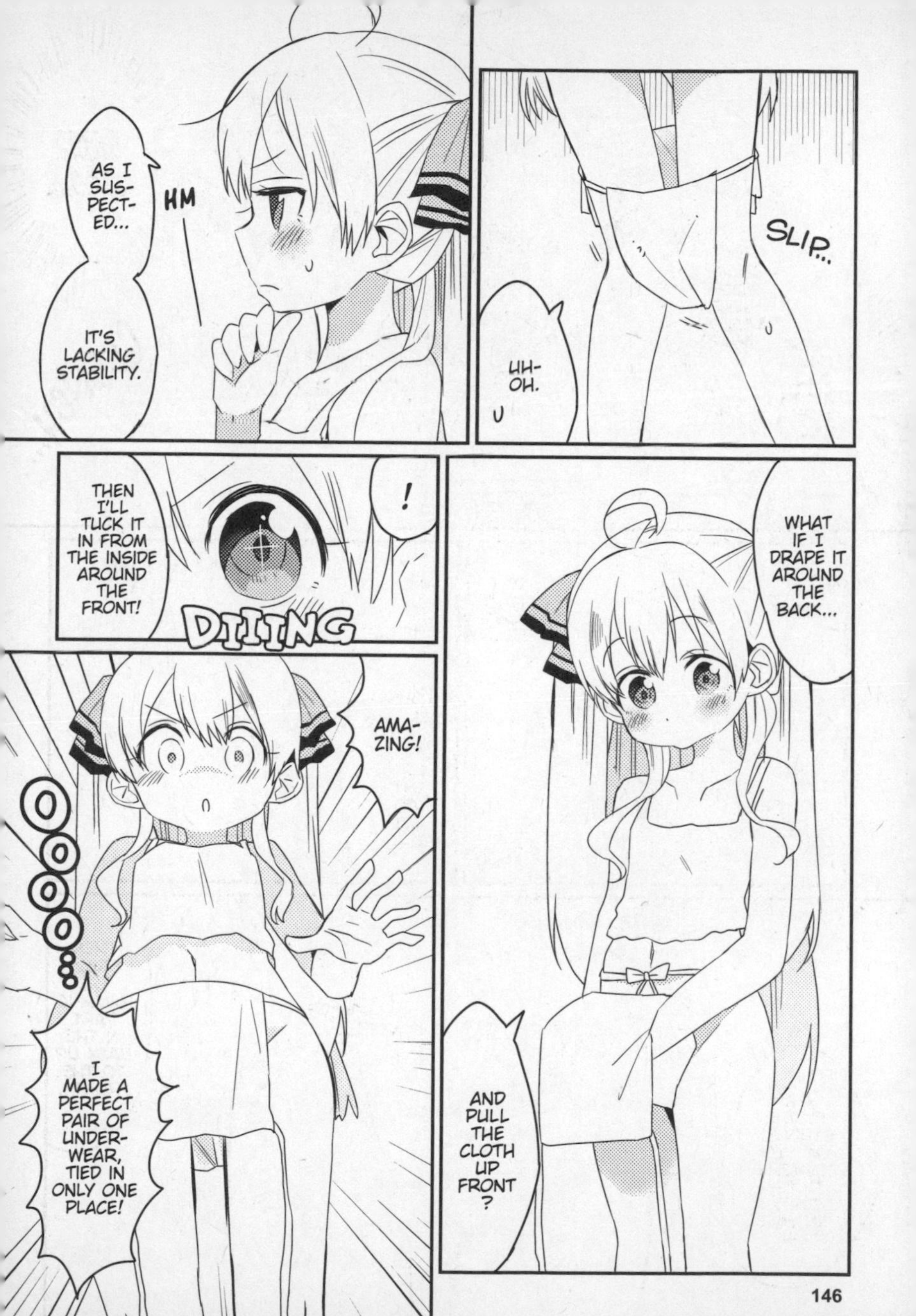
SLIP...
UH-OH.
AS I SUSPECTED...
HM
IT'S LACKING STABILITY.
WHAT IF I DRAPE IT AROUND THE BACK...
AND PULL THE CLOTH UP FRONT?
!
THEN I'LL TUCK IT IN FROM THE INSIDE AROUND THE FRONT!
DIIING
AMAZING!
OOOOO...
I MADE A PERFECT PAIR OF UNDERWEAR, TIED IN ONLY ONE PLACE!

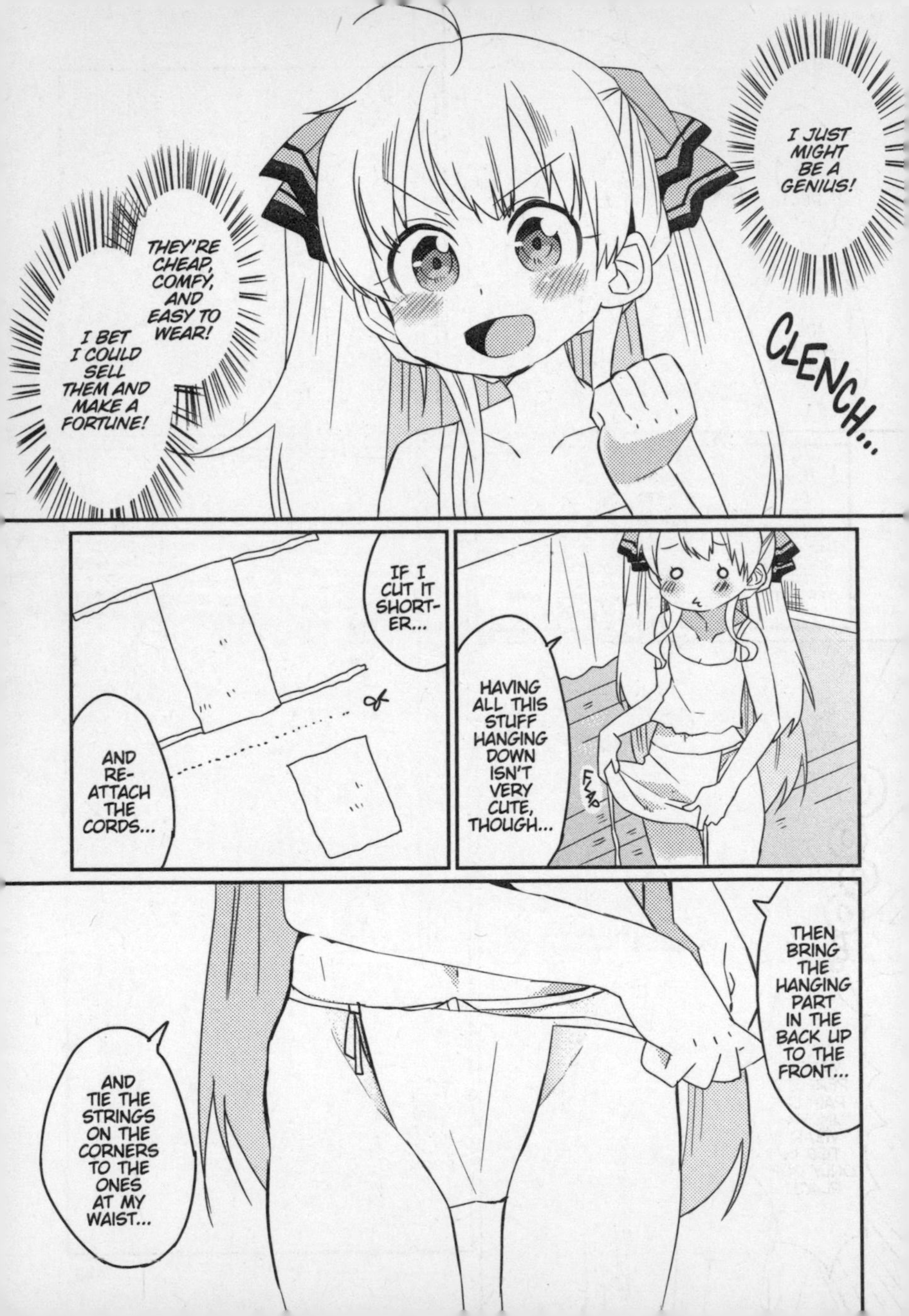
I JUST MIGHT BE A GENIUS!
CLENCH...
THEY'RE CHEAP, COMFY, AND EASY TO WEAR!
I BET I COULD SELL THEM AND MAKE A FORTUNE!
HAVING ALL THIS STUFF HANGING DOWN ISN'T VERY CUTE, THOUGH...
FLAP
IF I CUT IT SHORTER...
AND RE-ATTACH THE CORDS...
THEN BRING THE HANGING PART IN THE BACK UP TO THE FRONT...
AND TIE THE STRINGS ON THE CORNERS TO THE ONES AT MY WAIST...

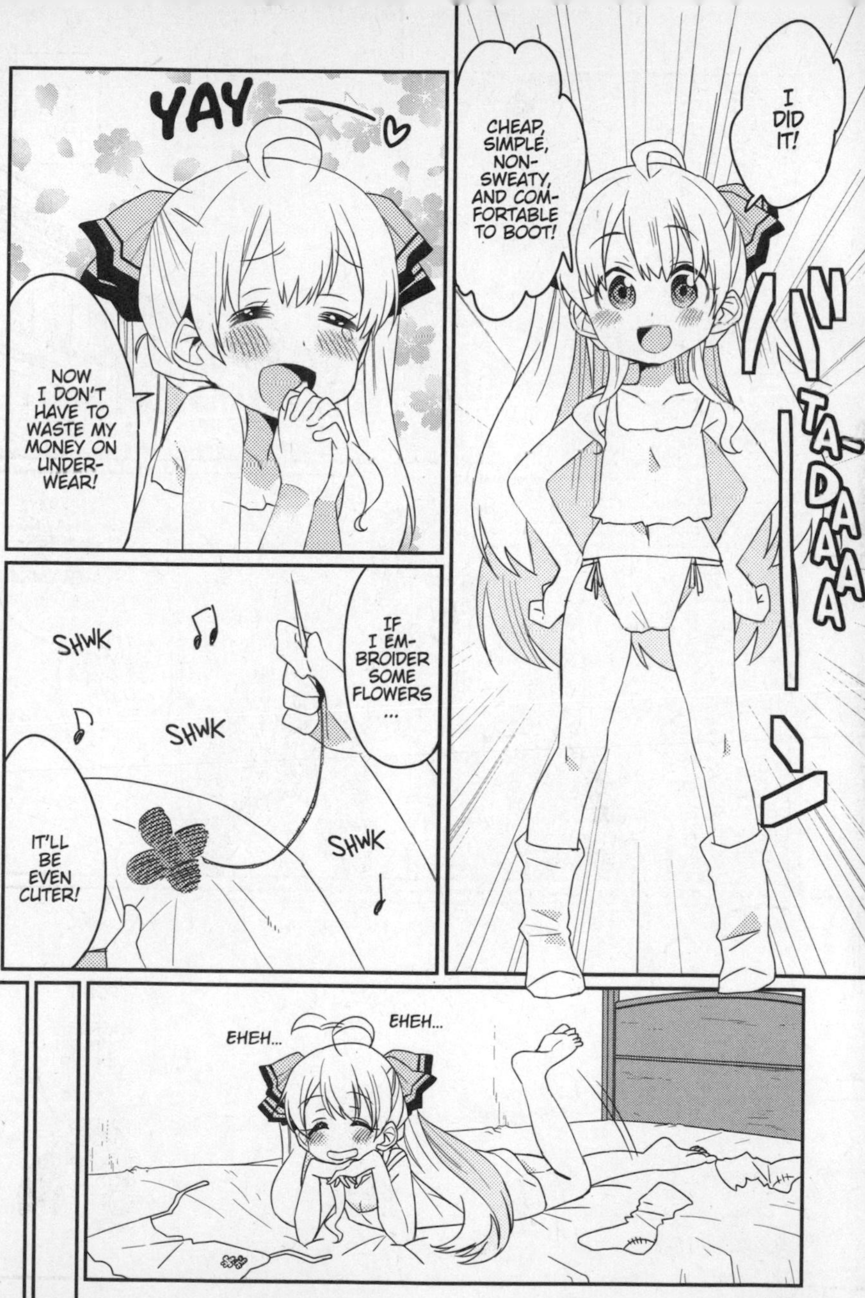
I DID IT!
CHEAP, SIMPLE, NON-SWEATY, AND COMFORTABLE TO BOOT!
TA-DAAAA
YAY
NOW I DON'T HAVE TO WASTE MY MONEY ON UNDERWEAR!
IF I EMBROIDER SOME FLOWERS...
SHWK
SHWK
SHWK
IT'LL BE EVEN CUTER!
EHEH...
EHEH...

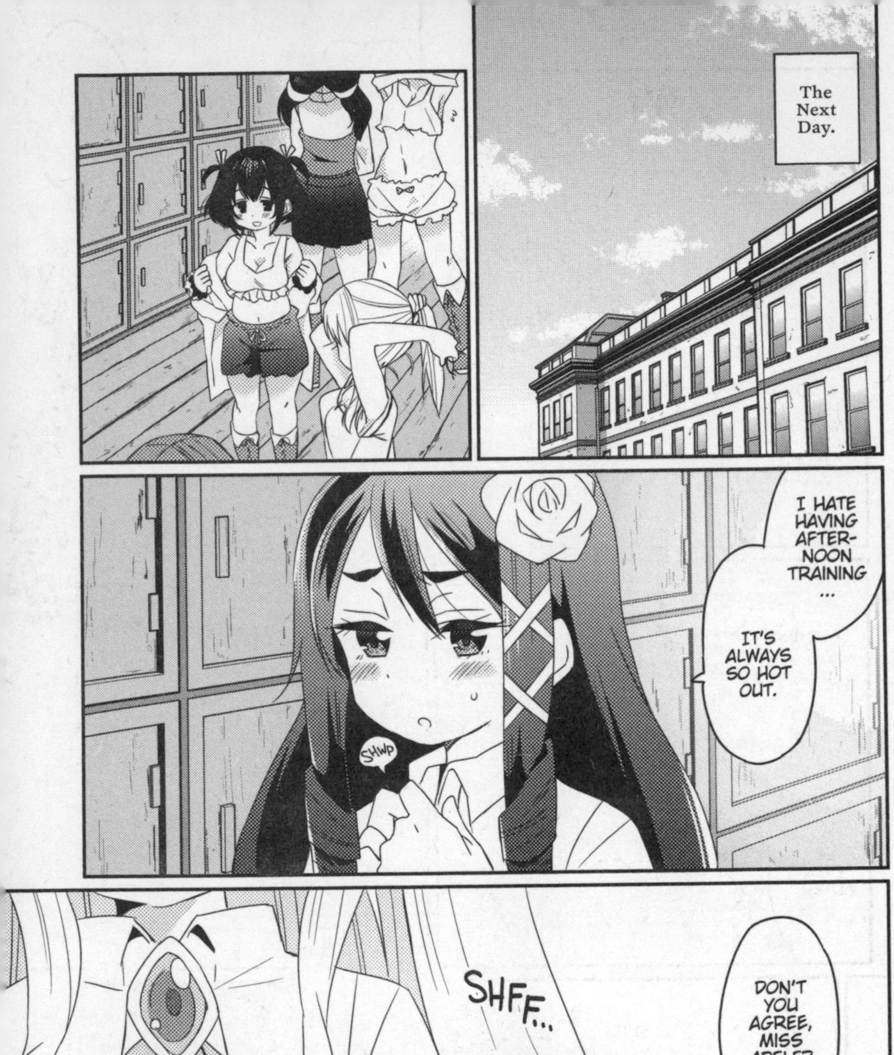
The Next Day.
I HATE HAVING AFTER-NOON TRAINING ...
IT'S ALWAYS SO HOT OUT.
SHWP
DON'T YOU AGREE, MISS ADELE?
SHFF...

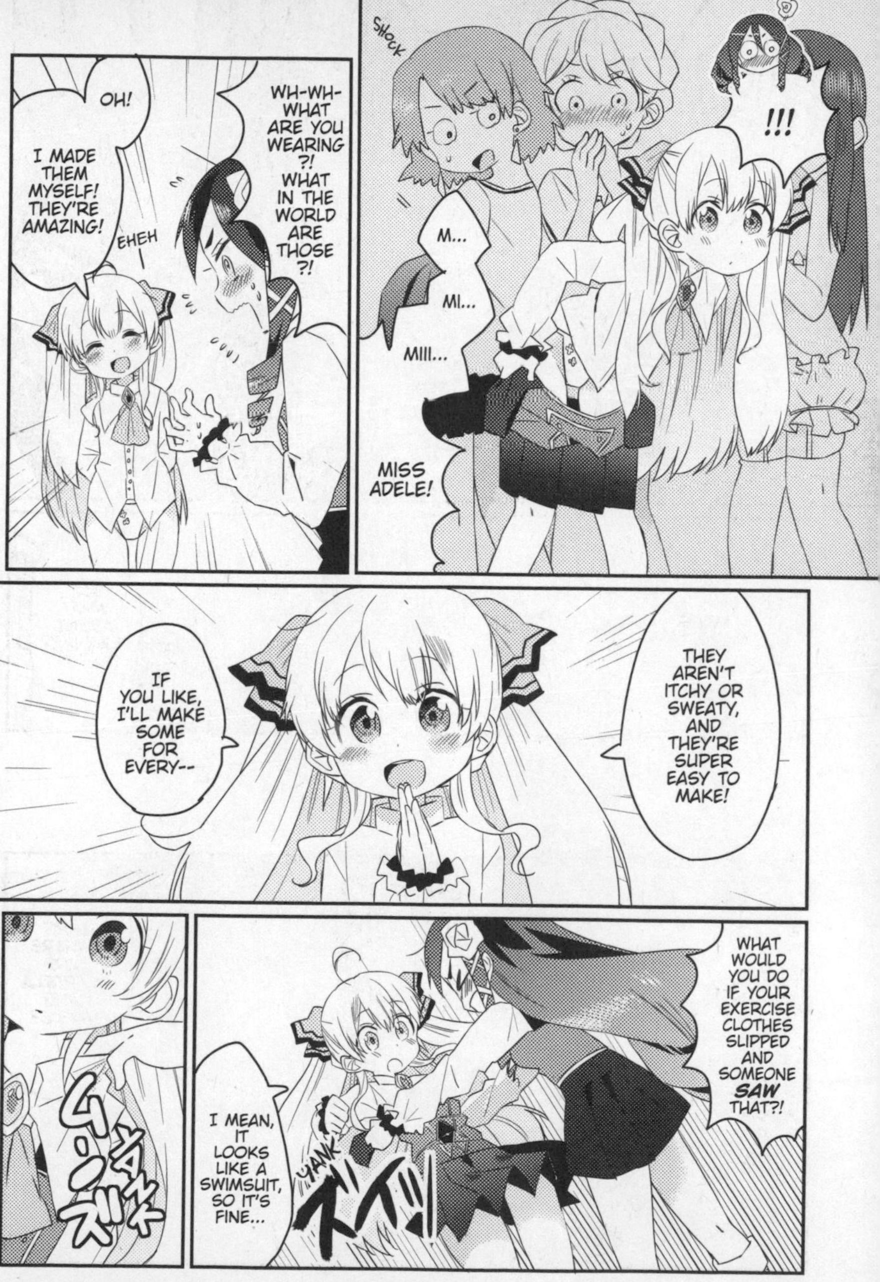
SHOCK
!!!
M...
MI...
MIII...
MISS ADELE!
WH-WH-WHAT ARE YOU WEARING?! WHAT IN THE WORLD ARE THOSE?!
OH!
I MADE THEM MYSELF! THEY'RE AMAZING!
EHEH
THEY AREN'T ITCHY OR SWEATY, AND THEY'RE SUPER EASY TO MAKE!
IF YOU LIKE, I'LL MAKE SOME FOR EVERY--
WHAT WOULD YOU DO IF YOUR EXERCISE CLOTHES SLIPPED AND SOMEONE *SAW* THAT?!
I MEAN, IT LOOKS LIKE A SWIMSUIT, SO IT'S FINE...
YANK
YANK

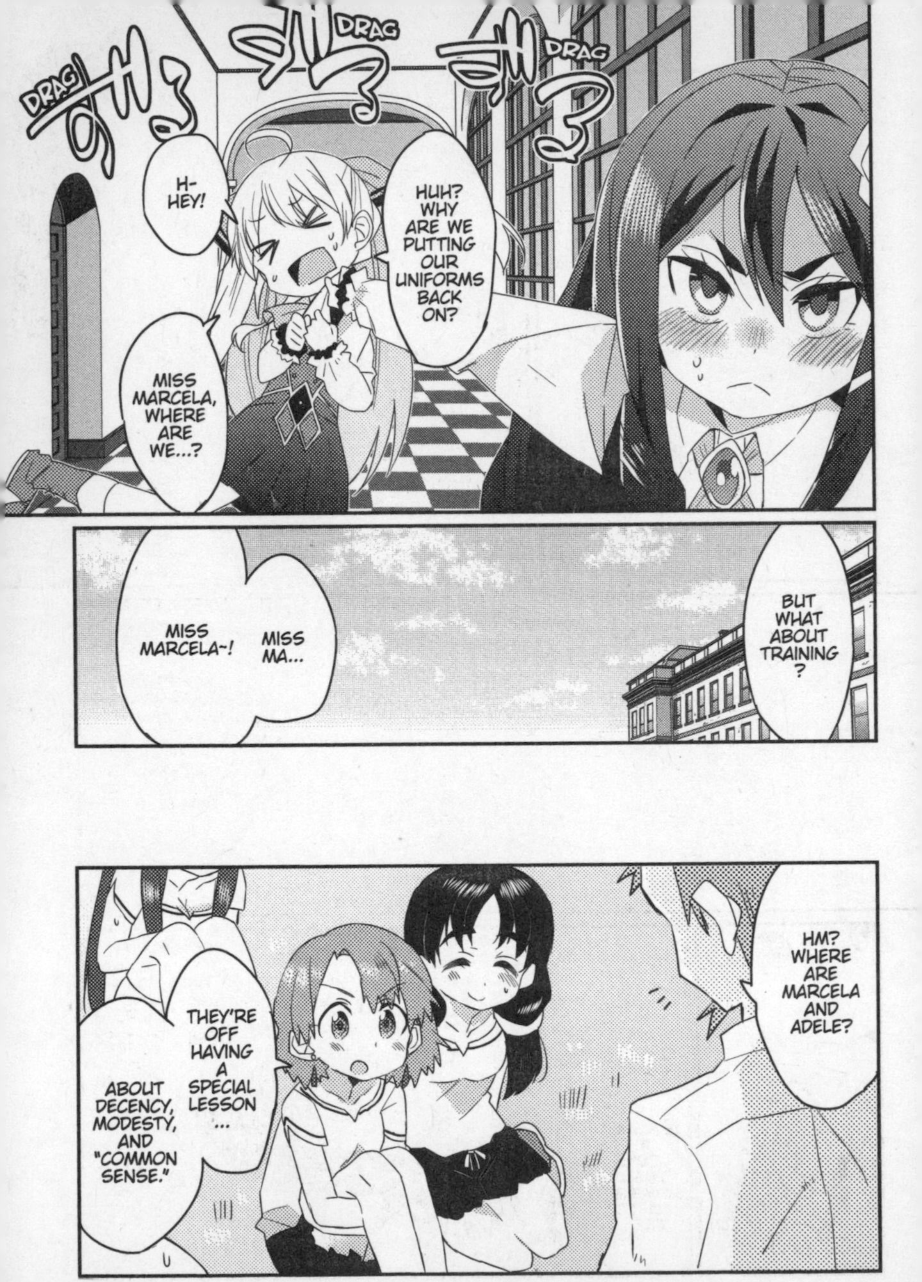
DRAG
DRAG
DRAG
HUH? WHY ARE WE PUTTING OUR UNIFORMS BACK ON?
H-HEY!
MISS MARCELA, WHERE ARE WE...?
BUT WHAT ABOUT TRAINING?
MISS MA...
MISS MARCELA~!
HM? WHERE ARE MARCELA AND ADELE?
THEY'RE OFF HAVING A SPECIAL LESSON...
ABOUT DECENCY, MODESTY, AND "COMMON SENSE."

Didn't I Say to Make My Abilities Average in the Next Life?!

BONUS STORY
Didn't I Say to Make My Abilities Average in the Next Life?!

The Next Generation

"Damn it... We haven't snagged a single girl yet?"

"Yo, don't be such a creep! You make it sound like we're pick-up artists!"

"O-oh yeah, sorry..."

These were the students of the thirteenth class of the Hunters' Prep School. Just like the class before them—the class which contained, among others, the Crimson Vow—the time had come for the students to begin the social process of forming teams, in preparation for their life post-graduation.

In order to put together a proper team, several qualifications had to be considered: strength, professions, specialties, weaknesses, personalities...and of course, whether or not they were a cute girl.

Whenever these invitation wars began, skirmishes broke out among the most talented and attractive students.

For the most part, handsomeness wasn't a factor. Most girls sought not a man who set their hearts aflutter, but rather a "strong and reliable protector." At the outset of their careers, surviving as long as possible took priority. It was by no means unusual for them to put off searching for a lover until they had made it past their first three years: the period where the

chances of dying were at their highest for a new hunter.

And so, during an average year, the men and women all mingled, fussing over this and that before coming together to form parties of five or six members each. Those who didn't would join existing parties of more veteran hunters, or else they would return to their hometowns and search for a party.

This time, however, that pattern fell utterly apart.

"Join your party? Um, no thanks. We've already got a pre-arranged party of five."

"Yep, it's going to be us four, and later we're going to recruit another girl, a front-line fighter, from the guild."

The girls weren't aiming to form parties with boys, but to form all-female parties. Not a single girl, not a single handful of them, had any other plan.

The rise of the Crimson Vow was at the root of it.

Even as hunters, a profession that required quite a bit of individual skill, women were still taken lightly. If they were part of a party residing at a rented residence, there were scoundrels who would push all the cooking, cleaning, and washing upon the women of the party. They treated them as a shared resource among the party's men. However, the usual thinking was that a party of all women was reckless, so there were very few to be had. A party of nothing but rookie women hunters was rarer still.

But then the Crimson Vow had formed, and everything changed.

There was the Guerrilla Battle at Amroth, where twelve hunters, including the Crimson Vow, single-handedly defeated over forty enemy soldiers.

There was the capture of a live wyvern at Helmont.

The sudden surplus of rock lizard harvests was also said to be the work of the Crimson Vow.

Thanks to them, many young ladies began to think, "Oh? We can make a killing with just other women? We don't need men at all?" Plus, a party of all women would be more fun and far more convenient.

Indeed, the Crimson Vow had become a beacon of hope for women hunters across the land. For a portion of men, however, they were a harbinger of doom.

"This is bad. At this rate, our dream of having a party of us three and three ladies is gonna be..."

It was nearly dawn when a solution came to the three young men, who had fretted over their predicament the whole night. Indeed, it was the sort of stroke of brilliance that only occurred when riding the high of sleep deprivation.

"Why don't we go hunting as a group on our next rest day?"

"Hm? Those woods aren't that dangerous—not enough to bother bringing individual parties together, anyway."

The three young men, who had made this proposal to a party of four women—two sword fighters and two mages—shook their heads.

"No, we aren't talking about the woods the novices use. We mean the woods proper, where the C-rankers go. We'll earn more out there. Plus, it's the spot they use for pre-graduation field experience, so it shouldn't be *too* dangerous."

"Huh?"

The girls were hesitant, but the boys explained that, since they were close to graduation already, they more or less possessed the skills of a C-rank hunter. With a party of seven, pushing through the thinner parts of the forest should be no problem. The girls thought perhaps they *could* give it a go.

At any rate, the prey in the beginners' woods had already been thoroughly hunted, so their numbers were slim. By

contrast, no one went to the heart of the forest to hunt jackalopes, so they could expect a big haul. On top of that, if they were able to hunt some goblins, they would take home at least a small reward—though in truth, the members they had gathered would likely be enough to take on two or three orcs.

Orc meat sold for a good price. If they could catch just two of them, the pay would be good, despite the fact it would be split seven ways. If they managed to get three or more, however, they would never be able to carry them all home. This was one reason storage magic was so highly valued.

After discussing it for a short while, the girls finally gave an affirmative:

"All right, let's do it!"

The next rest day arrived.

In the woods where the C-rank and B-rank hunters made their living, seven students could be seen.

"There!"

Ka-shunk!

"Got it!!"

Thus far, they had captured five jackalopes and three large birds, and had proof of four goblin kills. Given they had achieved such results in a short time, they expected quite the bumper crop if they continued until evening.

Perhaps now's the time, the boys thought. So, one of them proposed:

"What do you girls think about goin' a little deeper in?"

"Huh? But if we go deeper, we'll run into higher-ranking monsters. We're supposed to stick to the thinner parts..."

That was the plan, but if no orcs emerged, all their plans would fall apart.

The intent, should they encounter orcs, was to leave the battle to the girls first, then swoop in to save them once they

were backed into a corner. That would prove that a party of just girls would never be strong enough—they needed men.

The girls' group consisted of two sword fighters, one mage specializing in attack magic, and one mage specializing in support magic, who also wielded a dagger. They weren't much, so if they came across orcs and took advantage of getting in the first blow, the battle would get tricky once the orcs engaged them. Even if they managed to fell one of them with an initial spell, there wouldn't be enough time afterwards to prepare anything powerful. Besides, felling an orc with a single blow from a sword, or even using most magic techniques, was difficult.

When the going got tough, the three men—two swordsmen and one lancer—would valiantly save the day.

It was the perfect plan.

The young women initially opposed it, but at the men's cajoling, and considering the fact that bagging even one or two orcs would give them a financial cushion and confidence boost, they finally agreed. They were optimistic they could manage a few orcs, so long as the seven of them worked together.

Then, in order to be certain the women would be the first to enter the fray, the men began to leave just a bit of a gap between their parties as they walked.

"............"

Finally, they appeared.

Not orcs but *ogres*. Four of them.

It was rare to go to a hunting ground and have the quarry one desired appear straight away, but four ogres were a much less desirable opponent for seven students—assuming they tried fighting them head-on, anyway.

And so, the three boys, who had already left a sizeable gap

between themselves and the girls, fled. They ran like bats out of hell, casting the girls aside—or rather, offering them up as decoys.

"Th-those jerks!"

The girls grumbled and grit their teeth, but it was already too late.

It was four ogres against the four young students. Though they had ignored the boys, the ogres wouldn't let the girls get away. Even if they tried to run, they wouldn't be able to shake off a pack of ogres.

"This is all my fault," the group's appointed leader apologized. "I let myself be played by those boys. I'm sorry..."

The other three simply grinned.

"What're you saying? We made the decision together, so we have to take responsibility together. Such is the path of we," one said, and then they all shouted the rest of the sentence in unison, "*the Vermilion Sisterhood*!"

Seeing that their prey showed no sign of fleeing, the ogres approached slowly.

"Heh heh," one girl began to laugh.

"Heh heh heh..." another joined in.

Suddenly, they were all laughing uproariously.

"We barely even know each other," said the first.

"Looks like we'll be upholding that promise after all, huh?" chimed the second.

"Yep. Though we may've been born at different times, in different places..."

"*We will all die on the same day, at the same place*!!"

"Let's do this," said the leader. "It won't be any fun if our very first battle is a loss. I wanna give 'em a run for their money."

"Yeah!!"

The ogres moved closer and closer. Then...

Clap clap clap clap clap clap!

"Huh??"

When the ogres were but a hair's breadth away from the girls, applause rang out from the trees.

Both ogres and girls looked about, thoroughly startled.

"The heavens smile upon the determination of young battle maidens! In the name of justice, we grant you our aid!"

A golden-haired beauty appeared from a gap between the trees.

For a moment the girls were overjoyed to see someone come to their aid, but it was only a single girl in her late teens, so the situation had barely improved. The newcomer was to going to end up dead on their behalf.

"There's no point, just run," one of the girls said. "When you get back to the city, go to the Hunters' Prep School, and tell them we fought valiantly! And let those jerks who up and left us here get what's coming to them!"

"Oh! You're the new students, then? What are you doing so far out before you've even graduated?"

A second beauty, this one with silver hair and around twelve years old, also appeared from out of the trees.

"No, you've gotta run! Hurry, while they're distracted with us!"

Unfazed by the desperate protests, the two newcomers proceeded straight toward the ogres. Just as one of the beasts tried to grapple the golden-haired girl...

Whoosh!

The blonde swung a blade. And then...

Slssh... Thud!

The ogre fell to the ground in two pieces, torso cut cleanly in half.

"What?" The four girls were stunned. They couldn't believe their eyes.

The golden beauty's sword had gone through the ogre like a hot knife through butter.

"Not again, Mavis! You can't cut them down just to look cool! It ruins the resale value! Pauline's gonna yell at us again!"

"S-sorry!"

The golden-haired Mavis tipped her head toward the smaller girl, whose cheeks were puffed out in a pout.

Meanwhile, the ogres continued to approach from behind.

"Look ou—"

Thnk, whoosh!

Rrrm, ka-thud!

The smaller girl leapt nimbly and swung her sword. One of the ogres' heads went rolling, its body falling to the ground a beat behind it.

In the next instant, Mavis rushed toward the remaining ogres, swooping from the side and then swinging around to their backs. Suddenly, a third ogre's head went rolling across the ground.

"How about it? Would you ladies like to take on the last one?" she offered.

The young students' reply was unanimous.

"Okay!!"

"Beaten to a pulp."

That was the best way to describe the scene.

The ogre was struck by an Ice Javelin, two short swords, and a dagger. Thanks to its thick hide, however, the ogre still lived and shoved back one of the swordswomen with its arms. In that moment of distraction, though, as the monster lowered its head, a sword came up through its neck. It wasn't enough

to send the ogre's head flying, but it sent this final ogre tumbling to the ground.

"W-we did it..."

"W-we beat an ogre. Just the four of us."

"We *survived.*"

"Am I the only one who got hurt?"

"Ah ha..."

"Ah ha ha ha ha ha!"

As the four of them laughed together, tears streamed down their cheeks. But then, through the trees...

"How are you two so fast?"

Two more girls appeared from out of the trees, both gasping for breath.

"Thank you for saving us. We can reward you properly in a day or so."

"Don't worry about it. You're following in our footsteps, aren't you? Consider that *our* repayment to the school. Plus, I bet you all don't have any money."

"Er, well—ah ha ha..." The girls scratched at the back of their heads, embarrassed.

"Seriously though," one of the girls said. "You guys are amazing! Halving an ogre in a single blow like that. Which class were you all part of?"

"Twelfth class. It'll be half a year since we graduated soon, actually."

"Whaaaaaaaat?" The four girls were stunned. "You—you were part of the twelfth class? And you're a group of four amazingly skilled female hunters. Don't tell me you're..."

"The Crimson Vow. Heard of us, then?"

"*Have* we??!"

After their talk, Mile stored away the four ogres, as well as the jackalopes and birds the boys had left behind, while

Pauline tended to the one injured swordswoman with her healing magic. The girls were slack-jawed to see such quick and complete healing being done before their eyes.

* * *

Later, at the Capital branch of the Hunters' Guild...

"These were hunted by those girls there. Please go ahead and process the payment for them," Reina said to the old man running the guild's materials purchasing counter.

"Oho, sure thing," the man replied. "Hunted so much they couldn't carry it, so you lent 'em a hand? You gals are good mentors."

"Ah ha ha, something like that."

As Mile pulled the items from storage, she muttered, "Okay—so, we've got some jackalopes, some birds, some goblin ears, and some ogres."

"Whoa, whoa, whoa!" The old man was taken aback. "Them girls really hunted all this?"

"Well, we did help them a bit from the sidelines, but for the most part, this was their work."

"Gotcha. Well, even if they did have help, whoever smelt it dealt it. I mean, from the looks of 'em, they took down at least one of these ogres on their own. This is a pretty spectacular ogre elimination, that's for sure."

As a specialist, the old man could gauge who had taken down what prey just by looking at the wounds. However, just as the Vow had requested, the entire kill was marked down on the students' records.

"By the way, did three boys from the school come by?" Reina asked in a lilting tone, as though it were something that had just occurred to her.

"Hm? Well, it's a rest day, so a lot of kids from the school

came through. But no, I don't think there were any groups of three boys."

"I see..."

"Just out of curiosity," Mile said. "Supposing there were some young men who, I don't know, strong-armed some young ladies into going into a dangerous, uncharted place—saying they had something to show them, maybe—and suddenly an opponent they didn't expect—hypothetically, mind you, hypothetically speaking—something like four ogres appeared. And say those young men ran off, leaving those young ladies behind as bait, and in order to save their reputations they didn't *report* the incident or call for help for them. If such scoundrels existed, what might their punishment be?"

From behind them, something broke. *Crack! Crash! Crackle...* It almost sounded like glass. Not long after, one of the veteran hunters called out, "What'd you just say there, little miss?"

"Hm?"

"I said, what'd you just say?"

When Reina and the others turned, a dead silence fell over the populated guild hall. Every last hunter present stared straight at them, their faces frightening.

"Ah, well, I was just asking if something should *happen* to young men who run away and leave girls behind when four ogres appear."

"One. Two. Three. Four. There're four ogres there, ain't there?"

"Y-yes, so there are."

"And there next to ya, there's four rookie girls, ain't there?"

"Y-yes, so there are."

The silence rang loudly throughout the hall. But then...

"Bwah..."

"Ah ha..."

"Bwah ha ha ha ha ha ha!"

"Ah ha ha ha ha ha ha!"

"Is the guild master in?"

Amidst fits of laughter, the man stopped and turned to the receptionist, his tone serious. The receptionist silently nodded, and the man ascended the stairs to the second floor.

"Wh-what the heck was that?" Reina, who had been swept up in the moment, muttered as she watched the man walk away.

The old man at the counter said softly, "It was his daughter. She was part of a party of five young guys and two women before she turned up dead. Apparently, the women were the ones to die. The men came back unharmed, claiming they fought bravely and tried to protect them. Not one of us believed them. None of them had even a scratch on 'em. Three days later, those guys set off on a job, and haven't been seen since. Will probably *never* be seen. That was three years ago, after all..."

"............"

"A lot of the guys here've got daughters, and a lot of those daughters are hunters, too. Hunter men tend to treat women pretty lightly and push a lotta busy work on them, but it's because we're sweet on 'em. In return, we put our lives on the line to protect them from danger. Both sides know this, so it's all in good fun.

"But there are dumbasses out there who don't know how to fulfill even the minimum of their responsibilities. And when guys spit in the face of this fragile order, whaddya think happens?"

Here and there, the men who had gripped their glasses so hard in anger they shattered were being tended to by the

healing-proficient mages.

"What happens?" asked Reina.

"Hm? What happens with what?" the old man replied.

"What happens when men run away and leave women behind?"

"Never mindin' if they're students, proper E or F-rank hunters—or even if they're just newbies or registered as F-ranks for practice. They're still full-fledged members of the guild. So, they'll be evaluated, and it'll be put down in their record.

"There's nothin' wrong with runnin' off and leaving yer friends to rot when you encounter a strong opponent. Any sensible human being values his own life over everyone else's, so no one can tell him he's gotta throw his life away. However, if he doesn't report it, and loses out on the chance to send help, *that* we can't abide. It's not bad enough that we can sic the authorities on 'im, but it definitely flies right in the face of the code.

"It'll be noted on their record they lack the ability to evaluate danger, lack general judgement, and don't have much in the way of solidarity, camaraderie, morals, and a lotta other things. Since graduation's comin' up, I'm pretty sure they won't be expelled, but I don't think they'll be takin' the grad exam. They'll be deemed 'lacking the qualifications of a C-rank hunter.'"

"Well, don't you think that's rather unsatisfying?" asked Reina. The four female students nodding in agreement.

"Hey now, never said I was finished."

"Oh?"

The old man continued, "This kinda talk gets around fast, and folks don't quickly forget. Not surprisin', since this is a matter concerning their own lives. You really think anyone will want to buddy up with guys who'd toss their allies away

like nothin'? You think any merchant's gonna hire a guy like that to guard 'em? Folks can check a hunter's evaluation record before joinin' a party with them or hirin' them for guard duties.

"Plus, even if it doesn't go as far as that, there are lists that are passed around among the merchants: which hunters can be relied on, which hunters to absolutely avoid, which hunters you'd recommend for supplyin' water and providin' delicious food and so forth."

As he said the last part, he glanced Mile's way.

"Yer guild record follows you for life. I mean, you could always run off to a foreign country, change yer name and start again as an F-rank, but other than that, it takes a long time to wipe any stink off that you got at the start of yer career. You can ruin folks' faith in an instant, and it can take years t' earn that back. At this rate, they wouldn't even be startin' from zero—they basically got a net minus. Anyway, ain't no one they can pray to, to make their lives fun ones. Not even if they pledged themselves to some evil god or demon king."

"So, how do you all feel about that?" asked Reina.

The four girls nodded, thoroughly satisfied.

Still...it was the lives of four young girls that had been at stake, and such a punishment was perhaps still too light.

Just then, one of the guild staff called to them.

"Pardon me. The guild master would like to speak with you."

They were going to meet the guild master. For a group of rookie hunters, this was incredibly nerve-wracking. It was as good as a university freshman having the dean personally call on them on the first day of the term. Though the Crimson Vow thought nothing of it, this was by no means "normal."

"Well, we'll be going then!"

Ignoring the students, who were quaking in their boots, the Crimson Vow turned to make a hasty exit. The staff member stopped them.

"This means you too, ladies."

There was no escape.

"Yes ma'am..."

* * *

"There wasn't anyone that bad in our class, was there?" Mile asked on the way home.

"Nah, I don't think so," Mavis answered.

"There are *tons* of criminals and human trash among hunters!" Reina cut in. "The fact we didn't have any creeps in our class was a fluke. Honestly, if you two go around with your heads in the clouds like that, you're gonna end up making friends with some bad guys. You know what? I'm gonna gather up all the bad guys I can find, so both you dunces can get a taste of what the real world is like."

"No way! What kind of a bloodbath would that be?"

"Oh, gimme a break..."

"Hee hee hee."

"Pauline, what's with that creepy grin?"

"Gimme a *break*..."

Meanwhile, at the Hunters' Prep School, stocks among the male students were plummeting.

Not only were the boys involved looked upon with cold eyes, but all their brethren were as well. Promises to join with them, won through steady persuasion and proposals to form a "temporary party, just for a month," were taken back. The progress of wearing down the beautiful girls who were aiming to be solo hunters zeroed.

All the other girls had heard of the Crimson Vow's fearsome power—and their unbelievable coolness!—from the Vermillion Sisterhood.

There was Lady Mavis, the beauty with astounding steel; Mile, the darling rabbit with the venomous fangs; saintly Pauline, the goddess with the healing hands; and the high sorceress Reina, whose powers they hadn't witnessed but who seemed to be the party's leader and was probably the most powerful of them all.

"Like, I know for sure we aren't wrong here. All-female parties are like, *so* much prettier to look at, and like, *soooooooooooo* much more amazing."

The girls let out a sigh of admiration. However, they did realize one particular truth: Their powers weren't even a shred of what the Crimson Vow had.

They weren't sure they could make a living, or even survive, as that group did.

At least, not now.

The girls set into action. They would reexamine their party set-ups, and as the number of parties decreased, the number of members of each remaining party would rise. They would seek out other all-women parties they heard were forming up and seek their guidance as sisters. They would appeal to the veteran women hunters who were still stuck in male parties and scout them as their future leaders.

"All right girls, let's do this!"

"Yeah!!"

A deep grudge, meanwhile, was born against the three offenders.

First, by the other boys in the Hunters' Prep School's thirteenth class.

Second, by the veteran male hunters who had women

stolen from their parties.

Third, by all the men who could no longer enjoy the friendliness they had won with the all-women parties, and no longer enjoy the thrill of having the guidance of an older woman hunter.

Fourth, by the affiliates of the prep school, an institution whose name had been sullied.

And, most of all, by all the veteran hunters who valued women so dearly.

As far as everyone was concerned, that was the final nail in the coffin.

There was only one person overjoyed by this incident.

"This is amazing! Super amazing! Father, I want to go to the prep school, too!"

Indeed, her Highness, the Princess, who was at her father's side at the graduation exam and saw party after party made up solely of girls, was thrilled.

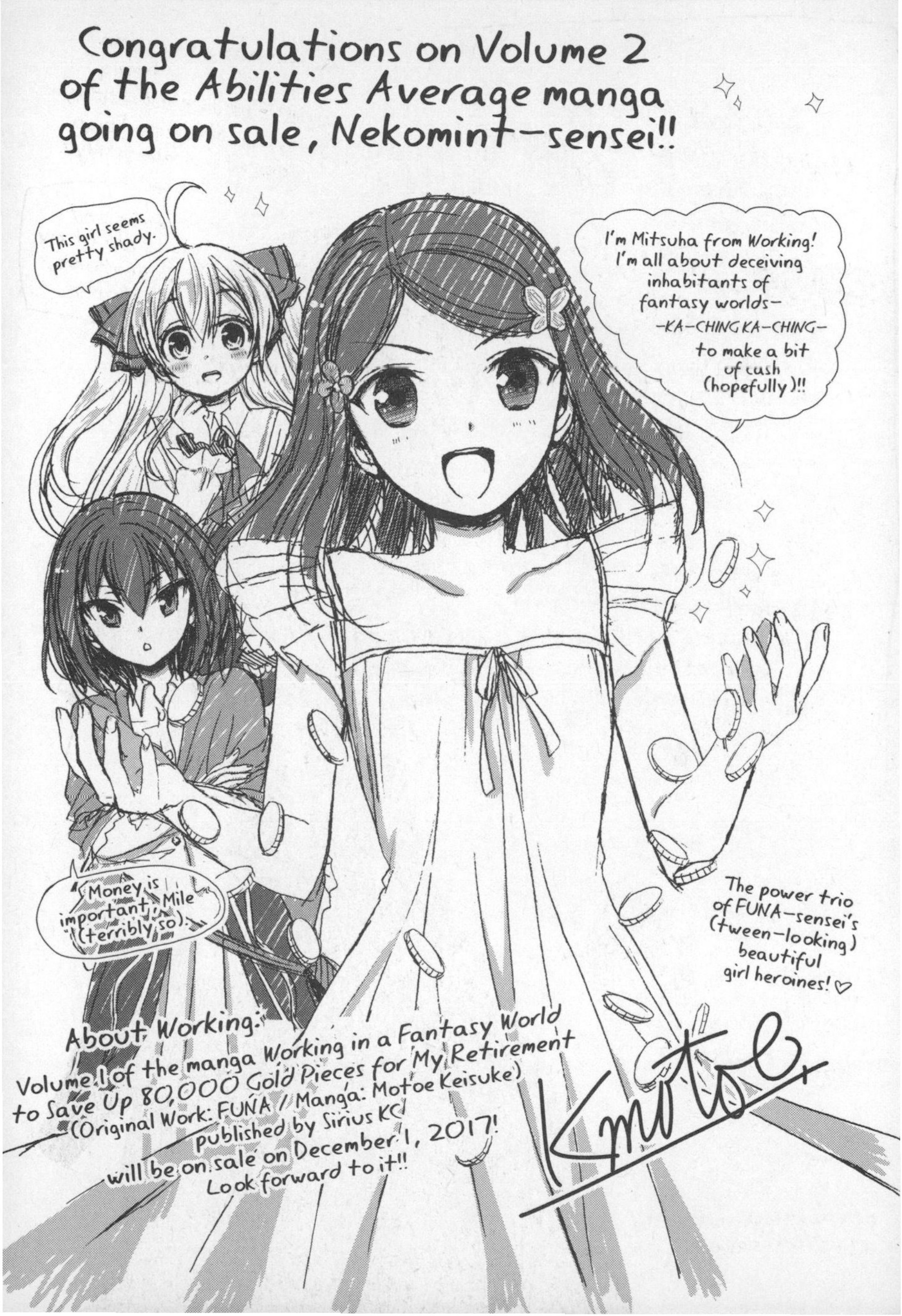
Congratulations on Volume 2 of the Abilities Average manga going on sale, Nekomint-sensei!!
I'm Mitsuha from Working! I'm all about deceiving inhabitants of fantasy worlds- -KA-CHING KA-CHING- to make a bit of cash (hopefully)!!
This girl seems pretty shady.
"Money is important," Mile (terribly so).
The power trio of FUNA-sensei's (tween-looking) beautiful girl heroines! ♡
About Working:
Volume 1 of the manga Working in a Fantasy World to Save Up 80,000 Gold Pieces for My Retirement (Original Work: FUNA / Manga: Motoe Keisuke) published by Sirius KC will be on sale on December 1, 2017! Look forward to it!!
K.motoe

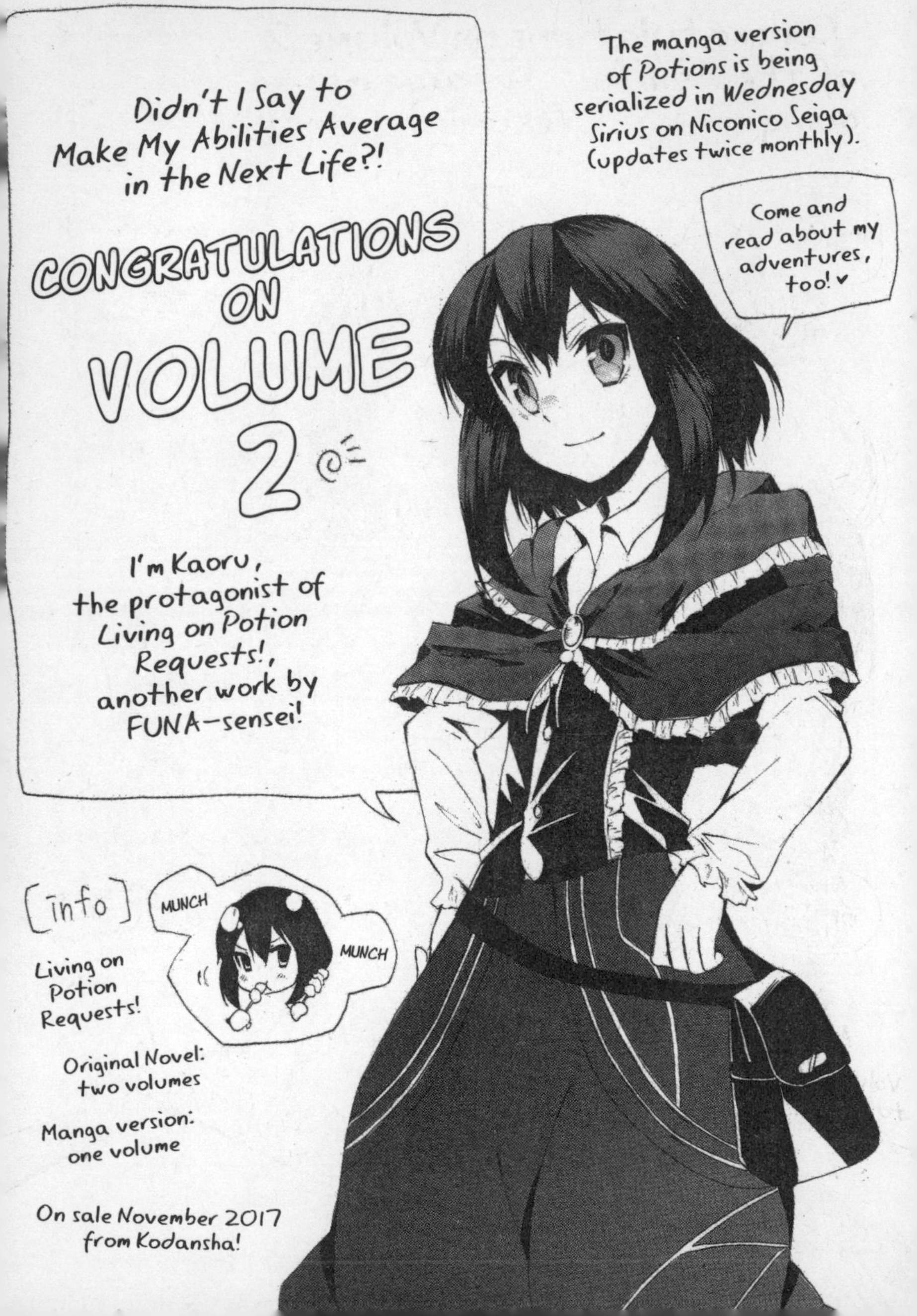

The manga version of Potions is being serialized in Wednesday Sirius on Niconico Seiga (updates twice monthly).
Come and read about my adventures, too!♥
Didn't I Say to Make My Abilities Average in the Next Life?!
CONGRATULATIONS ON VOLUME 2
I'm Kaoru, the protagonist of Living on Potion Requests!, another work by FUNA-sensei!
[info]
MUNCH
MUNCH
Living on Potion Requests!
Original Novel: two volumes
Manga version: one volume
On sale November 2017 from Kodansha!

Omake

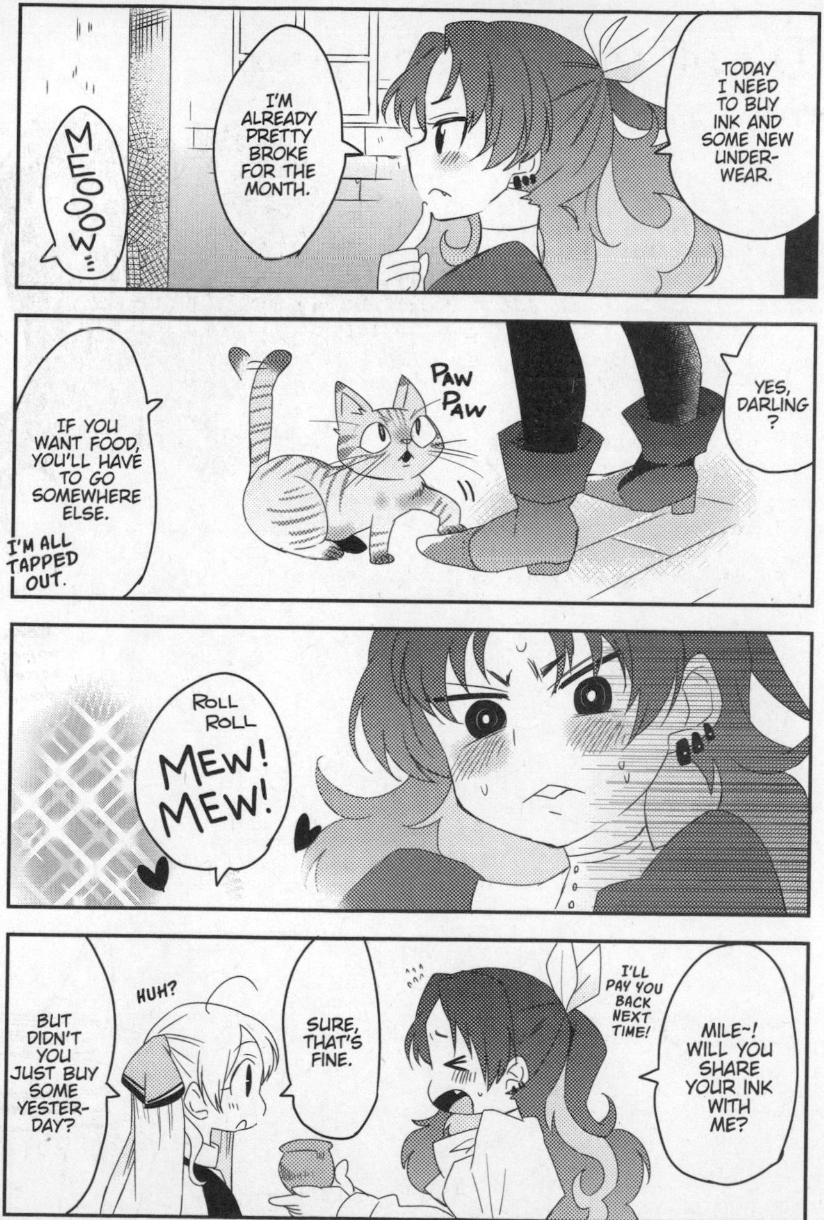
TODAY I NEED TO BUY INK AND SOME NEW UNDER-WEAR.
I'M ALREADY PRETTY BROKE FOR THE MONTH.
MEOOOW...
YES, DARLING?
PAW PAW
IF YOU WANT FOOD, YOU'LL HAVE TO GO SOMEWHERE ELSE.
I'M ALL TAPPED OUT.
ROLL ROLL
MEW! MEW!
MILE~! WILL YOU SHARE YOUR INK WITH ME?
I'LL PAY YOU BACK NEXT TIME!
SURE, THAT'S FINE.
HUH?
BUT DIDN'T YOU JUST BUY SOME YESTER-DAY?

Thank you for buying!

It's Volume 2!! I'm so happy!

I'll keep doing my best to introduce tons of people to the Average world!

When I'm drawing, I always think, "Man, it'd be great if I could use magic~!"

Thank you as always!

- Esteemed Originators: FUNA-sensei, Itsuki Akata-sensei
- Esteemed production and editing staff.

All the esteemed readers!

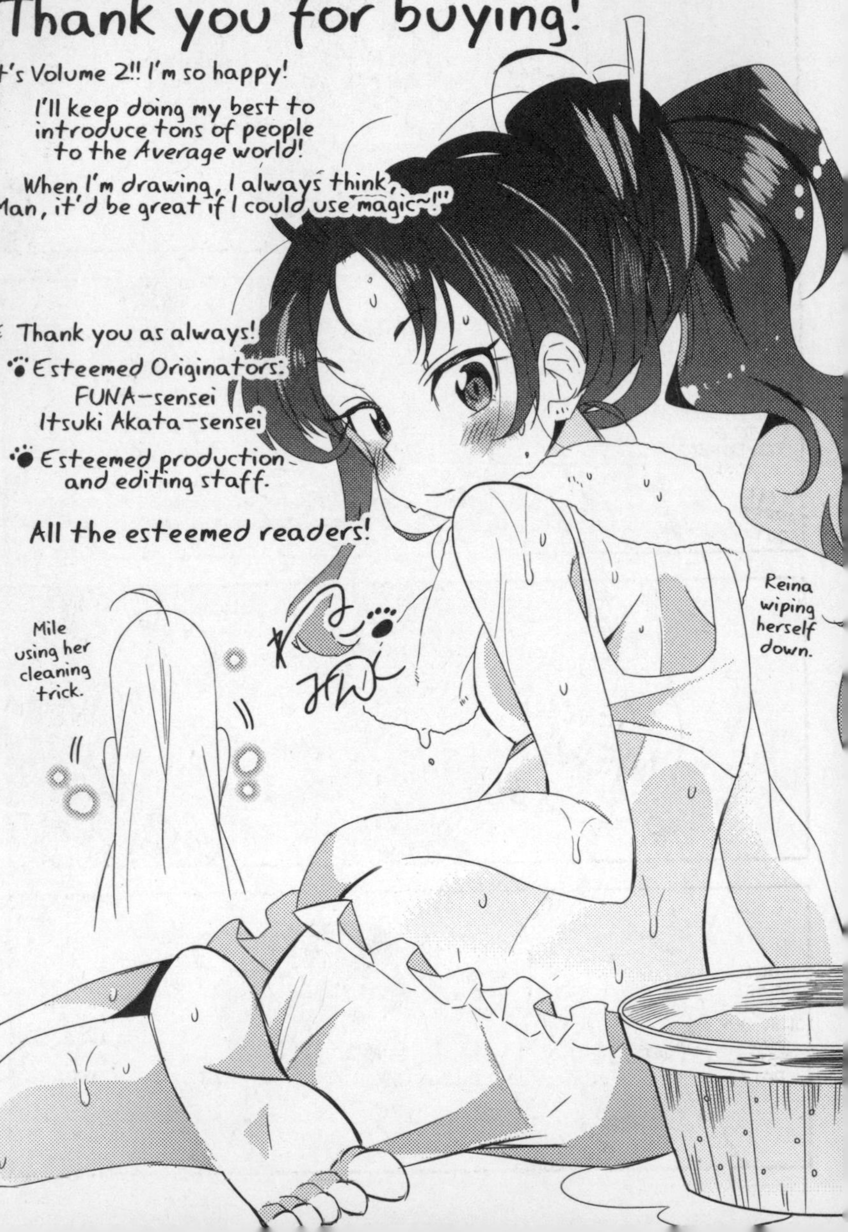
Mile using her cleaning trick.
Reina wiping herself down.

Now on sale from Seven Seas!

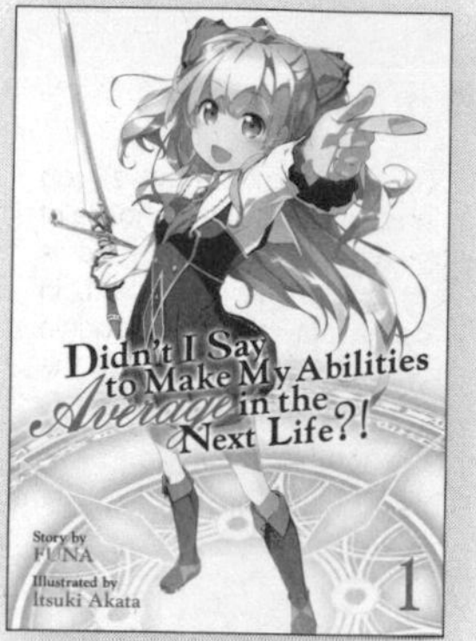
Didn't I Say to Make My Abilities Average in the Next Life?!
Story by
FUNA
Illustrated by
Itsuki Akata
1

Vol. 1

When gifted student Kurihara Misato dies right after her high school graduation, she meets God and has a peculiar request: to make her abilities average in the next life. But few things—especially wishes—ever go quite as planned. As she navigates her new life as a ten-year-old girl in a magic-filled world, she realizes God has a unique definition of average!

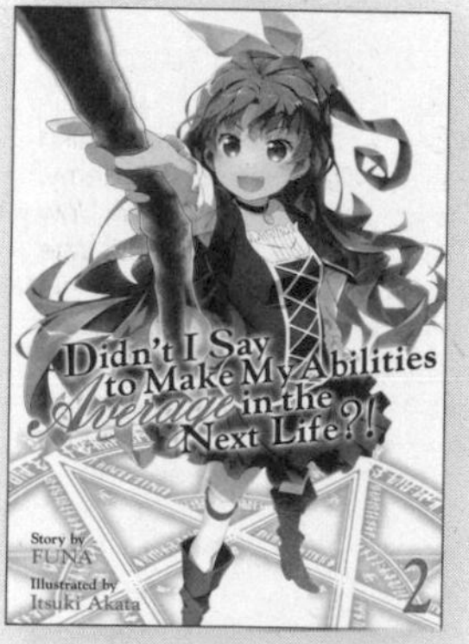
Didn't I Say to Make My Abilities Average in the Next Life?!
Story by
FUNA
Illustrated by
Itsuki Akata
2

Vol. 2

The newly graduated Crimson Vow are out in the world and determined to prove themselves. Mile, Reina, Pauline, and Mavis look for work as C-rank hunters, but when an exciting yet dangerous job comes along, the girls cannot resist! Can Mile see herself and her friends through this new challenge while still keeping her remarkable abilities hidden?

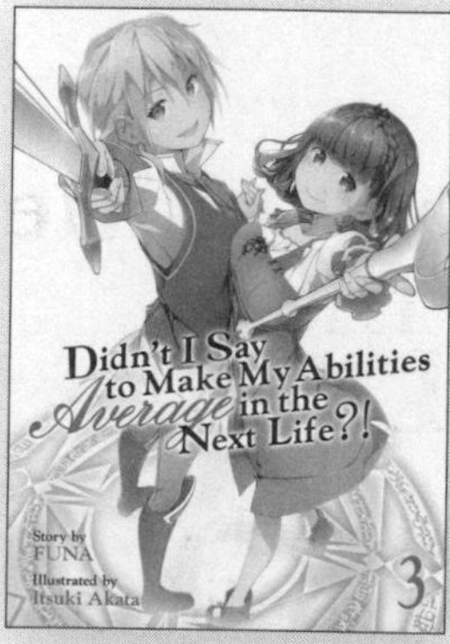
Didn't I Say to Make My Abilities Average in the Next Life?!
Story by
FUNA
Illustrated by
Itsuki Akata
3

Vol. 3

The Crimson Vow have fought fearsome bandits and monsters, but when the past catches up with Mavis and Pauline, they must confront something that swords and spells can't easily defeat. With the most dangerous job they have ever taken looming on the horizon, the very future of the party is at stake!

The smash hit original novels!

Vol. 4

When the Crimson Vow's newest job brings them up against not just a horde of beastmen but an elder dragon, Mile is forced to fight for her life in earnest, in what will become her greatest struggle yet! Can she dig deep and tap the combined power of her three selves to protect her friends?

∨

Vol. 5

Mile left Marcela, Aureana and Monika behind when she fled Eckland Academy, but when a job takes the Crimson Vow back into the Kingdom of Brandel, she can't pass up the chance to see her old friends. But the Wonder Trio aren't ready to let Mile go again now that they have her back! It's tug of war time, and Mile's in the middle! Will she be forced to choose one set of friends over the other?

∨

Didn't I Say
to Make My Abilities
Average in the
Next Life?!

Read the original light novels—
now in print and early digital editions!

Didn't I Say
to Make My
Abilities
Average in the
Next Life?!

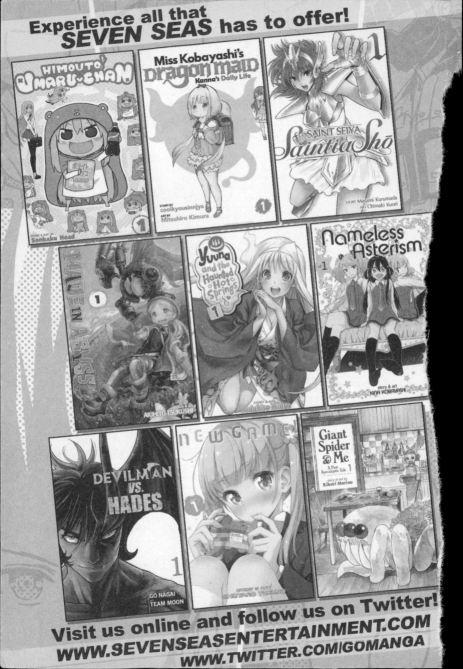

SEVEN SEAS ENTERTAINMENT PRESENTS

D[...] to Make M[...]
Average in [...]
Next [...]

story by **FUNA**   art [...]

Indian Prairie Library
401 Plainfield Road
Darien, IL 60561

TRANSLATION
Diana Taylor

ADAPTATION
Michelle Danner-Groves

LETTERING
Simone Harrison

COVER DESIGN
Nicky Lim

PROOFREADER
Danielle King
Stephanie Cohen

EDITOR
Jenn Grunigen

PRODUCTION ASSISTANT
CK Russell

PRODUCTION MANAGER
Lissa Pattillo

EDITOR-IN-CHIEF
Adam Arnold

PUBLISHER
Jason DeAngelis

WATASHI, NO[...]ERIKINOHI DE TTE ITTA YO NE! VOL. 2
© FUNA / Itsuki Akata 2016
© Nekomint 2017
Originally published in Japan in 2017 by EARTH STAR Entertainment, Tokyo.
English translation rights arranged with EARTH STAR Entertainment, Tokyo,
through TOHAN CORPORATION, Tokyo.

No portion of this book may be reproduced or transmitted in any form without
written permission from the copyright holders. This is a work of fiction. Names,
characters, places, and incidents are the products of the author's imagination
or are used fictitiously. Any resemblance to actual events, locales, or persons,
living or dead, is entirely coincidental.

Seven Seas books may be purchased in bulk for promotional, educational, or
business use. Please contact your local bookseller or the Macmillan Corporate
and Premium Sales Department at 1-800-221-7945, extension 5442, or by
e-mail at MacmillanSpecialMarkets@macmillan.com.

Seven Seas and the Seven Seas logo are trademarks of
Seven Seas Entertainment, LLC. All rights reserved.

ISBN: 978-1-626929-53-1

Printed in Canada

First Printing: December 2018

10 9 8 7 6 5 4 3 2 1

FOLLOW US ONLINE: **www.sevenseasentertainment.com**

READING DIRECTIONS

This book reads from *right to left*, Japanese style.
If this is your first time reading manga, you start
reading from the top right panel on each page and
take it from there. If you get lost, just follow the
numbered diagram here. It may seem backwards at
first, but you'll get the hang of it! Have fun!!

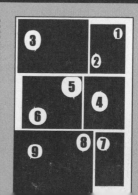